ENDORSEMENTS

Marlene's account of her journey and interaction with God differs from mine. And yet, in many ways similar. Both have come to an awareness of the hand of God actively engaging with his people in whatever way He chooses. Both have sought to understand those engagements, whether through events or visions, by pressing them through that sure Word of prophecy given by the breath of God in the Scriptures. Both have been received with the assumption that these are not simply gifts for us to treasure but are intended to benefit those to whom God has sent us.
I am intrigued. And I thank Marlene for sharing her story, heart, and passion to see people meet Jesus.

—Dennis Wilhite, Ed.D.
Assistant Professor, Instructional Mentor
John W. Rawlings School of Divinity
Liberty University

I love to read books where the author has personally encountered God. Marlene is one of these people, having had many visions and dreams. I find her interpretations of these encounters helpful and encouraging. The Lord is coming soon; this book will stir your heart to be ready for that great event!
Steve Long is the former Senior Leader of Catch the Fire Church in Toronto, where Marlene attends. He and His wife now serve as Ambassadors representing the church. They also serve as coaches and consultants for 45+ churches in Europe.
Steve is the author of several books, including The Faith Zone and My Healing Belongs to Me.

—Steve Long
Author, Ambassador
Catch the Fire Church, Toronto

The book is a must-read for everyone who wants to have an oversight of the Lord's dealings in our times. As much as end-time prophecy and His Second Coming have been a gripping fear in many people, as some authors and speakers have portrayed, your book comes with lots of excitement to prepare men and women for the Second Coming of our Lord. Thanks for being sensitive to the Holy Spirit and offering yourself to author this tremendous book.

—Rev. Jonathan E. Mudenyo
New Hope Christian Center, Kenya

His Second Coming

Reverend
Dr. Marlene Brown

His Second Coming by Reverend Dr. Marlene Brown
Published by Creation House Publication
A Strang Company 600 Rinehart Road
Lake Mary, Florida 32746 www.strangbookgroup.com
This book or parts thereof may not be reproduced in any form, stored in a retrieval system, or transmitted in any form by any means—electronic, mechanical, photocopy, recording, or otherwise—without prior written permission of the publisher, except as provided by United States of America copyright law.

All Scripture quotations are taken from the *Zondervan KJV Study Bible*, Kenneth Barker, ed. (Grand Rapids, MI: Zondervan, 2002). All rights reserved. www.Zondervan.com

Word definitions are taken from the *New International Encyclopedia of Bible Words* by Lawrence O. Richards (Grand Rapids, MI: Zondervan, 1991) also Crossroads eBible, Libronix Digital Library System. © 2007 Thomas Nelson, Inc. All rights reserved.

Design Director: Bill Johnson
Cover design by Justin Evans
Copyright © 2010 by Reverend Dr. BrownAll rights reserved
Library of Congress Control Number: 2009943069
International Standard Book Number: 978-1-7389250-1-8
First Edition
10 11 12 13 14— 9 8 7 6 5 4 3 2 1
Printed in the United States of America

The testimony of Jesus is the spirit of prophecy.

—Revelation 19:10

And he said, hear now my words: If there be a prophet among you, I the Lord will make myself known unto him in a vision, and will speak unto him in a dream.

—Numbers 12:6

Indeed, the Sovereign LORD never does anything until he reveals his plans to his servants, the prophets.

—Amos 3:7

Dedicated first to Jesus, the precious Lamb of God, my dear Savior and Redeemer!

Then to the Holy Spirit who guides me and teaches me all things;

Next to my parents, who taught me the ways of the Lord; Then to my husband and my two boys, Brandon and Brian;

Next to my sisters and brothers for their support, especially James;

And to all my brothers and sisters in Christ in every language and tongue, looking forward to Christ's return.

* * * *

In loving memory of my Grandmother Rebecca Clarke, You are greatly missed and greatly loved.

See you at the Marriage Supper

Table of Contents

Preface

Part I: His Second Coming

Chapter 1: His Second Coming	2
Chapter 2: The Nature of Prophecy	7
Chapter 3: Prophecy of Israel and Fulfillment of Prophecy	13
Chapter 4: Fulfillment of Prophecy in Our World Today	16
Chapter 5: The Destruction of Jerusalem	19
Chapter 6: Prophetic Vision of the Cross	26
Chapter 7: A Vision of Christ Jesus—the Son of God	33
Chapter 8: Prophetic Vision of Jesus's Second Coming	40
Chapter 9: Visions and Dreams for Men of Old	54

Part II: Walking in the Power of Salvation

Chapter 10: The Lord's Work	52
Chapter 11: Jesus Christ Reigns	60
Chapter 12: Prophetic Revelation Given of 666	65
Chapter 13: My New Relationship with Jesus	69
Chapter 14: Holiness unto the Lord	73
Chapter 15: What Can I Do to Be Saved?	77
Chapter 16: Sin and Its Origin	81
Chapter 17: You Must Be Born Again	87
Chapter 18: Your New Identity in Christ	104
Chapter 19: Salvation	107

Chapter 20: What Is Faith?   114

Chapter 21: Doubts of Your Salvation   119

Chapter 22: Significance of the Blood   122

Chapter 23: Cleansing Power of the Blood of Jesus   125

Chapter 24: Direct Communication to Jesus, Our High Priest   131

Chapter 25: Significance of the Cross   134

Chapter 26: The Cross Experience of Jesus   138

Chapter 27: Born Dead for 15 Minutes—The Cross   147

Chapter 28: The Resurrection of Christ   152

Chapter 29: Doubts About Christ's Resurrection   160

Chapter 30: Gone to Prepare a Place for You   166

Chapter 31: Signs of the End of the World   171

Chapter 32: The Self-Righteous   176

Chapter 33: The Importance of Baptism   181

Chapter 34: The Holy Spirit, or the Comforter   185

Chapter 35: Receiving The Holy Spirit   191

Chapter 36: Who Am I in Christ?   198

Chapter 37: How to Walk in Love Daily Through Christ   206

Chapter 38: The Power of Humility   211

Chapter 39: The Power of Forgiveness   215

Chapter 40: Are You an Addict Today?   230

Chapter 41: How We Should View Preachers   236

Chapter 42: Religion Versus Salvation   240

Chapter 43: Prepare to Meet Thy God   244

Chapter 44: Letter of Encouragement to Be on the Watch!   247

Part III: Prophetic Heavenly Visions of Christ with Interpretations

Chapter 45: Prophetic Vision of God's Heart for Young People	228
Chapter 46: Prophetic Vision of His Spoken Word	231
Chapter 47: A Prophetic Dream Within a Dream	236
Chapter 48: Prophetic Vision of Heaven (the Marriage Supper)	241
Chapter 49: Preparing for His Second Coming	253
About the Author	255
In Conclusion	258

Preface

This book, His Second Coming: Prophetic Visions of Christ and His Return, was written under divine inspiration from God through prayer and fasting. Its sole purpose is to encourage believers in their faith so that they hold firm to what they have for the return of Jesus Christ.

This book is very prophetic. Every aspect of the book has been written through divine inspiration and visions of dreams by the Holy Spirit. Its function is to enlighten all men and encourage and comfort believers as they prepare for the Second Coming of the Lord.

The prophetic visions and dreams are direct messages from Christ to share with the church and are interpreted by the living Word of God to enlighten the eyes of the believer that the coming of the Lord is at hand. The Lord's revelation of these prophetic visions in the heavens proves how close He is. The prophet Joel mentioned that in the last days, He would pour out His spirit upon all flesh, and the young men would have visions. These visions will help the reader focus on the Lord's coming and not be distracted by the cares and trials of this world or the philosophy of men. The Lord is coming back like the Scripture says, as King of kings and Lord of lords!

To all the nonbelievers: I have seen Jesus Christ in visions over fourteen times and counting. He has shown me His face of fire! Just like the Bible says, He is a consuming fire.

The Savior of all humankind is real, and He loves you with everlasting love; He is the lover of your soul.

Yes, we do not have much time to linger. We, the church, the Bride of Christ, must be ready and waiting for His glorious return. Yes, indeed, Jesus Christ lives. He is undoubtedly King of kings and Lord of lords. Who can be compared to Him?

The Scriptures were taken directly from the Holy Bible, containing the Old and New Testaments in the King James Version and the KJV Study Bible. You will find translations of the original tongue.

The Lord has inspired me to design this book so that the topics and Scriptures are helpful for sinners, new Christians, and old believers.

Scriptures in this book teach us how to live holy lives before the God of the universe and to reverence Him. And others that explain how we need to adore His only begotten Son, Jesus Christ. You will also find Scriptures that speak of Christ's love for us: His death, resurrection, and coming as King of kings and Lord of lords. And lastly, you will find Scriptures that reveal your new identity in Christ.

I pray that you will feed on the Word of God daily for your spiritual growth. Also, you will put God's saving work into action and obey God with deep reverence and fear. The Word of God works within you, giving you the desire to obey Him and the power to do what pleases Him. It is the Word of God that converts the heart or soul of man. May you find this book a blessing through Jesus Christ, our Lord. Amen!

Part I
His Second Coming

Dr. Marlene Brown

Chapter 1
His Second Coming

Behold, I come quickly: blessed is he that keepeth the sayings of the prophecy of this book.

—Revelation 22:7

His Second Coming is the phrase that is on almost every believer's lips, or at least those believers who are looking for His reappearance. Jesus told us in His Word that He was going to prepare a place for them and that in His Father's house are many mansions. He said, "If it were not so, I would have told you." Jesus continued to say:

> And if I go and prepare a place for you, I will come again, and receive you unto myself; that where I am, there ye may be also. And whither I go ye know, and the way ye know. Thomas, saith unto him, Lord, we know not whither thou goest; and how can we know the way? Jesus saith unto him, I am the way, the truth, and the life: no man cometh unto the Father but by me.
>
> —John 14:3–6

Today, we find scoffers mocking Christians concerning the coming of Christ. Some Christians also lose hope in His coming, while others become weary. Some people point out that they have been watching since they were children, and their parents have also been watching since they were children. Some point out that the disciples also watched for His eminent return and did not live to see it. They began to lose faith and care more for the things of this world than for the things of God. However, the Word of God says

His Second Coming

in Isaiah, "His ways are not our ways, saith the Lord: Neither His thoughts our thoughts our thoughts." Second Peter 3:3–4, 8–9 says:

> There shall come in the last days scoffers, walking after their own lusts, And saying, Where is the promise of his coming? For since the Fathers fell asleep; all things continue as they were from the beginning of the creation. But, beloved, be not ignorant of this one thing, that one day is with the Lord as a thousand years and a thousand years as one day. The Lord is not slack concerning his promise, as some men count slackness, but is longsuffering to us-ward, not willing that any should perish, but that all should come to repentance.

So, in other words, the Lord loves us so much that He is patient in His coming to see that all people come to repentance. Jesus also declares in His Word that His appearance will be like a thief in the night. So, the Scripture says that we should be diligent that we may be found by Him in peace, without spot, and blameless.

In Matthew 25:1–13, Jesus describes what His Second Coming will be like.

The Scripture says:

> Then shall the kingdom of heaven be likened unto ten virgins, which took their lamps and went forth to meet the bridegroom. And five of them were wise, and five were foolish. They that were foolish took their lamps, and took no oil with them: But the wise took oil in their vessels with their lamps. While the bridegroom tarried, they all slumbered and slept. And at midnight, there was a cry made, Behold, the bridegroom cometh; go ye out to meet him. Then, all those virgins arose and trimmed their lamps. And the foolish said unto the wise, Give us of your oil; for our lamps are gone out. But the wise answered, saying, Not so; lest there be not enough for you and us: but go ye rather

to them that sell, and buy for yourselves. And while they went to buy, the bridegroom came; and they that were ready went in with him to the marriage: and the door was shut. Afterward came also the other virgins, saying, Lord, Lord, open to us. But he answered and said, Verily I say unto you, I know you not. Watch, therefore, for ye know neither the day nor the hour wherein the Son of man cometh.

Here, we see that Jesus likened the church to virgins, foolish ones, and wise ones, all waiting for the bridegroom, Jesus Christ Himself, about to make His appearance. While waiting for Christ to appear, the church members, represented by the foolish virgins, lose their effectiveness. Their oil has run out. They have lost their anointing.

The oil, which is the precious anointing, destroys the yoke of bondage in our lives (Isa. 10:27). It is the anointing that makes us overcomers and conquerors, defeating the enemy. Jesus declared in His Word:

> He that overcometh, the same shall be clothed in white raiment; and I will not blot out his name out of the book of life, but I will confess his name before my Father, and before his angels. He that hath an ear, let him hear what the Spirit saith unto the churches.
>
> —Revelation 3:5–6

So let us not be like the scoffers thinking that the Lord has delayed His return. But instead, let us be on watch since Jesus declared that He would be coming unannounced, and we, the church, need to be found with oil in our lamps (that is, righteousness in our temples, which are our bodies waiting for the coming of our Lord).

Scripture declares that before that great day comes, some Christians will fall away from the faith so that Satan, the man of sin, can be revealed. Second Thessalonians 2:3 says:

Let no man deceive you by any means: for that day shall not come, except there come a falling away first, and that man of sin be revealed, the son of perdition.

What does "falling away" mean? Falling away means turning away from Christianity's faith in other religions. The Greek word for falling is *apostasia*, which means "to forsake."

This Scripture makes you wonder, how can a Christian or a child of God read the Word of God, then turn away from the faith? Some of these people even become atheists. They do not believe in God or His existence. What makes them turn their backs on the truth? Is it a lack of faith in the gospel or belief in the Word of God as the absolute truth?

To answer these questions, we need to ask ourselves, what is the validity of the Bible? And What is the nature of prophecy? I believe that answering these questions will help many to remain in the faith and to be empowered in it. Does prophecy have relevance to our society today? I firmly believe that the answers to these questions will help to encourage and strengthen many to hold on to their Christian faith. The Bible says it is not His will for any to perish but for all to have eternal life. So, let us go on a journey together as we seek to find out the true nature of prophecy and the validity of the Bible.

The Validity of the Bible

Before we go on a journey through the Bible to answer these questions, it is first imperative to note that the Bible is the living Word of God. It was inspired by God and written by forty holy men or prophets. Even though three separate languages were used to write the various books of the Bible, its contents and message remained the same throughout the ages.

The contents of the Bible consist of man's experience with the Highest God. It is a history book, yet more than a history book. It speaks of prophecies that have been fulfilled and prophecies to come. Second Peter 1:16 speaks of the validity of the Bible. Peter says:

> For we have not followed cunningly devised fables, when we made known unto you the power and coming of our Lord Jesus Christ, but were eyewitnesses of his majesty.

Here, Peter pointed out that he was among several eyewitnesses of Christ and that His coming is not based upon devised fables or tales. Peter continued by saying: "For he [Jesus] received from God the Father honor and glory when there came such a voice to him from the excellent glory, This is my beloved Son, in whom I am well pleased" (2 Pet. 1:17). "And this voice," Peter states, "which came from heaven we heard when we were with him in the holy mount. We also have a surer word of prophecy: whereunto ye do well that ye take heed, as unto a light that shineth in a dark place until the day dawn and the day star arise in your hearts: Knowing this first, that no prophecy of the Scripture is of any private interpretation. For the prophecy came not in old time by the will of man: but holy men of God spake as they were moved by the Holy Ghost" (2 Pet. 18–21).

His Second Coming

Chapter 2
The Nature of Prophecy

> *"You are my witnesses," declares the LORD, "and my servant whom I have chosen, so that you may know and believe me and understand that I am he.*
>
> —Isaiah 43:10

For us to understand the nature of prophecy, we need to take a closer look at the people of Israel. Israel was created to be a witness to God. The living God called Israel by the mouth of His prophets, His chosen people—a people that He chose to show forth His praise.

In Isaiah 43, we read God's promise to redeem his people, Israel. He kept reminding his people through the prophet Isaiah that He had created them to be His witnesses. He had made them so that He could be their king. He had created them so He could be their Savior, the Holy One of Israel, beside whom there is no other.

I particularly find this statement interesting because it says God created them to be His witness, that He is God, that He is alive, and that there is no other besides Him. He is using Israel to witness to other nations that He is God. This means He will be showing Himself mighty in the land of Israel and among the Jews so that their lives will forever be a witness to the world that there is a God, the true and living God, and beside Him, there is no other!

Let us read what the prophet Isaiah has to say concerning the Jews in Israel in Isaiah 43.

> But now thus saith the Lord that created thee, O Jacob, and he that formed thee, O Israel, Fear not: for I have redeemed thee, I have called thee by thy name; thou art mine. When thou passest through the waters, I will be with thee; and through the rivers, they shall not overflow thee: when thou walkest through the fire, thou shalt not be burned; neither shall the flame kindle upon thee, for I am the Lord thy God, the Holy One of Israel, thy Saviour.

Here, we read of the Lord's passion for Israel. He did not say that they would not be persecuted. However, He promises to be with them when they go through their various trials, represented by the waters, the rivers, and the fire.

In Exodus 13:17, we read the account of the children of Israel facing the Red Sea, having nowhere to turn with Pharaoh's men in pursuit of them. The Lord had to part the Red Sea for Moses and His children to pass through. The Word of God says He created Israel to be His witness that He is God, as He demonstrates His mighty power in their lives.

Let us turn to Exodus 13, where we read of Moses crossing the Red Sea. In verse 17, we read that Pharaoh had let the people go. We also read:

> And it came to pass when Pharaoh had let the people go, that God led them not through the way of the land of the Philistines, although that was near; for God said, Lest peradventure the people repent when they see war, and they return to Egypt: But God led the people about, through the way of the wilderness of the Red Sea.
>
> —Exodus 13:17–18

The children of Israel now went up out of the land of Egypt. Verse 20 says they took their journey from Succoth and encamped in Etham, at the edge of the wilderness.

His Second Coming

> And the Lord went before them by day in a pillar of a cloud, to lead them the way; and by night in a pillar of fire, to give them light; to go by day and night: He took not away the pillar of the cloud by day, nor the pillar of fire by night, from before the people.
>
> —Exodus 13:21–22

The pillar, I believe, represents God's visible presence. In Numbers 12:5, the Lord comes down as a pillar to speak to Miriam and Aaron. So, in Exodus 14, the Lord spoke to Moses, saying that he should instruct the children of Israel to encamp between Migdol and the sea. Now we see the Lord strategizing and making known to Moses how He would defeat Pharaoh and receive honor from Pharaoh and his host so that they may know He is God.

The Lord told Moses that Pharaoh would say that the Israelites were entangled in the land and the wilderness had shut them in. In verse 4, the Lord told Moses that He would harden Pharaoh's heart to follow after them; He would receive honor from Pharaoh and his men so that the Egyptians would know He is the Lord. And so, they did.

As we go further along in Exodus 14, we read that Pharaoh drew near:

> And when Pharaoh drew nigh, the children of Israel lifted up their eyes, and, behold, the Egyptians marched after them, and they were sore afraid: and the children of Israel cried out unto the Lord. And they said unto Moses, Because there were no graves in Egypt, hast thou has taken us away to die in the wilderness? Wherefore hast thou dealt thus with us, to carry us forth out of Egypt? Is not this the word that we did tell thee in Egypt, saying, Let us alone, that we may serve the Egyptians? For it had been better for us to serve the Egyptians than that we should die in the wilderness.

Dr. Marlene Brown

—Exodus 14:10–12

Here, the Lord brings them into the wilderness to show His strength and salvation. In verse 13, Moses said unto the people:

> Fear ye not, stand still, and see the salvation of the Lord, which he will show to you today: for the Egyptians whom ye have seen today, ye shall see them again no more forever. The Lord shall fight for you, and ye shall hold your peace.

> And the Lord said unto Moses, Wherefore criest thou unto me? speak unto the children of Israel that they go forward: But lift thou up thy rod, and stretch out thine hand over the sea, and divide it: and the children of Israel shall go on dry ground through the midst of the sea.

> And I, behold, I will harden the hearts of the Egyptians, and they shall follow them: and I will get me honor upon Pharaoh, and upon all his host, upon his chariots, and upon his horsemen. And the Egyptians shall know that I am the Lord, when I have gotten me honor upon Pharaoh, upon his chariots, and upon his horsemen.

Here, the Lord is bent on showing Pharaoh that He is God and that the children of Israel are His chosen vessel. Here, He wants to demonstrate to the children of Israel that even though they feared Pharaoh, Pharaoh will fear Him as the almighty God, and He will receive honor and respect from Pharaoh and his horsemen.

In verse 19, we read that the angel of God, which went before the camp of Israel, changed its position and went behind them.

> The pillar of the cloud went from before their face and stood behind them: And it came between the camp of the Egyptians and the camp of Israel, and it was a cloud and

His Second Coming

darkness to them, but it gave light by night to these: so that the one came not near the other all the night.

And Moses stretched out his hand over the sea, and the Lord caused the sea to go back by a strong east wind all that night, and made the sea dry land, and the waters were divided. And the children of Israel went into the midst of the sea upon the dry ground: and the waters were a wall unto them on their right hand, and on their left.

—Exodus 14:19–22

The Bible says the waters were a wall unto them on the right and left sides. That is truly amazing. Indeed, the children of Israel experienced the power and the strong arm of the mighty God. Indeed, their experience will be shared with their descendants for many generations. The story speaks of the mighty hand of the living God. It reveals how God showed forth His love and power by dividing the Red Sea into dry land.

The Scripture says the Egyptians pursued and went after them to the midst of the sea, even all Pharaoh's horses and chariots. The Scripture says:

In the morning watch, the Lord looked unto the host of the Egyptians, through the pillar of fire and of the cloud, troubled the Host of the Egyptians and took off their chariot wheels that they drave them heavily: so that the Egyptians said, Let us flee from the face of Israel; for the Lord fighteth for them against the Egyptians. And the Lord said unto Moses, Stretch out thine hand over the sea, that the waters may come again upon the Egyptians, their chariots, and their horsemen.

And Moses stretched forth his hand over the sea, and the sea returned to his strength when the morning appeared, and the Egyptians fled against it, and the Lord overthrew the Egyptians in the midst of the sea.

And the waters returned, and covered the chariots, and the horsemen, and all the host of Pharaoh that came into the sea after them; there remained not so much as one of them.

—Exodus 14:25–28

The Scripture declares, however:

But the children of Israel walked upon dry land in the midst of the sea, and the waters were a wall unto them on their right hand and on their left. Thus, the Lord saved Israel that day out of the hand of the Egyptians, and Israel saw the Egyptians dead upon the seashore. And Israel saw that great work which the Lord did upon the Egyptians: and the people feared the Lord, and believed the Lord, and his servant Moses.

—Exodus 14:29–31

Yes, indeed, God used Moses and the children of Israel to be his witness that He is God, and there is no other besides him. So, in Isaiah 43:10, the Lord confirmed His Word through the prophet Isaiah, who said that He had created Israel to be His witness.

The Scripture says:

Ye are my witnesses, saith the Lord, and my servant whom I have chosen: that ye may know and believe me, and understand that I am he: before me, there was no God formed, neither shall there be after me.

Christians who are turning away from the faith and who are doubting whether or not there is a God need to take a closer look at the prophecy of Israel and the fulfillment of prophecy.

His Second Coming

Chapter 3
Prophecy of Israel and Fulfillment of Prophecy

but, 'the Lord liveth who brought up the children of Israel from the land of the north, and from all the lands whither He had driven them.' And I will bring them back into their land that I gave unto their fathers.

—Jeremiah 16:15

It is prophesied by the prophet Ezekiel in Ezekiel 11:14 that God will scatter His people Israel but will also bring them back together from all parts of the world to the nation of Israel. Today, we see the fulfillment of this prophecy. The Jewish people are now returning home to the land of Israel in droves. Here are the words of the prophet Ezekiel:

> Again the Word of the Lord came unto me, saying, Son of man, thy brethren, even thy brethren, the men of thy kindred, and all the house of Israel wholly, are they unto whom the inhabitants of Jerusalem have said, Get you far from the Lord: unto us is this land given in possession.
>
> Therefore say, Thus saith the Lord God: Although I have cast them far off among the heathen, and although I have scattered them among the countries, yet will I be to them as a little sanctuary in the countries where they shall come.
>
> Therefore say, Thus saith the Lord God; I will even gather you from the people, and assemble you out of the countries where ye have been scattered, and I will give you the land of Israel.

Dr. Marlene Brown

—Ezekiel 11:14–17

The prophet Jeremiah received a similar word from the Lord concerning Israel. Here is the Word of the Lord concerning His people of Israel, as recorded in Jeremiah 16. The Scripture says:

> Therefore, behold, the days come, saith the Lord, that it shall no more be said, The Lord liveth, that brought up the children of Israel out of the land of Egypt. But, the Lord liveth, that brought up the children of Israel from the land of the north, and from all the lands whither he had driven them: ***and I will bring them again into their land that I gave unto their fathers.*** Behold, I will send for many fishers, saith the Lord, and they shall fish them; and after will I send for many hunters, and they shall hunt them from every mountain, and from every hill, and out of the holes of the rocks.
>
> —Jeremiah 16:14–16, emphasis added

Why would the Lord do this? This action speaks of God's faithfulness. The Lord is faithful to His Word. He had promised their forefathers that He would give them the land of Israel and wanted to show His faithfulness. In Jeremiah 30:1–4, the prophet Jeremiah prophesied the Word of the Lord, saying:

> The word of the Lord came to Jeremiah from the Lord, saying, thus speaketh the Lord God of Israel, saying, Write thee all the words that I have spoken unto thee in a book. For, lo, the days come, saith the Lord, that I will bring again the captivity of my people Israel and Judah, saith the Lord: and I will cause them to return to the land that I gave to their fathers, and they shall possess it. And these are the words the Lord spoke concerning Israel and Judah.

And so, we see the fulfillment of this prophecy today with the Jews returning home from all parts of the world, showing us the validity of the Bible, that it is the Word of the living God.

His Second Coming

As we continue to look at the fulfillment of prophecy from the Word of God, we also need to probe the Scriptures to see what prophecy there is concerning our world today and what is to come.

Dr. Marlene Brown

Chapter 4
Fulfillment of Prophecy in Our World Today

And ye shall hear of wars and rumours of wars: see that ye be not troubled: for all these things must come to pass, but the end is not yet.

—*Matthew 24:6*

We can see that our world today is heading for a fall. There is no peace; we constantly hear of war. We also hear of earthquakes, famine, and pestilence, such as the AIDS virus, and of weapons of mass destruction. Presently, we are aware of diplomatic efforts with North Korea and nuclear weapons.

What does the Bible have to say concerning these events? And what does the Bible say concerning war and rumors of war that will lead to the end of the world and the Second Coming of Christ? The Bible is very precise about what we should look for as signs in the world today concerning the Second Coming of Christ.

Everyone knows that we are in the last and final days, no matter how simple you are or whether you believe in a God or not! Here's what Jesus has to say about it.

In Luke 12, Jesus spoke to the people concerning the times that they were living in. This is what Jesus says:

When ye see a cloud rise out of the west, straightway ye say, There cometh a shower; and so it is. And when ye see

His Second Coming

the south wind blow, ye say, There will be heat; and it cometh to pass.

—Luke 12:54–55

Then He asks, why are we being such hypocrites? We can study the face of the sky and the earth, yet we cannot discern or tell how close it is to the world's end.

In Matthew 24, we read about Jesus teaching His disciples the various signs they should look for as precursors to His coming and the end of the world. The Scripture says that when Jesus came out from the temple, and His disciples came to Him to show Him the various buildings of the temple, He said unto them: "See ye not all these things? Truly, I say unto you: There shall not be left here one stone upon another that shall not be thrown down." This prophecy of Jesus was actually fulfilled in A.D. 70 when the Romans completely destroyed the temple during the reign of Titus.

The Scripture declares that as He went and sat on the Mount of Olives, which is a long north-south ridge that lies just east of Jerusalem, His disciples came to Him privately and asked Him:

Tell us, when shall these things be taking place? And what shall be the sign of thy coming and of the end of the world?

—Matthew 24:3

The Scripture says that the disciples had three basic questions on their minds. First, they wanted to know when the temple would be destroyed, as Jesus had said. Second, what would be the sign of His coming? And third, what would be the sign of the world's end? The first question is answered in Luke 21:20–24. The Scripture says when you shall see Jerusalem surrounded with armies, then know that the destruction of Jerusalem is near. Jesus continued to say that there would be distress in the land and wrath upon the people of Jerusalem. Verse 22 says, "For these days will be the days of vengeance that all things, which are written may be fulfilled."

Dr. Marlene Brown

Let us probe the Scriptures concerning Jerusalem's destruction and the Second Coming of Christ.

Chapter 5
The Destruction of Jerusalem

For I will gather all nations against Jerusalem to battle; and the city shall be taken, and the houses rifled, and the women ravished; and half of the city shall go forth into captivity, and the residue of the people shall not be cut off from the city.

—*Zechariah 14:2*

Zechariah 14 tells us what that day will be like in Jerusalem. Verse 2 says, "For I will gather all nations against Jerusalem to battle.

The city shall be taken, the house rifled, and the women ravished; half of the city shall go forth into captivity, and the residue of the people shall not be cut off from the city" (Zech 14:2–3). Zechariah 12 states all that burden themselves with it shall be cut in pieces, though all the people of the earth should gather against it.

Christ mentions in Luke 21:24, "that they shall fall by the sword and be taken away as prisoners into all the nations, and that Jerusalem shall be trodden down by the Gentiles until the times of the Gentiles be fulfilled."

Until the times of the Gentiles be fulfilled—what does that mean?

The Greek word for "times" is *kairos,* as used in this line, which means "a season." It also means a "fixed and definite time when things are brought to crisis; the decisive time or era waited for."

Strong's analysis describes the word *Gentiles* as *eth-nos.* This translates to mean "a nation" sixty-four times. It also means "a multitude of individuals of the same nature." In the Old Testament, the word *Gentiles* is used to describe people who are not worshiping the true God. However, because we have been grafted into the true vine, we are now called Gentile Christians, according to Apostle Paul.

"Be fulfilled" in Greek means *pleroo,* which is translated as "being full" fifty-one times and "fill" nineteen times. It also means to carry through to the end and complete all sayings, prophecies, and promises given by God through the prophets for them to receive their fulfillment.

Now let us look once more for the full meaning of the phrase "until the times of the Gentiles be fulfilled": it means that when the body of believers, who are the Gentiles, are filled with the presence and power of God and are entered into His kingdom, to complete God's mission on earth, and all fulfillment has taken place, then all of Israel shall be saved.

Through the fall of Israel, salvation came to the Gentiles to provoke the Jews into jealousy. As the Scripture declares in verse 26 of Romans 11, there shall come out of Zion the Deliverer, who shall turn away ungodliness from Jacob. "For as we the Gentiles in times past have not believed in God, yet we have now obtained mercy through their unbelief, even so, have the Jews not believed, that through our mercy that we have obtained through the Father, they will also receive this mercy" (Rom. 11:25–26, 30–31). And so, all of Israel will be saved. So, Jesus says in Luke 21:28:

> And when these things begin to come to pass, then look up, and lift up your heads; for your redemption draweth nigh.

Now, the disciples' second question was, "What shall be the sign of thy coming?" Jesus answers in Matthew 24:21–24, 30:

> For then shall be great tribulation, such as was not since the beginning of the world to this time, no, nor ever shall be. And except those days should be shortened, there should

His Second Coming

no flesh be saved: but for the elect's sake those days shall be shortened. Then if any man shall say unto you, Lo, here is Christ, or there; believe it not. For there shall arise false Christs and false prophets, and shall shew great signs and wonders; insomuch that, if it were possible, they shall deceive the very elect. And then shall appear the sign of the Son of man in heaven: and then shall all the tribes of the earth mourn, and they shall see the Son of man coming in the clouds of heaven with power and great glory.

The prophet Zechariah says in chapter 12, verses 9–11:

And it shall come to pass in that day, that I will seek to destroy all the nations that come against Jerusalem. And I will pour upon the house of David, and upon the inhabitants of Jerusalem, the spirit of grace and supplications: and they shall look upon me whom they have pierced, and they shall mourn for him, as one mourneth for his only son, and shall be in bitterness for him, as one that is in bitterness for his firstborn. On that day, there shall be a great mourning in Jerusalem.

This prophecy of Zechariah speaks of the vision that I had of Christ when I saw the sign of the Son of Man (Jesus), a double crucifixion of Christ on the cross in my vision, as He burst the sky from the East in the heavens. We will discuss this vision of Jesus's Second Coming as we continue through this book of prophecy.

So now we read of Christ telling us in Matthew that there will be great mourning when they see the Son of Man coming from heaven with power and great glory. Here, we also read the prophet Zechariah prophesying that when Christ returns, they will look upon Him whom they have pierced, and there will also be great bitterness and mourning.

Zechariah, the prophet, continues to prophesy in Zechariah 14, telling us exactly what that day is going to be like when Christ appears for the second time, standing on the Mount of Olives in Jerusalem.

> Then shall the Lord go forth, and fight against those nations, as when he fought in the day of battle. And his feet shall stand in that day upon the Mount of Olives, which is before Jerusalem on the east, and the Mount of Olives shall cleave in the midst thereof toward the east and toward the west, and there shall be a very great valley; and half of the mountain shall remove toward the north, and half of it toward the south.
>
> —Zechariah 14:3–4

Now, remember how, in Matthew 24, Jesus sat on the Mount of Olives and prophesied? Zechariah prophesied that when Christ returns to Jerusalem, His feet shall stand on that day upon the Mount of Olives. So no longer will He be sitting on the Mount, but standing as reigning King of heaven and earth.

Zechariah 14:5–9, 11 continues:

> And ye shall flee to the valley of the mountains; for the valley of the mountains shall reach unto Azal. Yea, ye shall flee, like as ye fled from before the earthquake in the days of Uzziah king of Judah: and the Lord my God shall come, with all his saints. And it shall come to pass in that day, that the light shall not be clear, nor dark: But it shall be one day which shall be known to the Lord, not day, nor night: but it shall come to pass, that at evening time it shall be light.
>
> And it shall be in that day, that living waters shall go out from Jerusalem; half of them toward the former sea, and half of them toward the hinder sea: in summer and in winter shall it be. And the Lord shall be king over all the earth: in that day shall there be one Lord, and his name one. And

His Second Coming

men shall dwell in it, and there shall be no more utter destruction; but Jerusalem shall be safely inhabited.

Now we know the time is coming when Jerusalem shall be at perfect peace. This will be when the Prince of Zion touches down on the Mount of Olives and puts an end to this war, making Jerusalem safe once more to be inhabited.

In Revelation 21, we read of a New Jerusalem coming down from God, beautifully prepared as a bride adorned for her husband. John says he saw this holy city. Let us read his prophecy concerning the New Jerusalem which is to come.

> And I, John, saw the holy city, new Jerusalem, coming down from God out of heaven, prepared as a bride adorned for her husband. And I heard a great voice out of heaven saying, Behold, the tabernacle of God is with men, and he will dwell with them, and they shall be his people, and God himself shall be with them, and be their God.
>
> And God shall wipe away all tears from their eyes; and there shall be no more death, neither sorrow, nor crying, neither shall there be any more pain: for the former things are passed away. And he that sat upon the throne said, Behold, I make all things new. And he said unto me, Write: for these words are true and faithful. And he said unto me, It is done. I am Alpha and Omega, the beginning and the end.
>
> —Revelation 21:2–6

These are prophecies spoken by God's prophet, which have yet to come to pass. As we read the times and the seasons we are living in, we see clearly the various signs that are leading up to the fulfillment of these prophecies about the Second Coming of Christ, thus proving and establishing the truthful nature of the Bible, that it is indeed the Word of the living God.

The third question from the disciples to Jesus was, "What will be the sign of the end of the world?" In Matthew 24:14, Jesus answers this question: "This gospel of the kingdom shall be preached in all the world for a witness unto all nations; and then shall the end come."

Today, we see the gospel of Jesus Christ entering through various doors that would have been impossible in times past, such as in India, China, Japan, Korea, Russia, Germany, France, Singapore, Thailand, Indonesia, Iraq, and so on. In Israel, especially in Jerusalem, the gospel goes forth like never before. Not only is the gospel going forth, but there is also a yearly gathering for an All Nations Convocation, joining together in Jerusalem for worship, praise, and prayer as they usher in the return of the Lord Jesus. Millions are being saved in Africa and other parts of the world. Jesus says that the gospel must be a witness in every part of the world unto all nations, then the end of the world will come. The enemy has been trying to keep the gospel of Christ at bay, but the Word of God says, "Upon this rock, I will build my church; and the gates of hell shall not prevail against it" (Matt. 16:18). His glory shall fill this earth as the waters cover the seas.

So yes, the Bible is a history book, but more than a history book. It is a book that is filled with prophecy concerning Jesus Christ, witnesses of Christ, the redemption of man, and the end of time. It is a book that is filled with holiness and righteousness, with words of life from the living God. It is a book of love, for it teaches us how to experience love because God is love.

Now that we have established the truth concerning the Holy Bible and its validity, let us go deeper into recent prophetic visions God gave me, along with their interpretations from the Holy Word of God, the Bible, concerning His Son's Second Coming. As Joseph mentions in Genesis 40:8, all interpretations belong to God, and the Scriptures declare that the testimony of Jesus is the Spirit of prophecy.

His Second Coming

It is the desire and the perfect will of the Father for me to write this book and to share this book with the entire body of Jesus Christ throughout the nations of the earth for the church to know and understand what the Spirit of the Lord is saying to the church at this time. That is, "Now is the time to be on the watch and be ready!"

The Lord Jesus wants His glory to be made known not only in the times of the apostles but also in our present time and the one to come so that man may know He is still the same God yesterday, today, and forever! He will be coming back whether man is ready for His imminent return or not, for the earth is the Lord's and the fullness thereof, whether theology teaches otherwise or not. His promise is sure, and His Word is true. The Lord Jesus wants me to share what He has shown me to strengthen the body of Christ so that my visions will inspire and empower you to hold on to your salvation until He comes. As Revelation says, let no man take your crown! As you read through the many topics given by the Holy Ghost, I pray that it will increase your love for Him, build up your faith to walk in the power of God's salvation and prepare you for His imminent return.

Dr. Marlene Brown

Chapter 6
Prophetic Vision of the Cross

A dream that I, Marlene, saw on November 24, 2000.

I woke up at 8:10 a.m.

And I will pour upon the house of David, and upon the inhabitants of Jerusalem, the spirit of grace and of supplications: and they shall look upon me whom they have pierced, and they shall mourn for him, as one mourneth for his only son, and shall be in bitterness for him, as one that is in bitterness for his firstborn.

—Zechariah 12:10

I dreamed that I was at a park. The park had a large open space with benches, similar to a park in Kingston, Jamaica, called Hope Gardens. I was standing in a section of the park when I saw a black man talking to a white girl. He was telling the girl that he was waiting for someone to bring him drugs to make him feel better. I overheard the conversation and said to him, "You know, drugs are not the answer. The devil wants you to take this drug to destroy yourself so you never get to know about God." The man then said to me, "I can't hear you . . . I will come a little closer."

When he came closer to me, I told him about this Pentecostal church that I was visiting. I asked him, "Why don't you come to church with me on Sunday?" The man turned to me and said, "Aren't you afraid I would hurt you?" I turned to him and said, "You wouldn't dare hurt me while I have a baby in my hand!" Suddenly, my eyes turned toward the sky, where I saw this very huge, thick, and massive, silver-looking cross moving toward us quickly. It kept

His Second Coming

getting bigger and bigger. It was huge, thick, and massive with a silver color. There was something inscribed on the front of the cross.

Then I touched the man and said to him, "Look! There is a cross in the sky!" I looked over my shoulder to see if the white girl was looking at the cross, too. The cross continued to get bigger and bigger coming toward me, and then suddenly a man appeared before the cross—he was huge—but I could not tell what his face looked like, nor his feet. My eyes were focused on his chest! His bosom was huge, thick, and massive with a beautiful color, with very long red and blue veins. It looked alive, like flesh, and my eyes were focused on his chest. I found myself jumping in the air with my hands stretched out to receive him. Then I heard a spirit say to me, "But you have not received the Holy Ghost!" Immediately, a thought came to my mind: "I wonder if my sister in Connecticut is watching." This thought distracted me for a second. Within the split second that my thoughts became distracted, the body became bigger and bigger, then went, *whoosh*! —disappeared past us. The *whoosh*! that the body made as it went past us was at such great speed that it shook my baby, Brandon, who was four months old at the time. He was lying beside me on my bed. The speed jerked my baby, and the baby's vibration woke me up. I got up and looked at the time. It was 8:00 in the morning.

Needless to say, I was in total shock and confused simultaneously because of the magnitude of what I saw. I could not believe what I had just seen! I did not know, nor had I heard, of the God of the universe visiting people in such a manner. Still shocked, scared, and confused, I began to thank God for such a powerful vision. I did not know what to do or how to handle it because I had recently given my life to the Lord.

I was so scared to sleep, fearing what I might see again. Because of the magnitude of what I saw, the thought of food made me sick! This vision immediately placed me into a lifestyle of fasting and prayer every day until noon or evening, as well as the continuous reading of God's Word.

Prophetic Vision of the Cross: Interpretations from the Bible

Many people could give interpretations concerning visions and dreams; however, the Scripture says in Genesis 40:8 that all interpretations belong to God. So, I find it very fitting to turn to the Word of God, the book of prophecy concerning this, and all interpretations are given to me to share with the body of Christ concerning Christ and His Second Coming.

Dream

> *I dreamed that I was at a park. The park had a large open space with benches, similar to a park in Kingston, Jamaica, called Hope Gardens. Standing in a park section, I saw a black man talking to a white girl. The black man told her he was waiting for someone to bring him drugs to make him feel better. I overheard the conversation, and I said to him, "You know, drugs are not the answer. The devil wants you to take this drug to destroy yourself so you never get to know about God."*

Interpretation

Jesus says in Luke 4:18–19:

> The Spirit of the Lord is upon me because he hath anointed me to preach the gospel to the poor; he hath sent me to heal the broken-hearted, to preach deliverance to the captives, and recovering of sight to the blind, to set at liberty them that are bruised, to preach the acceptable year of the Lord.

His Second Coming

This man needs to be delivered from the lies and strongholds of the enemy. He also needs to be delivered from drug addiction. We see clearly in our society today that drugs are destroying young people. Both young and old are being killed by this demon, this lying spirit that promises a better life, peace, joy, and wholeness from a feel-good drug. Know full well that this wholeness only comes from Jesus Christ, the righteous, the Son of the living God, and our identity is in Him. Jesus is saying here that only His cross can bring deliverance. Only His cross will bring authentic satisfaction and the peace of mind that the world is searching for. Jesus says in His Word, "If any man thirsts, let him come unto me and drink." Jesus says that out of his belly shall flow rivers of living water (John 7:37).

Jesus is saying here and reminding us that He became a curse for us. By being made a curse through His death on the cross, it became possible for the blessing of Abraham to come upon us, the Gentiles, through Him (Gal. 3:14). All blessings, freedom, and prosperity are found in Him.

The Scripture says it is not His will for any to perish, but for all to have eternal life through Jesus Christ our Lord (John 3:16).

Dream

Suddenly, I turned toward the sea, where I saw this huge, thick, and massive, silver-looking cross moving toward us quickly. It kept getting bigger and bigger. It was huge, thick, and massive with a silver color. There was something inscribed on the front of the cross.

Interpretation

Silver represents the pureness of God's Word. "The words of the Lord are pure words: as silver tried in a furnace of earth, purified seven times" (Ps. 12:6)

The silver cross means we must focus on God's Word, which is pure and without blemish. It is like silver purified seven times. We must focus on the blood of the cross for man's deliverance.

> For the preaching of the cross is to them that perish foolishness; but unto us which are saved, it is the power of God. For it is written, I will destroy the wisdom of the wise and will bring to nothing the understanding of the prudent. Where is the wise? Where is the scribe? Where is the disputer of this world? Hath, not God made foolish the wisdom of this world?
>
> For after that, in the wisdom of God, the world by wisdom knew not God; it pleased God by the foolishness of preaching to save them that believe. For the Jews require a sign, and the Greeks seek after wisdom: But we preach Christ crucified, unto the Jews a stumbling block, and unto the Greek foolishness; But unto them which are called, both Jews and Greeks, Christ the power of God, and the wisdom of God.
>
> —1 Corinthians 1:18–24

I believe that the Lord is saying here that we need to focus more on preaching the cross for man's deliverance. The Scripture says, "For I am not ashamed of the gospel of Christ: for it is the power of God unto salvation to everyone that believeth; to the Jew first, and also to the Greek. For therein is the righteousness of God revealed from faith to faith: as it is written, the just shall live by faith" (Rom. 1:16–17). The gospel of Christ brings deliverance; it brings forth salvation.

Dream

> *Then I touched the man and said to him, 'Look! There is a cross in the sky!" I looked over my shoulder to see if the white girl was looking at the cross, too. The cross continued to get bigger and bigger coming toward me, and*

His Second Coming

then suddenly a man appeared before the cross—he was huge—but I could not tell what his face looked like, nor his feet. My eyes were focused on his chest!

Interpretation

I believe that as Christ reveals His bosom to us, He is speaking of His heart and His love for mankind, which sent Him to the cross on behalf of us all.

> For God so loved the world, that he gave his only begotten Son, that whosoever believeth in him should not perish, but have everlasting life. For God sent not his Son into the world to condemn the world; but that the world through him might be saved. He that believeth on him is not condemned: but he that believeth not is condemned already, because he hath not believed in the name of the only begotten Son of God.
>
> —John 3:16–18

Dream

His bosom was huge, thick, and massive with a beautiful color, with very long red and blue veins in it. It looked alive as though it were flesh...

Interpretation

> And as they thus spake, Jesus himself stood in the midst of them, and saith unto them, Peace be unto you. But they were terrified and affrighted and supposed that they had seen a spirit. And he said unto them, Why are ye troubled? And why do thoughts arise in your hearts? Behold my hands and my feet that it is I myself: handle me, and see; for a spirit hath not flesh and bones, as ye see me have. And when he had thus spoken, he showed them his hands and his feet.

Dr. Marlene Brown

—Luke 24:36–40

His Second Coming

Chapter 7
A Vision of Christ Jesus—the Son of God

The second dream that I, Marlene, saw. It took place on December 5, 2000.

I woke up at 7:00 a.m.

And lo a voice from heaven, saying, This is my beloved Son, in whom I am well pleased.

—Matthew 3:17

I dreamed that I was walking to meet my mother and one of my sisters. The place was very dark, as if there were no light anywhere in the world. Then I found myself running and lifting in the air, shooting forward through the air and then falling to the ground again in a continuous motion.

While on the ground, I looked up in the sky and saw two men. Both of these men were looking down on me. One had a glow about his head, forming a semi-circle. I could not tell what clothes he was wearing because he seemed transparent—so I will say his clothes were white. The other man I could see much more clearly. He was standing a little distance from the man with a semi-circle of light around his head. His hair was extremely black and curly, flowing down to his shoulders. He was wearing a gown that was beautifully striped. The gown seemed to be made out of a shiny, silky material, which had the brightest colors of the rainbow. Both of his hands extended slightly forward toward me, with the palm of each hand facing forward. Somehow, this man caught my attention. I realized he was looking down on me—I wondered who this man was.

Suddenly, I heard a voice (not a spirit), which came from the air, say to me, "His name is called Jesus!"

I continued until I met my mother and my sister. I began to tell them about what I had seen on my way to them. I casually told them: "I found myself running and shooting through the air in a continuous motion when I saw two men in the sky. One of them had a semicircle about his head, which had a light-yellow glow, and his clothing was transparent white. The other was wearing a colorful and beautifully striped gown. He was standing at a distance away from the man with transparent white clothing. I began to wonder who this man was— the one with the gown that was beautifully striped, standing a distance away, his hands slightly stretched towards me. I then heard a voice from the atmosphere say to me, "His name is called Jesus."

We were heading home when I saw a man I know—I am not sure if it was my husband or another man—I kissed him goodbye and said to him, "Be careful because it is dangerous out there!" When I looked into the street, I saw people running here and there with long guns. They were not military; they were civilians, and it was a moment of war, not peace. He assured me that he would be careful.

On my way home with my mother and sister, I saw a man and a woman sitting by the side of the street. I approached them, but the Holy Spirit said, "Don't touch them! They are unclean." We continued on our journey . . . suddenly, I heard my baby speaking in his crib and woke up.

With this vision/dream, I was so disappointed to know that it was not happening in the present moment! I was disappointed to wake up to it. Yes, I had grown up in a Christian home, but I was unaware that such encounters are still happening for the Son of the Living God to visit man just as in biblical times. The experience was out of this world, and I didn't know what to make of it since I had not been exposed to other Christians having such encounters.

A Vision of Christ Jesus—the Son of God
Second Vision/Dream Interpretation

Dream

The place was very dark as if there were no light anywhere in the world; then I found myself running and lifting in the air, shooting forward through the air and then falling down to the ground continuously.

Interpretation

Isaiah 40:31 says:

But they that wait upon the Lord shall renew their strength and mount up with wings as eagles.

Dream

While I was on the ground, I looked up in the sky and saw two men. Both of these men were looking down on me. One of them had aglow about his head, which formed a semi-circle. I could not tell what clothes he was wearing because he seemed transparent, so I will say that his clothes were white. The other man I could see much more clearly. He was standing a little distance away from the man with a semi-circle of light around his head. His hair was extremely black and curly, flowing down to his shoulders. He was wearing a gown that was beautifully striped. The gown seemed to be made out of a shiny, silky material, which had the brightest colors of the rainbow.

Interpretation

Dr. Marlene Brown

In Genesis 37:3, the Bible speaks of Israel, who loved Joseph and made him a coat of many colors. The coat of many colors on Joseph shows the mark of his father's favor on him. The coat of many colors shows that God highly favors him (Jesus) and is royalty.

The rainbow garments declare that He (Jesus) is the Son of the Highest! He is King of kings and Lord of lords (Rev. 19:16).

Dream

Both of his hands extended slightly forward towards me, with the palm of each hand facing forward. Somehow, this man caught my attention. I realized that he was looking down on me—I began to wonder who this man was... Suddenly, I heard a voice (not a spirit), which came from the air, say to me, "His name is called Jesus!"

Interpretation

His name is called Jesus: In Matthew 1:18–25, the Scripture declares to us His birth, the reason for such a name (Jesus), and why He was born. The Bible says He shall be called Jesus, for He shall save His people from their sins.

The Scripture explains to us in Matthew 1:18–25:

> Now the birth of Jesus Christ was on this wise: When as his mother Mary was espoused to Joseph, before they came together, she was found with child of the Holy Ghost. Then Joseph her husband, being a just man, and not willing to make her a public example, was minded to put her away privily. But while he thought on these things, behold, the angel of the Lord appeared unto him in a dream, saying, Joseph, thou son of David, fear not to take unto thee Mary

thy wife: for that which is conceived in her is of the Holy Ghost. And she shall bring forth a son, and thou shalt call his name JESUS: for he shall save his people from their sins. Now all this was done, that it might be fulfilled which was spoken of the Lord by the prophet, saying, Behold, a virgin shall be with child and shall bring forth a son, and they shall call his name Emmanuel, which being interpreted is, God with us. Then Joseph being raised from sleep, did as the angel of the Lord had bidden him, and took unto him his wife: And knew her not till she had brought forth her firstborn son: and he called his name JESUS.

In John 20:31, the Scripture says:

But these are written, that ye might believe that Jesus is the Christ, the Son of God; and that believing ye might have life through his name.

The Bible says:

God also has highly exalted him, and has given him a name which is above every name: That at the name of Jesus, every knee should bow, of things in heaven, and things in earth, and things under the earth; And that every tongue should confess that Jesus Christ is Lord to the glory of God the Father.

—Philippians 2:9–11

Dream

We were heading home when I saw a man I know—I am not sure if it was my husband or another man—I kissed him goodbye and said to him, "Be careful because it is dangerous out there!" When I looked into the street, I saw people running here and there with long guns in their hands. They were not military; they were civilians, and it was a moment of war, not peace. He assured me that he would be careful.

Interpretation

Jesus says in Luke 21:9 that you will hear of wars and commotions, but you should not be terrified for these things must come to pass, "but the end is not by and by" (Luke 21:10). Then Jesus says, "Nation shall rise against nation and kingdom against kingdom." In Luke 21:26, Jesus continues by saying men's hearts will fail them for fear, "and for looking after those things that are coming on the earth: for the powers of heaven shall be shaken" (Matt. 24:29–31).

Dream

On my way back home with my mother and sister, I saw a man and a woman sitting by the side of the street. I approached them, but the Holy Spirit said, "Don't touch them! They are unclean." We continued on our journey ... suddenly, I heard my baby speaking in his crib and woke up.

Interpretation

This last part of the dream means that the Spirit of God will lead and guide me in my ministry.

> For as many as are led by the Spirit of God, they are the sons of God.
>
> —Romans 8:14

Psalm 32:8 says:

His Second Coming

I will instruct thee and teach thee in the way which thou shalt go: I will guide thee with mine eye.

The Bible admonishes us not to be quick to lay our hands on each other and that we should keep ourselves pure.

Dr. Marlene Brown

Chapter 8
Prophetic Vision of Jesus's Second Coming

The fourth vision that I, Marlene, saw. It took place on December 16, 2000.

I woke up at 11:45 p.m.

Behold, I come quickly, and my reward is with me, to give every man according as his work shall be. I am Alpha and Omega, the beginning and the end, the first and the last.

—*Revelation 22:12-13*

For this dream, the Lord placed me into a very, very deep sleep. If He had not done so, the first explosions in the heavens would have awakened me.

I dreamed that my sister and I, along with a few family members, were in an upstairs building. I am unsure if it was a hotel or a house; however, it had a big glass window.

I was standing there holding my four-month-old baby, Brandon, just looking ahead, when I noticed the clouds were clearing up. The cloud then began to form different animal shapes in the sky ... The human head on the animal body and so on ... I called my sisters and family, who were there at the time, to look at the different animal shapes in the sky.

While my family and I stood by the big glass window watching the various animal shapes in the sky, my head turned slowly to my right—to the east in the heavens. Suddenly, I saw that section of the

His Second Coming

heavens burst wide open with a mighty explosion of light tearing the heavens open! As I was watching this magnificent splendor in the heavens, I saw the Lord Jesus appear through this explosion of light that broke open the heavens on a big, thick, and massive wood-looking cross. The cross had a brownish color with white streaks in the wood. The wooden cross seemed very heavy and massive. I saw His entire beautiful body. His head was leaning to His right shoulder, and He had a wreath platted around His head. His hands were nailed on either side of the cross. The palms of His hands were opened. My eyes trailed from the top of His head down to His feet. Our Lord was naked; He was not wearing any form of clothing. His legs were placed one on top of the other and nailed from the instep.

At the foot of the cross, there was another cross, and the body of Jesus was also on it. *I saw the crucifixion twice.* The sky lighted up brightly with His presence. We were all looking at the different animal shapes in the sky when we saw Christ appear in all of His glory.

I turned to them and said, "Now, you believe me about seeing things in the sky? See ..." I was referring to the Lord making His appearance. I moved away from the window because, to me, this was the coming of the Lord. Everything seemed so real!

I exalt Your Name, Lord. I glorify Your Name. I magnify Your Name. Thank You, Jesus!

I went to a table in the house and stood still, listening to hear the Lord Jesus shout as if to say, **"The God of the universe is here; no more time for man!"** I knew in my spirit that there would be the sound of a trumpet! The glory of His presence then hit the lights that were in the house, and the place went into total darkness, and I stiffened! I somehow knew that the whole world was now in darkness! At this point, I curled over with my head down and my eyes tightly shut.

Dr. Marlene Brown

I then heard the thunder roll... and I stopped my breath and stiffened while clenching my fist, saying to myself: "This is it! This is it!" Thinking to myself that the great and final day is here, standing still while listening out for the Lord to make His shout! The moment and the feeling were so intense as I stood there. There was a feeling of bitterness and doom! There was a feeling that *time*, as we know it, had finally ended! ***There is no more time for man on Earth.***

As I stood there trembling with my fists closed and my back bent tensely, waiting for the Lord to shout and make His announcement to earth, nothing seemed to happen! I was taken into a second dream.

In this second dream, I was taken to a church. In this church, there was division in it. The pastor was preaching, but no one was listening. Things were contrary in the church. On one side of the church, they were selling food. After entering this church, I brought peace and unity through worship. Then I woke up.

I was totally scared and terrified of what I saw! The Lord Jesus is making His appearance on earth for the second time! I was not crying when I woke up; I was weeping! I thought that time had ended—that the finality on earth had come! I was also weeping, thanking God that He has given us a little more time—a little more time to get things right, a little more time for souls to be saved, a little more time for man to be holy. This speaks of His grace and, His mercy, and His kindness! He has not forgotten us; He is indeed coming again—much sooner than a man thinks or cares to imagine!

The first time that I saw a vision of Christ before I became strong in the faith, an individual asked me this question: "What is it that the Lord is trying to say to you?" My response was, "I am not sure!" It took this fourth dream to open my eyes to what the Lord Jesus was saying, but who am I that the Living God would choose me to inform the world what He is about to do on the earth for people to know of His coming? He says, *"Marlene, I am much closer than you think! You need to get yourself ready and let my people know that this is the time they need to be on the watch because I will be coming as a thief in the night?"* He will be coming at a time when we least expect it! In His Word, He reminded me that He is coming for a bride without spot or wrinkle (Eph. 5:27). He is also coming for a bride who is fully dressed, sparkling and spotless, without blame, full of joy and passion, ready to meet her bridegroom (2 Pet. 3:14).

The Lord has also opened my eyes to the world. He has shown me that many people still do not know Him! There are still many that need to be called into the fold. "The harvest field is ripe!" He said, "My laborers are few." He said in His Word that it is not His will for any to perish but for all to have eternal life. So, He said to my spirit, "Let the people know of My coming! Let them know that My coming is at hand! Let them know of what you see and hear of Me in these visions and dreams! Let them know that now is the time to be on the watch, lest I come as a thief in the night and find them sleeping, overtaken by the cares of this world."

I believe the Lord is reminding us that we should enter through the straight gate. He declared in His Word that "broad is the way, that leadeth to destruction, and many there be which go in Because strait is the gate, and narrow is the way, which leadeth unto life, and few there be that find it" (Matt. 7:13–14).

The Lord wants to remind us that we should hold strong, even in times of persecution. He said in His Word that if any man suffers as a Christian, let him not be ashamed but glorify God. For the time has come that judgment must begin in the house of God first. As Christians, He wants us to hold what we have in him fast and let no man take our crown. He said in His Word that if the righteous can scarcely be saved, where shall the sinners and the ungodly appear?

So, He wants us to be strong in Him and of good courage because our Redeemer is returning as King of kings and Lord of lords.

Fourth Prophetic Dream: Interpretation of Jesus's Second Coming

The interpretation of this dream/vision is found line upon line and precept upon precept.

Dream

For this dream, the Lord placed me into a very deep sleep. If He had not done so, then the first explosions in the heavens would have awakened me.

Interpretation

This deep sleep is one way in which God speaks to man. Then the Bible says God opened the ears of men and sealed their instructions. This can be found in Job 33:15–16.

We also see in Genesis 2:21 that the Lord God will put man in a deep sleep when He wants to perform a significant work on earth or to make Himself known to man. The Scripture says the Lord God caused a deep sleep to fall upon Adam, and he slept. Then He took one of the ribs and closed up the flesh. And with the rib that the Lord God had taken from man, He made a woman and brought her to the man. In Genesis 15:12-13, we also read of this deep sleep falling upon Abram; the Bible declared that "when the sun was going down, a deep sleep fell upon Abram; and, lo, a horror of great darkness fell upon him. And he said unto Abram, know of a surety that thy seed shall be a stranger in a land that is not theirs, and shall serve them; and they shall afflict them four hundred years."

I believe that the Lord God had to place me in this very deep sleep in order to reveal to me what He was about to do on earth. If He had not done so, the first explosion of light in the heavens would have awakened me.

His Second Coming

Dream

The cloud then began to form different animal shapes in the sky. The human head on the animal body and so on ... I called my sisters and family, who were there at the time, to have a look at the different animal shapes in the sky.

Interpretation

Someone may be saying that what I saw was totally out of the ordinary, with animals in the sky, especially human faces on animal bodies. So, to see the credibility of this dream/vision and its prophetic nature, we need to hear what the Bible says concerning animals in the heavens.

The Scripture says in Revelation 4:6–8:

And before the throne there was a sea of glass like unto crystal: and in the midst of the throne, and round about the throne, were four beasts full of eyes before and behind. And the first beast was like a lion, and the second beast like a calf, and the third beast had a face as a man, and the fourth beast was like a flying eagle. And the four beasts had each of them six wings about him; and they were full of eyes within: and they rest not day and night, saying, Holy, holy, holy, Lord God Almighty, which was, and is, and is to come.

The Lord appeared in my vision shortly after seeing these animals (beasts).

Dream

Suddenly, I saw that section of the heavens burst wide open with a mighty explosion of light tearing the heavens open! As I was watching this magnificent splendor in the heavens, I saw the Lord Jesus appear through this explosion of light that broke open the heavens.

Interpretation

Revelation 6:14 best describes the opening of the heavens. The Scripture says:

> And the heaven departed as a scroll when it is rolled together.

Matthew 24:25–27 also explains the explosion of light from the open heaven. The Scripture says:

> Behold, I have told you before. Wherefore if they shall say unto you, Behold, he is in the desert; go not forth: behold, he is in the secret chambers; believe it not. As the lightning cometh out of the east, and shineth even unto the west; so, shall the coming of the Son of man be.

Dream

I saw the Lord Jesus appear through this explosion of light that broke open the heavens on a big, thick, and massive wood-looking cross.

Interpretation

Zechariah 12:10 says:

> And they shall look upon me whom they have pierced, and they shall mourn for him, as one mourneth for his only son, and shall be in bitterness for him, as one that is in bitterness for his firstborn.

Dream

The cross had a brownish color with white streaks in the wood. The wooden cross seemed very heavy and massive. I saw His entire beautiful body. His head was leaning to His right shoulder, and He had a wreath platted around His head.

His Second Coming

Interpretation

The wreath seen here can be found in John 19:2, where the Scripture says the soldiers platted a crown of thorns, put it on His head, and put on Him a purple robe. Verse 5 says Jesus came forth, wearing the crown of thorns and the purple robe. Verse 6 says that when the chief priest and elders saw Him, they cried out, saying, "Crucify him, crucify him."

Dream

At the foot of the cross, there was another cross, and the body of Jesus was also on it. I saw the crucifixion twice. The sky lighted up brightly with His presence.

Interpretation

Seeing a double crucifixion of Jesus Christ is indeed a sign. Jesus declares:

And then shall appear the sign of the Son of man in heaven.

—Matthew 24:30

The double crucifixion is a sign and holds the key to the entire vision as it reveals the mystery concerning Jesus Christ's Second Coming.

The Revelation of the mystery of the doubled crucifixion is found in Genesis 41.

In Genesis 41, the Scripture speaks of Pharaoh having the same dream twice. He saw seven years of famine in one dream, then seven years of plenty in another. And it came to pass that in the morning, his spirit was troubled. Then he sent for the wise men and magicians to interpret, but none could interpret. Joseph was called in from the dungeon to interpret his dream. This is the interpretation that Joseph gave to Pharaoh.

In Genesis 41:25, Joseph said to Pharaoh, "The dream of Pharaoh is one: God hath showed Pharaoh what he is about to do."

In verse 28, Joseph said, "This is the thing which I have spoken unto Pharaoh: What God is about to do he showeth unto Pharaoh."

In verse 32, Joseph said, "And for that, the dream was doubled unto Pharaoh twice; it is because God establishes the thing, and God will shortly bring it to pass."

The prophetic vision of the doubled crucifixion of Jesus Christ means what God is about to do on the earth; He has shown it to me. It also means because the dream was doubled unto me (double crucifixion), God establishes it, and God shall shortly bring it to pass.

Jesus Christ, the righteous, the Son of the Living God, Savior of the world, is about to appear on His earth for the second time. The Scripture says that unto them that look for Him shall He appear the second time without sin unto salvation as King of kings and Lord of lords. And yes, in the Scriptures, He said that no man knows the day or the hour when He shall be appearing; only His Father in heaven. So, He admonishes us to be on the watch (Matt. 24).

Dream

We were all looking at the different animal shapes in the sky when we saw Christ appear in all of His glory.

Interpretation

The Scripture says in Revelation 1:7–8:

Behold, he cometh with clouds; and every eye shall see him, and they also which pierced him: and all kindreds of the earth shall wail because of him. Even so, Amen. I am Alpha and Omega, the beginning and the ending, saith the

His Second Coming

Lord, which is, and which was, and which is to come, the Almighty.

Dream

I turned to them and said, "Now, you believe me about seeing things in the sky? See..." I was referring to the Lord making His appearance. I moved away from the window because this was it to me—the coming of the Lord. Everything seemed so real! I exalt Your name, Lord. I glorify Your name. I magnify Your name. Thank You, Jesus!

Interpretation

James 5:7–8 says:

Be patient, therefore, brethren, unto the coming of the Lord. Behold, the husbandman waiteth for the precious fruit of the earth, and hath long patience for it, until he receives the early and latter rain. Be ye also patient; establish your hearts: for the coming of the Lord draweth nigh.

Dream

I went to a table in the house and stood still, listening to hear the Lord Jesus shout as if to say, "The God of the universe is here; no more time for man!" I knew in my spirit that there would be the sound of a trumpet! The glory of His presence then hit the lights that were in the house, and the place went into total darkness, cutting the power in the house, and I stiffened! I somehow knew that the whole world was in darkness! At this point, I curled over with my head down and my eyes tightly shut.

Interpretation

Second Thessalonians 1:7–10 says:

And to you who are troubled rest with us, when the Lord Jesus shall be revealed from heaven with his mighty angels, In flaming fire taking vengeance on them that know not God, and that obey not the gospel of our Lord Jesus Christ: Who shall be punished with everlasting destruction from the presence of the Lord, and from the glory of his power; When he shall come to be glorified in his saints, and to be admired in all them that believe (because our testimony among you was believed) in that day.

Dream

I then heard the thunder roll... and I stopped my breath and stiffened while clenching my fist, saying to myself, "This is it! This is it!" Thinking to myself that the great and final day is here, standing still while listening out for the Lord to make His shout!

Interpretation

The Word of the living God says:

For the Lord himself shall descend from heaven with a shout, with the voice of the archangel, and with the trump of God: and the dead in Christ shall rise first: Then we which are alive and remain shall be caught up together with them in the clouds, to meet the Lord in the air: and so shall we ever be with the Lord. Wherefore comfort one another with these words.

—1 Thessalonians 4:16–18

Hear, ye deaf; and look, ye blind, that ye may see Who among you will give ear to this? Who will hearken and hear for the time to come?

—Isaiah 42:18, 23

Dream

His Second Coming

The moment and the feeling were so intense as I stood there. There was a feeling of bitterness and doom!

Interpretation

Matthew 24:30 tells us that all the tribes of the earth will mourn when they see the Son of Man coming in the clouds of heaven with power and great glory.

Zechariah 12: 9-10 tells us that there will be bitterness for Jesus as one that is in bitterness for his firstborn when they look upon whom they have pierced. On that day, the Scripture says, there shall be a great mourning in Jerusalem.

Dream

There was a feeling that time, as we know it, has finally ended! No more time for man on Earth.

Interpretation

I believe the whole dream or vision is based upon the conclusion of what John saw. The destiny of man, the finality on earth as man knows it, the end of time!

Listen to what John saw in Revelation 10:4–7:

> When the seven thunders had uttered their voices, I was about to write: and I heard a voice from heaven saying unto me, Seal up those things which the seven thunders uttered, and write them not. And the angel which I saw stand upon the sea and the earth lifted his hand to heaven, And sware by him that liveth forever and ever, who created heaven, and the things that therein are, and the earth, and the things that therein are, and the sea, and the things which are therein, that there should be time no longer:

But in the days of the voice of the seventh angel, when he shall begin to sound, the mystery of God should be finished, as he hath declared to his servants and prophets.

Dream

As I stood there trembling with my fists closed and my back bent, tensely waiting for the Lord to shout and make His announcement to earth, nothing seemed to happen. I was taken into a second dream.

In this second dream, I was taken to a church. In this church, there was division in it. The pastor was preaching, but no one was listening. Things were contrary in the church. On one side of the church, they were selling food.

Interpretation

Jesus went into the temple, and began to cast out them that sold and bought in the temple, and overthrew the tables of the moneychangers, and the seats of them that sold doves; And would not suffer that any man should carry any vessel through the temple. And he taught, saying unto them, Is it not written, My house shall be called of all nations the house of prayer? But ye have made it a den of thieves.

—Mark 11:17

Dream

After entering this church, I brought peace and unity through worship. Then I woke up.

Interpretation

The Word of God says the Father is seeking true worshipers. This can be found in John 4:23–24. The Bible says:

But the hour cometh, and now is, when the true worshipers shall worship the Father in spirit and in truth: for the Father

His Second Coming

seeketh such to worship him. God is a Spirit: and they that worship him must worship him in spirit and in truth.

Comment

Yes, such a time is coming when there will be time no more, and the mysteries of God will be finished, just as He declared to His servants and prophets through the Holy War of God. Yes, indeed, the Bible is true. The Word of God is true and faithful. The end is fast approaching!

Jesus concludes in His Word by saying in Revelation 22:12–17:

> Behold, I come quickly; and my reward is with me, to give every man according as his work shall be. I am Alpha and Omega, the beginning and the end, the first and the last. Blessed are they that do his commandments, that they may have right to the tree of life, and may enter in through the gates into the city. For without are dogs, and sorcerers, and whoremongers, and murderers, and idolaters, and whosoever loveth and maketh a lie.
>
> I, Jesus have sent mine angel to testify unto you these things in the churches. I am the root and the offspring of David and the bright and morning star. And the Spirit and the bride say, Come. And let him that heareth say, Come. And let him that is athirst come. And whosoever will, let him take the water of life freely.

The grace of our Lord Jesus Christ, God's love, and the Holy Ghost's communion be with you all. Amen.

Dr. Marlene Brown

Chapter 9
Visions and Dreams for Men of Old

Jesus Christ, the same yesterday, today, and forever.

—Hebrews 13:8

I have several reasons for interpreting these dreams with the Bible, the Holy Word of God. If we look back even to the beginning of time in the Word of God, we will see that God has been visiting man through many visions and dreams and has been revealing Himself to them, even before the time of Joseph and Daniel.

We will look at God's handiwork within these individual lives as God spoke to them and began to show Himself strong through visions, dreams, and His spoken word. I believe the Lord Jesus reminds us that God is the same yesterday, today, and forever, as He only wants to find a man to prove himself strong within the earth.

Let us first have a look at the life of Abraham. For many years, the Word of the Lord came to Abraham when his name was still Abram. The Lord then gave Abram his first visitation in a vision. As we read Genesis 15:1—4, the Scripture says:

> After these things, the Word of the Lord came unto Abram in a vision, saying, Fear not, Abram: I am thy shield, and thy exceeding great reward. And Abram said, Lord God, what wilt thou give me, seeing I go childless, and the steward of my house is Eliezer of Damascus? And Abram

His Second Coming

said, Behold, to me thou hast given no seed: and, lo, one born is in my house is mine, heir.

And behold the Word of the Lord came to him, saying, This shall not be thine heir; but he that shall come forth out of thine own bowels shall be thine heir.

In verse 12, the Scriptures tell us of Abram having a great deep sleep. The Scriptures say that when the sun was going down, a deep sleep fell upon Abram: "and, lo, an horror of great darkness fell upon him. And he said unto Abram, know of a surety that thy seed shall be a stranger in a land that is not theirs, and shall serve them: and they shall afflict them four hundred years" (Gen. 15:12–13).

Then we read of Jacob dreaming dreams in Genesis 28:11–15. The Scripture says:

And he lighted upon a certain place, and tarried there all night, because the sun was set; and he took of the stones of that place, and put them for his pillows, and lay down in that place to sleep. And he dreamed, and behold a ladder set up on the earth, and the top of it reached to heaven: and behold the angels of God ascending and descending on it. And, behold, the Lord stood above it, and said, I am the Lord God of Abraham thy father, and the God of Isaac: the land whereon thou liest, to thee will I give it, and to thy seed; And thy seed shall be as the dust of the earth, and thou shalt spread abroad to the west, and to the east, and to the north, and to the south: and in thee and in thy seed shall all the families of the earth be blessed. And, behold, I am with thee and will keep thee in all places whither thou goest, and will bring thee again into this land; for I will not leave thee until I have done that which I have spoken to thee of.

The Scripture says Joseph awoke out of his sleep, and he said, "Surely the Lord is in this place, and I knew it not."

From Jacob's lineage, we read of Joseph, the son of his old age. Genesis 37:5 says that Joseph dreamed a dream, "and he told it his brethren: and they hated him yet the more." In verse 9, the Scripture says he dreamed yet another dream, told it to his brethren, and said, "Behold, I have dreamed a dream more; and, behold, the sun and the moon and the eleven stars made obeisance to me." It is important to note that every vision and dream that the Lord God gave to man has come to pass. Every vision and dream that is from heaven will shortly come to pass. Not only was Joseph gifted with visions and dreams, but the Lord also anointed him with the interpretation of dreams.

In chapter 41 of Genesis, Pharaoh has a dream and awakens from that dream; then, he falls asleep again and dreams a second time. Then, Pharaoh again realizes that it was another dream. And it came to pass that Joseph was called in to interpret Pharaoh's dream. Then Joseph says to him in verse 25: "The dream of Pharaoh is one: God hath showed Pharaoh what he is about to do." Joseph begins to interpret the dream to Pharaoh. Joseph explains to Pharaoh, saying, "Because the dream was doubled unto Pharaoh twice; it is because God establishes the thing, and God will shortly bring it to pass."

The visions, dreams, and interpretations continue in the book of Daniel. The Scripture declares: "In the second year of the reign of Nebuchadnezzar, Nebuchadnezzar dreamed dreams, wherewith his spirit was troubled, and his sleep brake from him" (Dan. 2:1). In Daniel 2, we read of Daniel seeking the Lord to interpret Nebuchadnezzar's dream after the magicians, astrologers, sorcerers, and Chaldeans of the court could neither reveal the dream to the king nor interpret the dream.

Then, the secret was revealed to Daniel as a vision of the night. So, Daniel blessed the God of heaven. Then Daniel answered and said:

> Daniel answered and said, Blessed be the name of God forever and ever: for wisdom and might are his: And he

His Second Coming

changeth the times and the seasons: he removeth kings, and setteth up kings: he giveth wisdom unto the wise, and knowledge to them that know understanding: He revealeth the deep and secret things: he knoweth what is in the darkness, and the light dwelleth with him. I thank thee, and praise thee, O thou God of my fathers, who hast given me wisdom and might, and hast made known unto me now what we desired of thee: for thou hast now made known unto us the king's matter.

—Daniel 2:20–23

As Daniel revealed the vision to the king, the king answered unto Daniel and said:

Of a truth, it is, that your God is a God of gods, and a Lord of kings, and a revealer of secrets, seeing thou couldest reveal this secret.

—Daniel 2:47

Yes, he is the same God yesterday, today, and forever. He still speaks to men through visions and dreams, and I am happy to be one of his dreamers. So, I go directly to God for the interpretations of His Word to hear what the Spirit of the Lord is saying to the church. The interpretations can be found in the Living Word of God line upon line and precept upon precept so that you will be strengthened in your faith and be filled with might in the inner man; you, the body of Christ, will be greatly encouraged to live the Christian life and be ready for His Second Coming.

Part II
Walking in the Power of Salvation

Dr. Marlene Brown

Chapter 10
The Lord's Work

Then He said to them, "The harvest truly is great, but the laborers are few; therefore pray the Lord of the harvest to send out laborers into His harvest.

—*Luke 10:2*

Yes, the Lord Jesus has called us to do His work. He said in His Word that the field is ripe for harvest, but His laborers are few. According to my visions/dreams, Jesus says, "Yes, I was crucified; yes, I laid down my life 2,000 years ago for you; but look, I have conquered death and hell. I am alive! Behold, I live forevermore!" I believe the Lord is saying, "Go tell my people that my Word is established, and that which I have promised shall shortly come to pass! I have promised that if I go, I will come again and receive you unto myself that you will be where I am there. I have asked the Father for you to behold my glory and for you to be with me where I am. Yes, let the people know that I am Lord! I will return as King of kings and Lord of lords!"

Jesus Christ, the healer from Galilee, came over 2,000 years ago in the form of a man as our Savior and Messiah to bear your sins and my sins on Calvary's cross so that through His blood, men could be saved. Next time, He will return not as Savior but as King of kings and Lord of lords. The last or final days are here! Therefore, be ready to meet Him—His coming at hand. "For though I preach the gospel, I have nothing to glory of for necessity is laid upon me; yea, woe is unto me, if I preach not the gospel!" (1 Cor. 9:16). Jesus pointed out in His Word that "whosoever therefore shall confess me before men, him will I confess also before my Father which is in heaven. But whosoever shall deny me before men, him will I also deny before my Father which is in heaven" (Matt. 10:32–33). I had a vision recently while I was lying on my sofa. I believe it was an open vision. I was lying on my back looking toward heaven when I saw the sky become a scroll with lots of writing. The writing kept going upward, fading away like writing on a computer screen. I could not read the writing very fast from where I lay. However, I knew within my spirit that Jesus was telling me in writing that He was coming soon. In my vision, I turned to my neighbor to tell him what the writings were saying—that Jesus says He is coming soon. Yes, it is all about confessing Christ, not being ashamed of Him, and letting people know He is coming again, just like he promised.

I thank the Most High God, the God of the universe, for commissioning me as one of the many disciples of His Word to preach and teach and be an example of who He is through my life and through this book.

God is real, He is excellent, He is mighty, and He will be coming again to judge the world with righteousness. He will be coming again with power and great glory. His coming is much closer than we think! Who shall be able to stand the great and terrible day of the Lord? Second Corinthians 5:11 says, "Knowing, therefore, the terror of the Lord, we persuade men." However, never forget his goodness. The day of salvation is now! Now is the acceptable time. Now is the day of salvation. He loves you with an everlasting love. It is not His will for any to perish but for all to have everlasting life. However, time is running out much faster than you think. Do not let "too late!" be your cry.

The Lord is good; He is full of compassion and tender mercy. His love toward us surpasses all wisdom and understanding. Yet, though He is full of love, compassion, and tender mercies, He is a jealous God. He is jealous when we love other things above Him, love our very life more than Him, or even fail to pick up our cross to follow Him. He tells us that if we pick up our cross to follow Him and lose our lives in the process, we should not worry. We are guaranteed eternal life, and not only eternal life but also a crown of righteousness awaits us. This He promises in Revelation 2:10–11:

> Fear none of those things which thou shalt suffer: behold, the devil shall cast some of you into prison, that ye may be tried; and ye shall have tribulation ten days: be thou faithful unto death, and I will give thee a crown of life. He that hath an ear, let him hear what the Spirit saith unto the churches; He that overcometh shall not be hurt of the second death.

For the Scripture says in John 3:16–17:

> For God so loved the world, that he gave his only begotten Son, that whosoever believeth in him should not perish, but have everlasting life. For God sent not his Son into the world to condemn the world; but that the world through him might be saved.

This is the great, abundant love that God has for you. He sent His only Son to die for your sins, whatever sins they might be so that through His blood, you can have forgiveness of your sins. However, when our sins are forgiven, Jesus Christ is saying, "Pick up your cross and follow Me if you want to inherit eternal life," according to Matthew 10:38–39:

> And he that taketh not his cross, and followeth after me, is not worthy of me. He that findeth his life shall lose it; and he that loseth his life for my sake shall find it.

Many scientists today and many movie stars are seeking a solution for eternal life. They spend billions of dollars on different kinds of experiments and keep trying other products. They want to discover the fountain of youth. However, the Bible says that dust you are, and to dust, you shall return. For the children of God, however (that is, the righteous), Jesus Christ gave us the formula for receiving eternal life. In Luke 10:25–28, we read about a lawyer and

Mosaic Law teacher who wanted to test the Lord concerning eternal life. He questioned Christ thoroughly, saying:

> Master, what shall I do to inherit eternal life? He said unto him, What is written in the law? How readest thou? And he answering said; Thou shalt love the Lord thy God with all thy heart, and with all thy soul, and with all thy strength, and with all thy mind; and thy neighbour as thyself. And he said unto him, Thou hast answered right: this do, and thou shalt live.

In Mark 10:17–27, another formula is given:

> And when he was gone forth into the way, there came one running, and kneeled to him, and asked him, Good Master, what shall I do that I may inherit eternal life? And Jesus said unto him, Why callest thou me good? There is none good but one, that is, God. Thou knowest the commandments, Do not commit adultery, Do not kill, Do not steal, Do not bear false witness, Defraud not, Honour thy father and mother. And he answered and said unto him, Master, all these have I observed from my youth.
>
> Then Jesus beholding him, loved him and said unto him, One thing thou lackest: go thy way, sell whatsoever thou hast, and give to the poor, and thou shalt have treasure in heaven: and come, take up the cross, and follow me. And he was sad at that saying and went away grieved: for he had great possessions.
>
> And Jesus looked round about, and saith unto his disciples, How hardly shall they that have riches enter into the kingdom of God! And the disciples were astonished at His Words. But Jesus answereth again, and saith unto them, Children, how hard is it for them that trust in riches to enter into the kingdom of God!

It is easier for a camel to go through the eye of a needle than for a rich man to enter into the kingdom of God. And they were astonished out of measure, saying among themselves, Who then can be saved?

And Jesus looking upon them saith, With men it is impossible, but not with God: for with God all things are possible.

There are so many formulas in the Scriptures for eternal life.

The God of the universe loves you so much that He wants to give you eternal life. Man was made for this purpose until Satan came and deceived Adam and Eve in the Garden of Eden, which resulted in their disobedience to God. Their disobedience brought forth sin, which resulted in spiritual and physical death. They were also driven out from the Garden of Eden, which had the Tree of Life.

The God of the universe hates wickedness; He hates sin. For this reason, He destroyed the world once before with water. Genesis 6:5–7 tells us:

> And God saw that the wickedness of man was great in the earth and that every imagination of the thoughts of his heart was only evil continually. And it repented the Lord that he had made man on the earth, and it grieved him at his heart. And the Lord said, I will destroy man whom I have created from the face of the earth; both man, and beast, and the creeping thing, and the fowls of the air; for it repenteth me that I have made them.

When the Lord God of the universe said it repenteth Him that He made man, He meant that He was grieved. He meant that He was sorry that He made us because of our wickedness. The Hebrew word for *repent* is *nacham*, which is pronounced *naw-kham'*. This means "to be sorry or to regret."

His Second Coming

The Bible points out that God did not destroy the whole earth because Noah and his three sons found grace in the sight of God. The Bible said that Noah was a just man and perfected in his generation. His three sons were Shem, Ham, and Japheth. The earth, however, was corrupt before God and full of violence. When God looked down upon the earth, He saw that the earth was full of violence and was corrupt! Every soul other than Noah and his family had corrupted itself before God.

God then said to Noah, "The end of all flesh is come before Me; for the earth is filled with violence through them; and, behold, I will destroy them with the earth."

In today's society, we see how the earth is getting more and more corrupt, with violence and sodomy on every hand. Many people are saying, however, that God is a God of love and that He would not destroy us. What they fail to realize is that our God is holy! He is the holiest of holies. He cannot bear to look on sin. Habakkuk 1:13 says God's eyes are too pure to behold evil. This is the very reason why He could not look at His own Son when He became a curse with your sins and mine.

The Bible says Jesus became sin itself for us so that we can become the righteousness of God in Him (2 Corinthians 5:21). When Jesus was covered in sin, for the first time, He felt the rejection of His Father. For the first time, He felt what it was like to be separated from His Holy God due to the curse of sin. Christ has redeemed us from the curse of the law, being made a curse for us: For it is written, cursed is everyone who hangs on a tree (Galatians 3:13). So, He cried out on the cross, "My God, My God, why have you forsaken me?" So, if the God of the universe rejected His own Son because of sin, what will He do to us? He is a just God, and He is a holy God. The Word of God says in Jeremiah 9:24:

> But let him that glorieth glory in this, that he understandeth and knoweth me, that I am the Lord which exercise

lovingkindness, judgment, and righteousness, in the earth: for in these things I delight, saith the Lord.

The God of the universe knew that man needed a Savior! He also knew that the blood of bulls and goats that had been sacrificed under Mosaic law could no longer be offered as a sacrifice for sin. The question is, why not? The answer is that it could not get rid of the sins of the people once and for all. The sacrifices that kept happening year after year by the priest for himself and the people could not make man righteous. If they could, then they would have ceased to be offered, and the high priest and the people would have no more consciousness of sin. However, in those sacrifices, there was always a remembrance of sin made year after year (Heb. 10:1-4). The significance of the blood is for the forgiveness of sins. "And almost all things are by the law purged with blood; and without shedding of blood is no remission [or forgiveness]" (Heb. 9:22).

The God of the universe needed blood that was spotless and without blemish. He was tired of burnt offerings to purify the flesh; He needed one sacrifice—a Lamb whose blood was clean enough, pure enough, and without spots or blemish, to take away the world's sin once and for all. Hebrews 10:6 tells us, "In burnt offerings and sacrifices for sin thou hast had no pleasure." For this reason, God sent His son. Only the blood of His son is pure and clean enough to take away the sins of the entire world. Jesus would be the precious Lamb that would take away the sins of the world according to John 1:29:

> The next day, John seeth Jesus coming unto him, and saith, Behold the Lamb of God, which taketh away the sin of the world.

When Jesus came into the world and was crucified on the cross, He took on your sins and my sins—every sin that man can think of, has done, and will do. Jesus became a curse as he hung on the tree with our sins. His heavenly Father, the God of the universe, could not look on His Son. He turned away from him as His eyes were too

His Second Coming

holy to look upon sin. The spotless Lamb of God was so filthy with our sins that His heavenly Father punished Him. Yes, God punished Jesus for our sins. For the first time, Jesus knew separation from God. The emptiness, the loneliness, the bitterness, the rage, the anger— all that sin depicted—and His Father turned His back on Him. Habakkuk 1:13 says, "For the eyes of God are too pure to behold evil." So how could this Holy God look upon His beloved Son who became sinned? He had to turn away from Him. Jesus paid the penalty for sins and appeased the wrath of God towards us! Isaiah 53:11 says, "He shall see of the travail of his soul, and shall be satisfied: by his knowledge shall my righteous servant justify many; for he shall bear their iniquities."

Matthew 27:46 tells us that Jesus cried out with a loud voice, saying, "Eli, El, lama sabachthani?" That is to say, "My God, my God, why hast thou forsaken me?" Yes, at that moment, He was now bearing your sins and mine. At that moment, the work was accomplished! For shortly after, Jesus cried, "It is finished!" as it is written in John 19:30. He had completed the work that His Father had sent Him to do. He had paid the price for the sin of man. He had made an atonement for sin by the shedding of His blood. Man is now redeemed. Man is now reconciled to the Father.

When Jesus went to the cross, He paid the total price for your sins and my sins, whatever they might be, so that the world through Him might be saved!

> For God so loved the world, that he gave his only begotten Son, that whosoever believeth in him should not perish, but have everlasting life. For God sent not his Son into the world to condemn the world; but that the world through him might be saved.
>
> —John 3:16–17

Dr. Marlene Brown

Chapter 11
Jesus Christ Reigns

That at the name of Jesus every knee should bow, of things in heaven, and things in earth, and things under the earth;

—Philippians 2:10

It is my heart's desire for everyone to get to know the sweetness of God's love and how Jesus can take the vilest sinner, wash him in His own blood, and make him into a new creature, spiritually born again.

He makes us free from the fears of tomorrow, the guilt of our past, and any bondage or shackles that had us captive, setting us free.

I was in a sinful state when I met Jesus. He came into my heart, soul, mind, and body. He cleansed my soul from all unrighteousness and made my being clean and pure enough to see His glory (the pure in heart shall see God). This same Jesus can visit your life and make you clean. He will visit you as He visited me if only you ask Him to cleanse you from all unrighteousness and wash you in His blood, making your heart circumcised before Him.

I know many people worship their own god or images, but I can tell you there is only one God: The God of the universe. He is the true and living God. One does not need to worship other gods that do not speak or hear. This is how the psalmist describes it.

> Wherefore should the heathen say, Where is now their God? But our God is in the heavens: he hath done whatsoever he hath pleased. Their idols are silver and gold, the work of men's hands. They have mouths, but they

His Second Coming

speak not: eyes have they, but they see not: They have ears, but they hear not: noses have they, but they smell not: They have hands, but they handle not: feet have they, but they walk not: neither speak they through their throat. They that make them are like unto them; so is every one that trusteth in them.

—Psalm 115:2–8

My God, the true and living God, sent His Son into the world to be crucified for your sins and mine, and the Son died and rose again after three days, buried in the grave. Yes, Jesus Christ lives! My eyes have seen His glory! He reigns forevermore! I was not there 2,000 years ago when He was crucified and rose again, but in the year 2000, he visited me several times over. I was not there when they nailed Him to the cross, but my eyes have seen Him on the cross in the heavens. I was not there when He was on earth, but He visited me in the sky many times with one of His many angels. Yes, indeed, Jesus Christ lives; He reigns; He conquers death and hell! He lives forevermore. He is the King of all kings and the Lord of all lords! There will never be an end to His dominion!

The God you worship today, has He risen from the dead? Is He still in the grave waiting for the Day of Judgment? My God, who is my Savior, lives! He has the power over death, and He has conquered the grave. He also has the keys to death and hell! In Revelation 1:18, Jesus says to John:

> I am he that liveth, and was dead; and, behold, I am alive forever more, Amen; and have the keys of hell and of death.

If you are wondering today what my vision/dream means, it simply means that the coming of the Lord is at hand. It simply means that redemption draweth nigh. It means that this is the time for souls that are sleeping to wake up and those that are spiritually dead to become alive unto righteousness.

I now see clearly that the coming of the Lord is so close; I can feel it in my being. The rapture of the church is so close. Soon after the church's rapture, the world will face the Great Tribulation; that is when the mark of the beast will be branded on people, and people will not be able to buy or sell unless they have this mark on their right hand or their forehead.

I had a dream recently where I saw people buying loaves of bread in long lines. These same people were all bundled together on the ground in a marketplace where they had been sleeping and waiting since the night before. I thought they were market people waiting to sell their food in the morning. However, to my amazement, these same people, mostly women, got up and began to form long lines buying loaves of bread. Some people bought seven loaves! What is this vision saying? Is it prophetic in nature? It sure is! According to the Word of God, I truly believe what will be coming on the earth will be much worse than forming long lines to buy bread. The Bible tells us of a time that will be coming on earth when there will be a great food shortage, even wheat to make bread, which will result in great famine and pestilence! I believe the Lord, in his goodness, only showed me a bird's eye view of what the coming days will be like.

Interpretation of People Forming Long Lines to Buy Bread

I believe this is the interpretation of what I saw. It is taken from Revelation 6:5–8. The Scripture says:

> And when he had opened the third seal, I heard the third beast say, Come and see. And I beheld, and lo a black horse; [the black horse symbolizes famine] and he that sat on him had a pair of balances in his hand. And I heard a voice in the midst of the four beasts say, ***A measure of wheat for a penny***, and three measures of barley for a penny; and see thou hurt not the oil and the wine. And when he had opened the fourth seal, I heard the voice of the fourth beast say, Come and see. And I looked, and behold a pale horse: and his name that sat on him was Death, and Hell followed with

His Second Coming

him. And power was given unto them over the fourth part of the earth, to kill with sword, and with hunger, and with death, and with the beasts of the earth.

John heard a voice say, *"A measure of wheat for a penny!"* This is speaking about massive food shortages and inflated prices to at least ten times their normal level. I believe we are leading up to that time.

Pretty soon, there will be a global recession—this recession will be so great that economists will have no answer, resulting in massive unemployment. Their economic tools will not work as it will be unprecedented, and it will be worldwide! The global financial crisis will make it even more devastating for the poor and developing nations to access any finances needed. This will undoubtedly result in devastating famine and pestilence worldwide, leading to economic catastrophe. This global crisis will call for a global solution. The world's nations will then call in their heads from the G8 Summit, central bank leaders and representatives from the EU and IMF, and other financial experts to come together to solve this economic crisis, but none will be able to come up with a viable solution. This will call for a global currency so that the dollar, the pound, the euro, and all other national currencies will be made into one—a currency for a cashless society where only microchips will be acceptable legal tender. This will lead to a One World Government, which will lead to the Antichrist on earth. The nations will be in such a panic that they will eagerly agree to have one Commander-in-Chief, just as in a war, which will cause the Antichrist to arrive on the scene. When this Antichrist comes on the stage, he will cause many to be deceived; they will believe that he has the power to restore peace and hope and that he has the solution to fix the economy by having people take his mark on their forehead or their right hand to buy and sell. This number will be 666. The Bible says it is the number of man. This is what the Bible has to say about the Antichrist in Revelation 13:13-18:

And he doeth great wonders, so that he maketh fire come down from heaven on the earth in the sight of men, And deceiveth them that dwell on the earth by the means of those miracles which he had power to do in the sight of the beast; saying to them that dwell on the earth, that they should make an image to the beast, which had the wound by a sword, and did live. And he had power to give life unto the image of the beast that the image of the beast should both speak, and cause that as many as would not worship the image of the beast should be killed. And he causeth all, both small and great, rich and poor, free and bond, to receive a mark in their right hand, or in their foreheads: And that no man might buy or sell, save he that had the mark, or the name of the beast, or the number of his name. Here is wisdom. Let him that hath understanding count the number of the beast: for it is the number of a man, and his number is Six hundred threescore and six.

If, within my dream, people were forming long lines to buy bread, how much more terrible would it be when a man cannot buy or sell without this mark? Listen to the prophetic dream that the Lord Jesus gave me on June 4, 2001, in the next chapter.

His Second Coming

Chapter 12
Prophetic Revelation Given of 666

My eleventh heavenly dream: a dream that I, Marlene, saw on Monday, June 4, 2000.

And that no man might buy or sell, save he that had the mark, or the name of the beast, or the number of his name.

— Revelation 13:17

Before I share my dream with you, I would like to share with you the frame of mind that I was in. I got a powerful warning for Sharon, and I heard the voice of God; that day, I could not contain myself. Days upon days, I kept reliving the whole experience of hearing the voice of God. You will read about this experience later on in this book. After leaving the church that Sunday evening, I began to speak to the Lord while driving my car. I said to Him: "Father, if you have any warning for me to tell anyone, or whatever you want me to do, I will do it no matter what. I will not disobey you like others . . ." My conversation with Him went like that. Monday morning, this was the vision/dream that I received.

I dreamed that I was in a room by myself. I was standing by the bed looking at an open Bible. The Bible was opened in Matthew, where you find the Scriptures written in red. As you all know, red lettering represents Jesus speaking. Suddenly, I noticed three powerful-looking locks about eighteen inches above the Bible on the bed. I stood there looking at the locks and at the Bible. The first and the third locks were closed. The middle lock was three-quarters closed. I heard a voice in the spirit within my dream that said to me that the locks represented the number 666. I remember saying to myself in the dream, "Why am I looking in Matthew for 666?"

I kept repeating this in my dream: "666?" Then, looking at the locks, I could see how they had the form of the number 666.

It was also revealed to me that when the middle lock closes, the time of 666 will be here.

I ran out of the room to call my sister and a few people to have them look at the locks above the Bible. However, when we came back to the room where the Bible and the locks were, the locks had disappeared, leaving the Bible!

I started to turn the pages of the Bible vigorously, searching for the locks, but I could not find them.

Then I woke up from this dream.

Does this mean that the rapture of the church is much closer than we think? It is said that the rapture of the church will take place before the Great Tribulation. More importantly, what does the Lord Jesus say about the number 666?

Revelation 14:9–11 says:

> And the third angel followed them, saying with a loud voice, If any man worships the beast and his image, and receives his mark in his forehead, or in his hand, The same shall drink of the wine of the wrath of God, which is poured out without mixture into the cup of his indignation; and he shall be tormented with fire and brimstone in the presence of the holy angels, and in the presence of the Lamb: And the smoke of their torment ascendeth up forever and ever:

His Second Coming

and they have no rest day nor night, who worship the beast and his image, and whosoever receiveth the mark of his name.

Thank God the church will be out of the world before that time comes, as God hath not appointed us to wrath, but to obtain salvation by our Lord Jesus Christ (1 Thess. 5:9). The word *wrath* in the Greek is *orge*, which means movement or agitation of the soul.

The Scripture says that Satan, however, will not be able to overcome everyone on the earth, and there will be those who do not take the mark and make it out of the great tribulation. John saw these saints and says in Revelation 15:2: "And I saw as it were a sea of glass mingled with fire; and them that had gotten the victory over the beast, and over his image, and over his mark, and over the number of his name, stand on the sea of glass, having the harps of God."

I believe it is God's heart for me to share these prophetic visions and dreams with the world to witness and testify to His people concerning Christ's Second Coming. So many people take the Second Coming of Christ as a myth, not reality.

The Lord is about to make His appearance. Are you ready for the Rapture to be with the Lord? Are you prepared to be at the marriage supper? Are you passionately looking for Him? This does not mean that we should stop living or wanting to be prosperous on earth; it does mean that we need to support the gospel financially like never before. Can you not discern the signs of the times?

Whether the coming of the Lord will be in the next ten, twenty, or even fifty years, or much sooner, I do not know. However, these prophetic visions tell me His church, His body, needs to be ready in case the end is near. As we all know, the Bible says, "Without holiness, no man shall see God."

Dr. Marlene Brown

May we all heed these prophetic visions and dreams as the peace of God keeps your hearts and minds through Christ Jesus our Lord, for the testimony of Jesus is the spirit of prophecy (Rev. 19:10).

The blessings of God be with you all. Amen.

His Second Coming

Chapter 13
My New Relationship with Jesus

Abide in me, and I in you. As the branch cannot bear fruit of itself, except it abide in the vine; no more can ye, except ye abide in me.

—John 15:4

It is a great honor and privilege for the Lord Jesus to entrust me with his Word and revelation of things to come. It is not by works, lest any man should boast, but the precious gift of God. My relationship with Christ is now on a personal level. It never ceases to amaze me how Jesus Christ left His throne in heaven and became poor so that we can become rich!

Yes, because of His love for mankind, He left His Father, the one true and living God, the Most High God, and came down to earth in the form of man; laid down His life and was crucified so that His blood can be used as an atonement for sin. His blood cleanses us from all unrighteousness so that we can become the righteousness of God in Him and be called the children of God and sons of God. Christ knew no sin, yet He made Himself sin because of His great and matchless love for us. Neither was there any guile in His mouth right to the end. By giving His life, He paid the price for our sins, and greater love than this has no man.

This revelation of truth allows me to talk to my heavenly Father regularly. I am living proof of how rich His blood is and how Christ's blood cleanses you from all unrighteousness, turning you into a new creature. Once, I was blind, but now I can see clearly. I now see the light of the world. The light of the world is Jesus. The veil has been removed from my eyes. If you should hear the voice of God speaking to your heart today through this book or another source, please let me encourage you not to harden your heart but to turn or return to Him and allow Him to take complete control of your life. Tomorrow is promised to no man. If it were possible to ask all the dead who died in sin whether they had known that they would die that day, they would have given their life to the Lord and worshiped Him while they were alive; I know the answer would be yes.

Once a man is placed in the grave, it is over until the Day of Judgment. There can be no more repentance from sin. The final step is to meet your Maker. The prayer that is being prayed at your funeral cannot save you. We need to accept Christ while we are alive so that we can have forgiveness of sin. The Bible says we were all born in sin because of one man, Adam, and through the grace of God, we can now have the forgiveness of sin through one man, Christ Jesus.

Since I was born again, my journey with the Lord has not been easy. Several times, I have come under attack by the enemy both in my daily life and in my dreams. In my dreams, I have seen Satan, the devil, as the dragon of whom Revelation speaks. Revelation 12:7–10 says:

> And there was war in heaven: Michael and his angels fought against the dragon, and the dragon fought and his angels, And prevailed not; neither was their place found any more in heaven. And the great dragon was cast out, that old serpent, called the Devil, and Satan, which deceiveth the whole world: he was cast out into the earth, and his angels were cast out with him. And I heard a loud voice saying in heaven, Now is come salvation, and strength, and the kingdom of our God, and the power of his Christ: for the accuser of our brethren is cast down, which accused them before our God day and night.

His Second Coming

This dragon was spitting fire out of his mouth at people as they tried to escape from him. I have also seen him as a fallen angel in the air. They looked like men (Satan's angels took on human form, says Genesis 6:2). They were trying to draw Christians through the power of their eyes to prevent these Christians from serving Christ so that these Christians would be in their group. They tried to pull me towards them through the power of their eyes. The only way we could defeat them was by joining hands with other Christians in a circle to form unity and strength and then deciding within ourselves that we would die for Christ. When we decided in the dream to join hands and stick together and purposed within our hearts to die for Christ, the fallen angels lost their power. No wonder Paul teaches us that we need to die to ourselves daily. Their power is in the flesh. Once we decide to die in the strongholds of the flesh and live for Christ, even if it costs our lives, their power is broken. For this reason, Jesus says we need to take up our cross to follow Him. Why? Because the Bible says, the devil goes around like a roaring lion seeking whom he may devour. These attacks are nothing new to the children of God. Jesus Himself was also attacked by this wicked enemy while He was fasting in the wilderness for forty days. The Scripture says that as Jesus was leaving the wilderness, weak and tired from lack of food, the devil tempted Him, as it is written in Luke 4.

I have also seen Satan wrestling me for the Bible. This dream I received in October 2009. We were actually standing before each other with our backs bent and the Bible on the floor, wrestling in the spirit for the Bible. After this dream, I understood the profound significance of making the Bible a part of my daily walk with the Lord. I understood that Satan plans to prevent us from reading God's Word because God's power is in His Word! All blessings and glory and prosperity are in His Word! The way to salvation is in the Bible and no other book! So, the Scripture says, "We wrestle not against flesh and blood, but against principalities and powers and rulers of this world" (Eph. 6:12).

So, let me encourage you to begin reading the Bible again this day. Let me encourage you to fight the strongholds of Satan that place busyness in your day to prevent you from reading God's Word. As Christians, we need to fight the good fight of faith and lay hold of eternal life (1 Timothy 6:12). The apostle Paul, through many conflicts, trials, and shipwrecks, declared, "I have fought a good fight, I have finished the race, I kept the faith (2 Timothy 4:7). It is essential to fight the issues that Satan placed before us. Satan placed us within a zone of busyness so that we neglect the word, prayer, and solitude before the Lord. It is essential to understand that it is in our quiet time with the Lord that the Holy Spirit begins to minister to us and reveal issues that need to have dwelt within our lives. The presence of the Lord also transforms us more into the image of Christ. His presence also strengthens us and helps us to remain steadfast and strong under trial. Blessed is the one who perseveres under trial (designed by temptations or afflictions) because, having stood the test, that person will receive the crown of life that the Lord has promised those who love him (James 1:12).

His Second Coming

Chapter 14
Holiness unto the Lord

Who shall ascend into the hill of the Lord? or who shall stand in his holy place? He that hath clean hands, and a pure heart; who hath not lifted up his soul unto vanity, nor sworn deceitfully.

—Psalm 24:3-4

We serve a mighty God! We serve a holy God! We serve a great God! We serve a God of love! We serve a jealous God! We serve a merciful God! Moreover, He says in His Word, "You must be Holy, for I am Holy." The Most High God should be worshiped in the beauty of holiness, spirit, and truth.

O come, let us sing unto the Lord: let us make a joyful noise to the rock of our salvation. Let us come before his presence with thanksgiving and make a joyful noise unto him with psalms. For the Lord is a great God and a great King above all gods. In his hand are the deep places of the earth: the strength of the hills is his also. The sea is his, and he made it: and his hands formed the dry land.

O come, let us worship and bow down: let us kneel before the Lord, our maker. For he is our God; we are the people of his pasture and the sheep of his hand. Today if ye will hear his voice, Harden not your heart, as in the provocation, and as in the day of temptation in the wilderness: When your fathers tempted me, proved me, and saw my work. Forty years long was I grieved with this generation, and said, It is a people that do err in their heart, and they have not known my ways: Unto whom I swear in my wrath that they should not enter into my rest.

—Psalm 95:1–11

O sing unto the Lord a new song: sing unto the Lord, all the earth. Sing unto the Lord, bless his name; shew forth his salvation from day to day. Declare his glory among the heathen, his wonders among all people. For the Lord is great and greatly to be praised: he is to be feared above all gods. For all the gods of the nations are idols: but the Lord made the heavens. Honor and majesty are before him: strength and beauty are in his sanctuary. Give unto the Lord, O ye kindreds of the people, give unto the Lord glory and strength. Give unto the Lord the glory due unto his name: bring an offering, and come into his courts. O worship the Lord in the beauty of holiness: fear before him, all the earth Let the field be joyful, and all that is therein: then shall all the trees of the wood rejoice Before the Lord: for he cometh, for he cometh to judge the earth: he shall judge the world with righteousness, and the people with his truth.

—Psalm 96:1–9, 11–13

The Lord reigneth; let the earth rejoice; let the multitude of isles be glad thereof. Clouds and darkness are round about him: righteousness and judgment are the habitations of his throne. A fire goeth before him and burneth up his enemies round about. His lightnings enlightened the world: the earth saw, and trembled. The hills melted like wax at the presence of the Lord, at the presence of the Lord of the whole earth. The heavens declare his righteousness, and all the people see his glory. Confounded be all they that serve graven images that boast themselves of idols: worship him, all ye gods Ye that love the Lord, hate evil: he preserveth

His Second Coming

the souls of his saints; he delivereth them out of the hand of the wicked. Light is sown for the righteous, and gladness for the upright in heart. Rejoice in the Lord, ye righteous; and give thanks at the remembrance of his holiness.

—Psalm 97:1–7, 10–12

O sing unto the Lord a new song; for he hath done marvelous things: his right hand, and his holy arm, hath gotten him the victory. The Lord hath made known his salvation: his righteousness hath he openly shewed in the sight of the heathen. He hath remembered his mercy and his truth toward the house of Israel: all the ends of the earth have seen the salvation of our God. Make a joyful noise unto the Lord, all the earth: make a loud noise, and rejoice, and sing praise. Sing unto the Lord with the harp; with the harp, and the voice of a psalm. With trumpets and sound of cornet make a joyful noise before the Lord, the King. Let the sea roar, and the fulness thereof; the world, and they that dwell therein. Let the floods clap their hands: let the hills be joyful together Before the Lord; for he cometh to judge the earth: with righteousness shall he judge the world, and people with equity.

—Psalm 98:1–9

The Lord reigneth; let the people tremble: he sitteth between the cherubims; let the earth be moved. The Lord is great in Zion, and he is high above all the people. Let them praise thy great and terrible name; for it is holy. Exalt ye the Lord our God, and worship at his footstool; for he is holy. Moses and Aaron among his priests, and Samuel among them that call upon his name; they called upon the Lord, and he answered them. He spake unto them in the cloudy pillar: they kept his testimonies and the ordinance that he gave them. Thou answered them, O Lord our God: thou wast a God that forgavest them, though thou tookest vengeance of their inventions. Exalt the Lord our God, and worship at his holy hill; for the Lord our God is holy.

—Psalm 99: 1–3, 5–9

When we were in the world of sin, we did things according to the world:

We danced according to the world. We sang according to the world, talked according to the world, and lived according to the world. Now, we are no longer children of the world but children of the Most High God, who is holy.

So then, if we are children of the heavenly Father, we should talk according to His Word, sing praises to His Name, walk according to His Word, and be holy as Christ is holy. If we give up this world of sin and begin to walk with Christ, we will gain so much, according to Revelation 21:6–8. It mentions that not only would we inherit all things, but we would also not experience the second death.

> And he said unto me: It is done. I am Alpha and Omega, the beginning and the end. I will give unto him that is athirst of the fountain of the water of life freely. He that overcometh shall inherit all things; and I will be his God, and he shall be my son. But the fearful, and unbelieving, and the abominable, and murderers, and whoremongers, and sorcerers, and idolaters, and all liars, shall have their part in the lake which burneth with fire and brimstone: which is the second death.

Let us, therefore, draw near to Him with a true and faithful heart and serve the Lord in the beauty of holiness, for the Lord comes to judge the earth with righteousness and the people with equity.

His Second Coming

Chapter 15
What Can I Do to Be Saved?

And saying, The time is fulfilled, and the kingdom of God is at hand: repent ye, and believe the gospel.

—Mark 1:15

The Lord wants you to repent. To repent means "to feel regret, to change one's mind about something; to change one's way of thinking." Return to the ways of the Lord, for the Scripture says in Isaiah 55:8,

"My thoughts are not your thoughts; neither are your ways my ways, saith the Lord." The Lord says He came not to call the righteous but sinners to repentance (Matt. 9:13). Luke 13:3 says, "Except ye repent, ye shall all likewise perish." Why choose to live in sin and die when we can have eternal life? The Word of God says, "The wages of sin is death, but the gift of God is eternal life through Jesus Christ our Lord" (Rom. 6:23). The pleasure of sin is only for a season, for but a short while. Jesus says that if you confess your sins, He is faithful and just to forgive you. Not only will He forgive you, but also cleanse you from all unrighteousness (1 John 1:9). The Scripture says that one may have a zeal of God but lack the righteousness of God, and in so doing, begin to establish one's own righteousness rather than submitting to the righteousness of God.

The Scripture says, "If thou shalt confess with thy mouth the Lord Jesus, and shalt believe in thine heart that God hath raised him from the dead, thou shalt be saved. For with the heart, man believeth unto righteousness, and with the mouth, confession is made unto salvation. For the Scripture saith, "Whosoever believeth on him shall not be ashamed" (Rom. 10:9–11). For whoever calls upon the name of the Lord shall be saved.

Seek God. Humble yourself and ask Jesus to forgive you of your sins. Jesus Christ paid the full price for them on a Roman cross almost 2,000 years ago. We all have sin. We are all guilty before God. Receive the gift of God today—His forgiveness and His unending love. The joy of being forgiven and in fellowship with God is deep and permanent, and there is none like it. It is joy unspeakable and full of glory; half has never been told.

The promises and gifts of God are endless. There are so many promises and gifts and so much grace and mercy with our Lord Jesus. Whatever you need in this life, Jesus said you could ask Him or the Father for it, and it will be given to you if you believe. The Word of God declares that His Word is truth and life, so we can put all confidence and trust in it. So, Jesus encourages us in Matthew 7:7–11:

> Ask, and it shall be given you; seek, and ye shall find; knock, and it shall be opened unto you: For everyone that asketh receiveth; and he that seeketh findeth; and to him that knocketh it shall be opened. Or what man is there of you, whom if his son ask for bread, will he give him a stone? Or if he ask for fish, will he give him a serpent? If ye then, being evil, know how to give good gifts unto your children, how much more shall your Father which is in heaven give good things to them that ask him?

The Good Lord wants to give you a beautiful gift today; He wants to make you free from sin. He said in His Word that the wages of sin is death, but the gift of God is eternal life through Jesus Christ our Lord (Rom. 6:23). God wants to give you eternal life! Jesus says in His Word, "In my Father's house are many mansions: if it were not so, I would have told you. I go to prepare a place for you" (John 14:2).

His Second Coming

I am now happy since I have given my life to the Lord Jesus and accepted His salvation. I have no more fear of dying or any other fear that the enemy would try to bring upon me. I know without a shadow of a doubt that when I die, I will go to the place that Christ prepared after He paid the penalty for my sins.

John, who is also our brother and companion in the tribulation and in the kingdom and patience of Jesus Christ, writes in Revelation 1:9–11 of this place that the Lord has gone to prepare. John says he was "in the Spirit on the Lord's day," on the isle of Patmos, for the Word of God and the testimony of Jesus Christ, when he saw this vision. He said he heard behind him a great voice, "as of a trumpet," which said, "I am Alpha and Omega, the first and the last," and, "What thou seest, write in a book and send it unto the seven churches which are in Asia" (Rev. 1:10–11). In Revelation 21:2–7, the prophet continues to say:

> And I, John saw the holy city, new Jerusalem, coming down from God out of heaven, prepared as a bride adorned for her husband. And I heard a great voice out of heaven saying, Behold, the tabernacle of God is with men, and he will dwell with them, and they shall be his people, and God himself shall be with them, and be their God. And God shall wipe away all tears from their eyes; and there shall be no more death, neither sorrow, nor crying, neither shall there be any more pain: for the former things are passed away. And he that sat upon the throne said, Behold, I make all things new. And he said unto me, Write: for these words are true and faithful. And he said unto me: It is done. I am Alpha and Omega, the beginning and the end. I will give unto him that is athirst of the fountain of the water of life freely. He that overcometh shall inherit all things, and I will be his God, and he shall be my son.

The Lord is faithful to His promises. The things of this world will dim and lose their value, and they are only for a short while. But there is a new world that awaits believers who are in Christ. Why not repent from your sins today and be baptized to receive the free gift of salvation? Invite Jesus Christ into your heart today. The Bible says there is no other name given under heaven whereby men can be saved, only the name of Jesus (Acts 4:12). At the name of Jesus, every knee shall bow, and every tongue shall confess that He is Lord! (Philippians 2:10-12)

Chapter 16
Sin and Its Origin

Wherefore, as by one man sin entered into the world, and death by sin; and so death passed upon all men, for that all have sinned:

—Romans 5:12

Sin is an offense or revolt against God. It is deliberate defiance, wickedness, or ungodliness. Sin came into the world because of one man's disobedience, whose name is Adam: And death by sin; and so, death passed upon all men, for that all have sinned. The Bible says that all have sinned and fall short of the glory of God.

In Genesis 2, the Scripture describes how man was formed from the dust of the ground, life was breathed into his nostrils, and he became a living soul. The Scripture goes on to tell us that God commanded the man: "Of the tree of the knowledge of good and evil, thou shalt not eat of it; for in the day that thou eatest thereof thou shalt surely die" (Gen. 2:17).

Genesis chapter 3 describes the event between a man and the devil, which allowed sin to be on earth today, causing us to be eternally separated from God and making us all sinners.

> Now the serpent was more subtle than any beast of the field which the Lord God had made. And he said unto the woman, Yea, hath God said, Ye shall not eat of every tree of the garden? And the woman said unto the serpent, We may eat of the fruit of the trees of the garden: But of the fruit of the tree which is in the midst of the garden, God

hath said, Ye shall not eat of it, neither shall ye touch it, lest ye die.

—Genesis 3:1–3

Now, the Scriptures declare that God commanded Adam not to eat the fruit and also not to touch the fruit of the tree in the midst of the garden, according to the words of Eve.

And the serpent said unto the woman, Ye shall not surely die: For God doth know that in the day ye eat thereof, then your eyes shall be opened, and ye shall be as gods, knowing good and evil.

—Genesis 3:4–5

I find this statement that Satan made to Eve very interesting. Was he trying to make the true and living God out to be a liar? Or was he trying to tell Eve that he had their interest at heart? That he loves them and wants the best for them? That they could trust him? No wonder the Lord says all liars shall have their part in the lake of fire. This is how the enemy works. He tries to persuade us from the truth in our minds, presenting a situation that seems like a better way out, but without showing us the end of it because the end is death. Jesus describes his character in John 8:44 and the character of anyone who serves him. Jesus said in His Word that if the Spirit of God does not dwell within you, then your father is the devil, and you will find yourself doing his works, which is the lust of the world. Jesus said that the devil was a murderer from the beginning and abode not in the truth because there is no truth in him. Jesus explains that when the devil speaks, he speaks of himself, for he is a liar and the father of lies. Even today, people choose to remain in sin rather than accept the gift of the true and living God. The Word of God says that God plans to bless and not harm you. However, people believe that if they should come to Christ, they will be poor and poverty-stricken. The enemy is still selling them lies, and they are still being deceived like Eve, believing that God is withholding from them and He does not want them to prosper. This is the stronghold that the enemy put on our minds from the beginning of time, and he is still playing head games today. But I am here to tell you that Jesus came to give you life and for you to have this abundant life right here on earth and eternal life in heaven.

The account in Genesis continues: "When the woman saw that the tree was good for food, and that it was pleasant to the eyes, and a tree to be desired to make one wise, she took of the fruit thereof, ate, and gave unto her husband with her; and he did eat. And their eyes were opened, and they knew that they were naked; they sewed fig leaves together and made themselves aprons." Here, I can see in the spirit the enemy laughing at God, believing that he had destroyed men with sin forever. He thought he had gotten back at God for throwing him out of heaven. He felt that he had made man disobedient to the Most High God forever, and there would be no way God would communicate with His children anymore because of sin in them. He thought that because of their disobedience, which caused them to sin, God would cut Himself off from His creation forever! In the same manner in which he was cast down due to sin in his heart. But Satan did not know of the master plan that God had for us from before the foundation of the world. He did not know that God would send forth his Son in the likeness of sinful flesh to redeem us from sin, to save mankind from their sins, and to reconcile us back to the Father. Blessings, glory, majesty, and power be unto the Most High God for this master plan. Amen. So, the Scriptures go on to tell us:

> And they heard the voice of the Lord God walking in the garden in the cool of the day: and Adam and his wife hid themselves from the presence of the Lord God amongst the trees of the garden. And the Lord God called unto Adam, and said unto him, Where art thou? And he said, I heard thy voice in the garden, and I was afraid, because I was naked; and I hid myself.

Dr. Marlene Brown

—Genesis 3:8–10

Now we see why the Scripture says disobedience is the spirit of witchcraft. We also see that when we are disobedient to the Highest God, it causes the spirit of fear to come upon us, and this fear breathes torment. For the first time, man has been fearful of facing Father God. The Scripture says that God has not given us that spirit of fear but one of love, power, and a sound mind. Not only does sin breathe fear, but it also brings with it nakedness. That holy blessed covering has been removed because of sin. Physically, he could see his nakedness.

The Scripture says in verse 21 that the Lord God made coats of skins and clothed them. The man now needs both physical and spiritual covering. In some churches, we still find women needing physical covering; this is even more prevalent in the entertainment industry, as their eyes have become blinded to sin. Many in the entertainment industry believe that the fewer clothes they wear, the better they will look and feel. What a lie Satan has sold them, and they buy it!

The Scripture continues: "So God said to them; 'Who told thee that thou wast naked? Hast thou has eaten of the tree, of which I commanded thee that thou shouldest not eat?'" (Gen. 3:11). I can sense the fury of God when He asks Adam this question:

> And the man said, The woman whom thou gavest to be with me, she gave me of the tree, and I did eat. And the Lord God said unto the woman: What is this that thou hast done? And the woman said: The serpent beguiled me, and I did eat.
>
> —Genesis 3:12–13

Here, we notice that no one is taking the blame for their disobedience toward God. Adam blames the woman God gave him, and the woman blames the serpent for deceiving her.

And the Lord God said unto the serpent, "Because thou hast done this, thou art cursed above all cattle, and every beast of the field; upon thy belly shalt thou go, and dust shalt thou eat all the days of thy life: And I will put enmity between thee and the woman, and between thy seed and her seed; it shall bruise thy head, and thou shalt bruise his heel." Unto the woman he said, "I will greatly multiply thy sorrow and thy conception; in sorrow thou shalt bring forth children; and thy desire shall be to thy husband, and he shall rule over thee." And unto Adam he said: "Because thou hast hearkened unto the voice of thy wife, and hast eaten of the tree, of which I commanded thee, saying, Thou shalt not eat of it: cursed is the ground for thy sake; in sorrow shalt thou eat of it all the days of thy life; Thorns also and thistles shall it bring forth to thee; and thou shalt eat herb of the field; In the sweat of thy face shalt thou eat bread, till thou return unto the ground; for out of it wast thou taken: for dust thou art, and unto dust shalt thou return."

—Genesis 3:14–19

Here, it is evident that the Most High God is furious with Adam because He had given Adam a specific command and expected him to be in total control and total obedience to Him, not to pass the blame onto anyone else.

Today, the Lord speaks to our hearts, and many of us still pass the blame onto others. We are still blaming our husbands or wives, our sons, our bosses, our mothers, our fathers, and our friends for keeping us from total obedience to God, but God is saying to us, "I gave you a specific command for you to be in total obedience to me through the blood of My Son Jesus Christ!"

The Bible goes on to say:

Behold, the man is become as one of us, to know good and evil: and now, lest he put forth his hand, and also take of the tree of life, and eat, and live forever: Therefore the Lord God sent him forth from the garden of Eden, to till the ground from whence he was taken. So he drove out the man; and he placed at the east of the garden of Eden Cherubims, and a flaming sword which turned every way, to keep the way of the tree of life.

—Genesis 3:22–24

Yes! They committed sin against the God of the universe by disobeying His Word, so when Eve conceived and brought forth children—and we are all her children—they were marked with sin, and because of sin, we die a spiritual and physical death. This was and still is the plan of Satan—to steal, kill, and destroy humanity. But today, we have good news! Jesus, the Son of the living God, came to earth to bring us life again—eternal and everlasting life. He said in His Word that He comes to bring us life and for us to have this life more abundantly (John 10:10). Jesus went so far as to lay down His life for us, His sheep. He has given us this new life in Him as the second Adam. The first Adam brought us death; the second Adam, Jesus Christ, now brings us life, reconciling us to the Father. Glory be to His holy name.

For as by one man's disobedience many were made sinners, so by the obedience of one shall many be made righteous. That as sin hath reigned unto death, even so, might grace reign through righteousness unto eternal life by Jesus Christ our Lord.

—Romans 5:19, 21

His Second Coming

Chapter 17
You Must Be Born Again

Jesus answered, 'Most assuredly, I say to you unless one is born of water and the Spirit, he cannot enter the kingdom of God."

—John 3:5

The New Birth

Jesus declared that you must be born again to enter into the kingdom of heaven! But who is this Jesus that speaks with such authority about heaven? Heaven is the place where Jesus lives! Jesus says I came down from heaven, not to do my own will; but the will of him who sent me (John 6:38). He had an identity and existed long before entering the earth as a man. He was in existence as God before he became a man.

He was the *"Word"* or *Logos* of God. The Word became flesh, human, and began to live amongst men. John, the Beloved, the one that rested on Jesus' bosom at the Table (John 13:23), clarifies the actual existence and divine nature of Jesus in his gospel. He was the closest to Jesus of all his disciples.

The Word Became Flesh

John states, "In the beginning was the "Word," λόγος, *lógos*, and the Word, λόγος, *logos*, was with God, and the **Word** was "**God**." John cross-references to Genesis Chapter 1: "In the beginning, God created the heavens and the earth. This Scripture in Genesis is in the Torah and the Old Testament.

Dr. Marlene Brown

The author, Goodspeed, asked the question, "Is the 'Word' the prophetic, revelatory Word of Jehovah which came to the prophets (Jeremiah 1:4; Joel 1:1, etc.), or is it the metaphysical 'word' or *Logos* (reason) of stoic philosophy?[1] *Logos* meant the act of speaking or the spoken word. **"Word," as used in this context, denotes the personal wisdom, power, and knowledge of God working in union with God.** He is the cause of life on earth, both spiritual and physical.

In him, the "Word," or the Logos, was life, which gives men light (John 1:4). The Logos that existed with God the Father entered the world with the knowledge of his pre-existence.

The "Word," the Logos, refers to Christ Jesus (John 1:1-5; Rev. 19: 13), which proves the preexistence of Christ. He is eternal, just like the Father and the Holy Spirit that make up the Trinity (1 John 5:7). God created all things through him (Colossians 1:15-18). Knowing God and accepting Jesus Christ as your Lord and Savior will guarantee your eternal salvation, as Jesus is God and was sent by God the Father on the earth. For this reason, the very word that Jesus speaks brings forth life (Matthew 8:8). The Psalmist spoke of Jesus in Psalms 107:20 and said, He sent forth his word and healed them of their diseases. The words of Jesus have power and authority over sicknesses and diseases. Jesus said: "The words that I speak, they are Spirit and they are life" (John 6:63). When Jesus rose from the grave, he said to his disciples, "Everything must be fulfilled about me that was written in the Law of Moses, and the prophets and the Psalms" (Luke 24:44).

"He made all things; without him was not anything made that was made. In him was life, and life was the light of men. And the light shineth in darkness, and the darkness comprehended it not" (John 1:3-5). Jesus Christ, the Logos, is God's only expression and

---

[1] Johnson Goodspeed, "The Gospel of John." 48 no. 4(Oct., 1916): 255-260, accessed June 7, 2014.

character. He represents God's nature and upholds all things by His powerful Word (Hebrews 1:3).

Consequently, as the God-man and the representative of God, he has great authority in heaven. Therefore, as the captain of man's salvation, Jesus declared to one and all, "You must be born again to enter into the kingdom of heaven." Listen in on Jesus's conversation with Nicodemus, a great ruler in Israel. The Scriptures unfold to us:

> There was a man of the Pharisees named Nicodemus, a ruler of the Jews. This man came to Jesus by night and said to Him, "Rabbi, we know that You are a teacher come from God, for no one can do these signs that You do unless God is with him."
>
> Jesus answered and said to him, "Most assuredly, I say to you, unless one is born [a]again, he cannot see the kingdom of God."
>
> Nicodemus said to Him, "How can a man be born when he is old? Can he enter into his mother's womb a second time and be born?"
>
> Jesus answered, "Most assuredly, I say to you, unless one is born of water and the Spirit, he cannot enter the kingdom of God.
>
> That which is born of the flesh is flesh, and which is born of the Spirit is Spirit. Do not marvel that I said to you, 'You must be born again.' The wind blows where it wishes, and you hear its sound but cannot tell where it comes from and where it goes. So is everyone who is born of the Spirit."
>
> Nicodemus answered and said to Him, "How can these things be?"
>
> Jesus answered and said unto him, "Art thou a master of Israel, and knowest not these things? Truly, truly, I say unto thee, We speak that we do know, and testify that we have

seen; and ye receive not our witness. If I have told you earthly things, and ye believe not, how shall ye believe, if I tell you of heavenly things? And no man hath ascended up to heaven, but he that came down from heaven, even the Son of man which is in heaven."

—John 3:1-13

Examine Yourself

- Am I born again?
- Have I received the Holy Spirit from God?
- Am I a sinner?
- Do I need a Savior?
- Will the Law of Moses (The Ten Commandments) make me holy?
- What will reconcile my heart back to God?
- Can my good works save me from the wrath of a Holy God?
- What if my good works fall short of God's standard? What then?
- Will God forgive me of my sins?
- How will God forgive me?
- If I were to die right now, what is my assurance of heaven? Will my religion save me?
- Is there assurance to escape hell?

Below, you will find the answers to the questions of this life. Jesus has made a way for you!

Keynotes:

- Jesus declared to the Jews; you are from below: I am from above (John 8:23); my Father has sent me to earth (John 6:38-46; John 20:21; John 8:29). Therefore, I know the way to heaven! Jesus says to Nicodemus he is the only one that reveals things about heaven. Jesus is the only one who ascended to heaven. Furthermore, he is the only one who came down from heaven (John 3:13). Therefore, Jesus is qualified to say, listen to me and my words: and not the words of another!

- Jesus declared, "I am the way, the truth, and the Life: No man comes to my Father in heaven except you come through me" (emphasis added John 14:6-11).

Come to Me – Not Religion

Jesus declared: "Come to Me, all who are weary and heavily burdened [by religious rituals that provide no peace], and I will give you rest [*refreshing your souls with salvation*]. Take My yoke upon you and learn from Me [*following Me as My disciple*], for I am gentle and humble in heart, and YOU WILL FIND REST (renewal, blessed quiet) **FOR YOUR SOULS**: For My yoke is easy [to bear], and My burden is light" (Matthew 11:28-30 Amplified Bible).

The prophet Isaiah bids you turn to Jesus the Messiah. Isaiah said,

> Let every one that thirsts, come you to the waters, and he that hath no money; come you, buy, and eat; yea, come, buy wine and milk without money and without price. Wherefore do you spend money for that which is not bread? And your labor for that which satisfies not? Listen diligently unto me, and eat you that which is good, and **let your soul** delight itself in fatness.
>
> —Isaiah 55:1-2

Only Jesus can fill the longing soul, not a dead religion that promises life but has no power to give it! Within Jesus, life exists. He is the creator of life. He has living water that can fill the soul with spiritual goodness. Men and women, boys and girls, are turning to drugs and alcohol and material things of this world, which satisfy the soul only for a short while. Then, the soul enters back into its dark and empty place. Only Jesus can satisfy the soul. Therefore, Jesus cried out to the Jews on the feast's last and greatest day. Jesus stood up and loudly said, "If anyone is thirsty, let him come to Me and drink (John 7:37). Jesus promised to release streams of living water by the Holy Spirit of God to anyone who believes in him. What does it mean to believe in Jesus? It means to believe that He is the Son of God, Christ the Messiah, the Savior of the world.

Come to Jesus for your Salvation – Be Rescued from Sin

It is evident in many Scriptures that Jesus implores men and women, boys and girls, Jews and Gentiles, to come to Him to be saved! You may ask the question, why do I need to be saved? You need to be saved from your sins! To be rescued from an eternal hell, where the fire does not quench, and the worm does not die! Jesus wants to *give your soul* peace and rest. He desires to grant you eternal life. For this reason, God had to become man to save you from your sins. It costs Jesus his life to prevent man from entering the place. It is a place that is prepared for the devil and his angels. However, having the seed of sin will cause a man to enter that place if the blood of Jesus does not cleanse the soul from its sins. Therefore, Jesus declared:

"Search the scriptures; for in them ye think ye have eternal life: and they are they which testify of me. And ye will not come to me, that ye might have life." (John 5:39-40)." For had ye believed Moses, ye would have believed me; for he wrote of me! But if ye believe not his writings, how shall ye believe my words?" (John 5:46-47).

Jesus spoke of his pre-existent nature to Jews and Gentiles, but no one received his message. Jesus says: "For as the Father raiseth up the dead, and quickeneth (give life) to them; even so the Son quickeneth (make alive) whom he will. For the Father judgeth no man but hath committed all judgment unto the Son: All men should honor the Son, even as they honor the Father. He that honoureth not

His Second Coming

the Son honoureth, not the Father which hath sent him. Verily, verily, I say unto you, *He that heareth my Word,* and *believeth on him that sent me, hath everlasting life, and shall not come into condemnation; but is passed from death unto life"* (John 5:21-24).

Sent by God the Father

The Scripture states, "But when the fullness of the time has come, God sent forth his Son, made of a woman, made under the law, to redeem them that were under the law, that we might receive the adoption of sons." (Galatians 4:4-5). God enters into a woman's womb. Nothing is impossible with God! He entered the womb of his creation, a virgin woman. He then clothed himself with human flesh and became a man. The process is known as the "hypostatic union." It is a term that refers to the Divine nature of Jesus, who is/was fully God and yet fully man (the God-man). It refers to the combination of the Divine and human nature of Christ. When God put on human flesh, the process was the incarnation.

It is essential to understand that the hypostatic union or the incarnation does not refer to a man taking on God's status, but rather, *God condescending to man's status and becoming the God-man*. He took on a form that is lower than angels. The Scriptures say that he wants to identify with his brethren and taste death for everyone to bring many sons and daughters into heaven (Hebrews 2:8-10).

What a beautiful Savior! Though Jesus identified with God and is God's very image and expression, he took on human flesh to reveal God's loving nature to humanity. Therefore, to see Jesus is to see the Father. To love Jesus is to love the Father. Jesus declared that he and his Father are one in nature. Therefore, Jesus said that as you honor the Father, you must honor the Son (John 5:22-23).

Why Did God Desire to be Human?

The Scriptures say: "Since the children have flesh and blood, he too shared their humanity so that by his death he might break the power of him who holds the power of death—that is, the devil: and free those whom all their lives were held in slavery by their fear of death. For surely it is not angels he helps, but Abraham's descendants. For this reason, he had to be made like them, fully human in every way, so that he might become a merciful and faithful high priest in service to God and that he might make atonement for the sins of the people. Because he suffered when tempted, he can help those tempted" (Hebrews 2: 14-18). *What a wonderful Savior!*

The Scripture says:

"And God raised us up with Christ and seated us with him in the heavenly realms in Christ Jesus so that in the coming ages he might show the incomparable riches of his grace, expressed in his kindness to us in Christ Jesus" (Ephesians 2:6-7).

> O, the depth of the riches, both of the wisdom and knowledge of God! How unsearchable are his judgments and his ways past finding out! For who hath known the mind of the Lord? or who hath been his counselor? Or who hath first given to him, and it shall be recompensed unto him again? For of him, and through him, and to him, are all things: to whom be glory forever. Amen.
>
> —Romans 11:33-36

Jesus Conceived by the Holy Spirit

The Scriptures say:

> But while Joseph thought about these things, behold, an angel of the Lord appeared to him in a dream, saying: 'Joseph, Son of David, do not be afraid to take to you Mary, your wife, for that which is conceived in her is of the Holy Spirit. And she will bring forth a Son, and you shall call His name JESUS, for He will save His people from their sins.' So all this was done that it might be fulfilled, which

was spoken by the Lord through the prophet, saying, the virgin shall be with child, and bear a Son, and they shall call His name Immanuel,' which is translated, 'God with us.'

—Matthew 1:20-23

A Savior for All People was Born, Regardless of Race, Culture, or Religion

The Scriptures declared, "Now, there were in the same country shepherds living out in the field, keeping watch over their flock by night. And behold, an angel of the Lord stood before them, and the glory of the Lord shone around them, and they were greatly afraid. Then the angel said to them, 'Do not be afraid, for behold, I bring you good tidings of great joy which will be to all people... for there is born to you this day in the city of David a Savior, who is Christ the Lord.'" (Luke 2:8-11).

Keynotes:

- Good works cannot save the soul.
- God says self-righteous acts are filthy rags before him.

The soul is dead because of sin and needs life! Sin is a lethal drug. It kills the soul. People have become walking dead! The conscience is destroyed! It needs to become alive once more to serve the living God. The Scriptures say: "We have all become like one who is unclean, and all our righteous deeds are like a polluted garment. Like the wind, we all fade like a leaf, and our iniquities take us away" (Isaiah 64:6). The word filthy came from the Hebrew word iddah, which means "the bodily fluids from a woman's menstrual cycle." This word refers to a woman's feminine cycle. The feminine process of a woman makes her unclean. All self-righteous acts are like a soiled feminine product before God –useless before the Holy God! Why? The good works are done from a corrupted heart of hatred, jealousy, malice, anger, murder, adultery, fornication, theft, immoral behavior, etc. All these acts are sinful before God, so the heart requires cleansing.

The nature of the heart is corrupted by sin. Sin needs to be atoned. What does that mean? Something must be done to make up for all the wrong that the soul did towards the holy God. How? The soul needs to be cleansed from sin, and restitution needs to be made to God. Sinful man needs to be reconciled to God. The soul must be restored to its original state of holiness and righteousness.

Blood Atoned for the Soul

How does blood atone for the soul? The Sovereign God told Moses he had provided blood to make atonement for the soul. It is the blood that cleansed the soul from sin. For the life of man is within the blood. Blood within the body of man gives the body life. The blood of man is tainted with sin by Adam's fallen race. Therefore, man's soul needs cleansing by the blood that is pure and holy to give the soul life once more. Therefore, God told Moses that he had provided blood to make atonement for the soul (Leviticus 17:11). It is imperative to note, however, that Moses used the blood of animals as a covenant seal before the children of Israel and the Sovereign God Yahweh. Moses used the blood of animals as commanded by God. He sprinkled it on the people and said, "This is the blood of the covenant that the LORD has made with you in accordance with all these words" (Exodus 24:7).

The blood of animals could not make the heart perfect before God (Hebrews 10:4). Bullocks and goats couldn't take away sin once and for all. The blood of animals was just an introduction or a shadow of things to come until the real Lamb, Jesus Christ, the God-man, came. Therefore, when Jesus Christ came into the world, he said, sacrifices and burnt offerings you have no desire, but a body, you have prepared me (Hebrews 10: 5). God has prepared Jesus a body to be the ultimate sacrifice for the sins of the whole world. The soul of Jesus was then made as an offering for sin (Isaiah 53:10). Jesus is the perfect Lamb of God, whose blood is holy and pure to be made as a sin offering for man. John the Baptist testified of him and said, "Behold the Lamb of God who came to take away the world's sin (John 1:29). The blood of Jesus is potent to cleanse your heart and make your conscience alive once more before the living God. His blood will give life to the soul and cleanse the soul from all unrighteousness. Jesus says he proceeded forth and came out from God to partake of flesh and blood so that his blood can atone for your sins (John 8:42; Hebrews 2:14-15). God told Moses it is the blood that makes atonement for the soul. (Leviticus 17:11). When Jesus shed his blood, he took his blood directly to heaven. He placed it upon God's mercy seat for the forgiveness of your sins and cleansing of the soul (Hebrews 9:23-28).

Jesus Christ shed his blood as a lamb and as a spotless Lamb of God to pay the price for the world's sin (John 1:29). This payment is valid only when an individual or a person directly accepts the gift of salvation by faith in Christ Jesus.

How Can that Be?

Each individual must ask Jesus to forgive them of their sins. Secondly, the individual needs to ask Jesus to come into their heart and cleanse them with his blood that was shed as payment for sins. The individual must repent, turn away from their sins, and do them no more. Next, the individual needs to place their trust in the finished work of what Jesus did for them on the cross. Each person must accept this gift by faith by asking Jesus to come into their heart and be the Lord of their Life and Savior of their soul. The process is experiential. The Holy Spirit of Jesus will enter the believer's heart and transform the sinner's stony heart into a heart of flesh. A trade will be made. Jesus will give the believer his robe of righteousness and become sin for the believer (2 Corinthians 5:21). Jesus then takes the punishment of sin to himself and dies in the believer's place. On the third day, he rose from the grave to justify the believer (Romans 4:25). ***Therefore, being justified by faith, we now made peace with God through our Lord Jesus Christ*** (Romans 5:1). ***For***

by grace you are now saved: Not of yourself, it is the gift of God: Not of works; lest any man should boast (Ephesians 2:8-9). The believer now identifies with Jesus' death, burial, and resurrection. Therefore, as Jesus rose from the dead and died no more, the believer will rise to meet the Lord in the air at His Second Coming. The event is confirmed. The expectation of his coming is imminent. Therefore, we await him with great joy and anticipation for his arrival.

The Sinful Nature

The Scripture says, For all have sinned and fallen short of God's glory, regardless of race, religion, and culture (emphasis added Romans 3:23). Is this Scripture true? Have you sinned? What does that mean? Humankind has fallen short of the standard of the Holy God. We have missed his righteous requirements. We sinned not because we are human but because our forefather, Adam, sinned by disobedience to God. Therefore, all of humanity thus inherits a sinful nature. The good news is that Jesus Christ can change this sinful nature. Jesus Christ has become sin for us who knew no sin so that we can be made the righteousness of God in him (2 Corinthians 5:21). For the "wages of sin is death: But the gift of God is eternal life through Jesus Christ our Lord" (Romans 6:23). Concepts of religion will not deliver. Ideologies of religion will not save. What does this mean to you?

Consequently, you must be born again! (John 3:3) Not by human intervention, sex between a man and a woman. *You must be born again from above by the Holy Spirit of God.* Jesus declared, *"Unless a man is born again, he cannot see the kingdom of heaven."* For this reason, Jesus Christ became a man to bring us to God through the blood of his cross. He is the only mediator between God and man (1Timothy 2:5). Therefore, Jesus said unto them, "I am the way, the truth, and the life; no man comes to the Father except by me" (John 14:6). *Is Jesus being exclusive?*

His Second Coming

Yes, he is. Who gave him such authority? His heavenly Father! Jesus came down from heaven to earth. He knew the way and had the power and authority to teach men the way to heaven.

Jesus stated several times over that he is from above and not of this earth. Jesus told the Jews, "You are from below, I am from above; you are of this world, I am not of this world!" They did not believe that Jesus was God the Messiah, the world's Savior; therefore, Jesus said to them, "You will die in your sins; for unless you believe that I am He, you will die in your sins." The people said to him, "Who are You?" Jesus said to them, "What have I been saying to you from the beginning? "I have many things to speak and to judge concerning you, but He who sent Me is true; and the things which I heard from Him, these I speak to the world." They did not realize that He had been speaking to them about the Father. So, Jesus said, "When you lift up the Son of Man (the crucifixion), then you will know that I am He, and I do Nothing on My own initiative, but I speak these things as the Father taught Me. "And He who sent Me is with Me; He has not left Me alone, for I always do the things that are pleasing to Him." As He spoke these things, many came to believe in Him."

—John 8:23-30

Assurance of Salvation

Is it possible for you to have the assurance of eternal life? Yes. God had made it possible for you to walk with the assurance and confidence of salvation. The Scripture declares, "If you confess with your mouth the Lord Jesus and believe in your heart that God has raised Him from the dead, you will be saved. For with the heart one believes unto righteousness, and with the mouth, Confession is made unto salvation. The Scriptures say, "Whoever believes on Him will not be put to shame" (Romans 10:9-11). For God so loved the world, that he gave his only Son; that whosoever believes in him, will not perish, but have everlasting life. God did not send his Son into the world to condemn the world, but for the world through him might be saved (John 3:16-17). Once saved, the Scriptures say we no longer live for ourselves but now live for Christ. The Scriptures explain it in this manner, "And he died for all those who live should no longer live for themselves but for him who died for them and was raised again" (2 Corinthians 5:15).

Subsequently, we say yes to Jesus by opening our heart's doors to let him in. Jesus said, "Behold, I stand at the door and knock: if any man hears my voice and opens the door, I will come into him and sup with him, and he with me" (Revelation 3:20). The Scripture declared, while it is said: "Today if you hear His voice, do not harden your hearts as in the rebellion" (Hebrews 3:15). Jesus has appeared to put away sin by the sacrifice of Himself. Men are appointed to die once, but after this, they face judgment. Even so, Christ was offered once to bear the sins of many. To those who eagerly wait for Him, He will appear a second time, without sin, for Salvation (Hebrews 9:25-28). Therefore, we rejoice in our salvation.

This section is a prayer for salvation. The prayer is simple yet very effective if the prayer is prayed with sincerity and in truth. Ask Jesus to come into your heart and cleanse you from all unrighteousness to receive the forgiveness of your sins! This prayer to Jesus is the first step toward your transformation of being born again. The next step is to be baptized in water and join with other believers, known as his church. Jesus is the head of the church. He died for this body of believers, none other. Therefore, to be a part of his body, you must repent, turn away from your sins, and ask Jesus to cleanse you from all unrighteousness.

A SINNER'S PRAYER FOR SALVATION

Dear Heavenly Father,

***I come before you as a sinner.** Thank you for sending Jesus to earth to die for me to pay the price for my sins. Please forgive me for my sins. Jesus, as of this day, **I repent** and do them no more! Please wash me in the blood that was shed for me. Please clean my heart from all unrighteousness. From this day, I repent of my sins and turn away from them.*

*Heavenly Father, I confess before you today that Jesus Christ is the Son of God. **I believe** He came down from heaven to earth to die a sinner's death on the cross to give his life as a ransom for my sins. I believe he rose on the third day to justify me before you. As of this day, I surrender my life to Jesus.*

*Come into my heart and life, and let your Holy Spirit live inside me. Teach me your way of holiness and righteousness. Purify my heart and my mind. From now on, **I choose you to be the Lord of my life and Savior of my soul**. Jesus, thank you for calling me out of darkness into the light of your glorious kingdom.*

Thank you for eternal life! Make me your very own both now and forever more. Amen.

****

If this prayer speaks to your heart and you mean it with all conviction, then humbly kneel before **the throne of grace by faith** and say this prayer **ALOUD** to Jesus. He promised that anyone who invited him into their heart and life, he would come into their hearts along with his Father, to be with them forever. Jesus promised he would never turn that person away. Jesus says, "All that the Father gives me shall come to me, and anyone that comes to me I will in no wise cast out, or turn away" (emphases added John 6:37)

Dr. Marlene Brown

When you say the prayer for salvation, the Holy Spirit of God enters your heart and begins to transform it. He will place a new Spirit and a right mind within you. If any man is within Christ, he is a new creature. Old things have passed away; behold, all things have become new (2 Corinthians 5:17). The new Spirit is the Holy Spirit of God. He is the same Spirit that raised Jesus from the dead! He now lives within you (Romans 8:11). The Holy Spirit will fill your heart with God's love, joy, peace, goodness, gentleness, and self-control.

Subsequently, Jesus Christ has removed your sins as far as the east is from the west (Psalms 103:12). Jesus remembers them no more (Hebrews 8:12). Your next step is to **read the Holy Bible daily for strength** and encouragement. As you read the Holy Bible, the Word of God will wash over your heart and clean it from the inside out (John 15:3). Jesus is now seeking obedience to His Word.

NEW BIRTH CERTIFICATE

I _____, received Jesus Christ into my heart to be my Personal Savior and Lord, on this day, _____. I am now a new person in Christ Jesus! Today I have become a child of God! I am a Christian, and I am born again from above by the Holy Spirit of God!

Congratulations!
You are now a new person in Christ

Dr. Marlene Brown

Chapter 18
Your New Identity in Christ

Therefore if anyone is in Christ [that is, grafted in, joined to Him by faith in Him as Savior, he is a new creature [reborn and renewed by the Holy Spirit]; the old things [the previous moral and spiritual condition] have passed away. Behold, new things have come [because spiritual awakening brings a new life].

—2 Corinthians 5:17

Amplified Bible

Jesus says heaven rejoices over one sinner that repents (Luke 15:7). Remember that the Scriptures say: "For by grace you have been saved through faith; and that not of yourselves, it is the gift of God; not as a result of works, so that no one may boast, for we are His workmanship, created in Christ Jesus for good works." (Ephesians 2:8-9). The Scripture says, "Knowing that the works of the law do not justify a man, but by the faith of Jesus Christ, even we have believed in Jesus Christ, that the faith of Christ might justify us, and not by the works of the law: for by the works of the law shall no flesh be justified" (Galatians 2:16).

NOW PUT ON THE NEW MAN

If you then be risen with Christ, seek those things above, where Christ sits on the right hand of God. Set your affection on things above, not on things on the earth. You are dead, and your life is hidden with Christ in God. When Christ, who is our Life, shall appear, you shall also appear with him in glory.

His Second Coming

Mortify therefore your members on the earth; fornication, uncleanness, inordinate affection, evil desire, and covetousness, which is idolatry: For which things' sake the wrath of God comes on the children of disobedience. You also walked in that manner sometimes when you lived in them. But now you also put off all these: anger, wrath, malice, blasphemy, filthy communications out of your mouth. Lie not one to another, seeing that you have put off the old man with his deeds; And have put on the new man, which is renewed in knowledge after the image of him that created him: Where there is neither Greek nor Jew, circumcision nor uncircumcision, Barbarian, Scythian, bond nor free: but Christ is all, and in all.

Put on therefore, as the elect of God, holy and beloved, bowels of mercies, kindness, humbleness of mind, meekness, long-suffering; Forbearing one another, and forgiving one another, if any man has a quarrel against any: even as Christ forgave you, so also do you. And above all these things, put on charity, which is the bond of perfection. And let the peace of God rule in your hearts, to which you are also called in one body; and be thankful. Let the Word of Christ dwell in you richly in all wisdom, teaching and admonishing one another in psalms, hymns, and spiritual songs, singing with grace in your hearts to the Lord. And whatever you do in word or deed, do all in the name of the Lord Jesus, giving thanks to God and the Father by him.

— Colossians 3:1-16

Additionally, Christians should be holy and without blame, walking in love (Ephesians 1:4). If you sin, confess it to Jesus: He is faithful and just to forgive your sins and cleanse you from all unrighteousness (1 John 1:9).

Furthermore, as Christians, we belong to a body of people, a community that belongs to Christ. We come together each week to become strengthened in the faith. In addition, you need to read His Word daily, which is the Bible. Jesus calls himself the "Word!" His "Word" will continue to strengthen you daily and allow you to grow from strength to strength. Pray daily by speaking to him as many times as you desire! Prayers are an honest conversation with God from your heart! Tell him about your worries, failures, and successes. Ask him for directions in your daily decision-making. As a Christian, it does not mean your life will be trouble-free. Jesus says, in this world, you will have trouble. But he says, "Be of good cheer, as he has overcome the world" (Matthew 9:2). Furthermore, Jesus says he will never leave you nor forsake you. He will be with you always, even to the end of time (Matthew 28:20).

Next, have a spirit of expectation for his return. Jesus says, be on the watch, for you do not know the day or the hour the Son of man shall appear! (Matthew 24: 42) His coming will be like a thief in the night. Jesus says: Unto them who are looking for him, shall he appear without Sin to Salvation. He is coming for those on the watch looking out for him. It is called the 'rapture" of the church.

May the grace of God be with you to gracefully walk in his salvation.

Chapter 19
Salvation

For by grace are ye saved through faith; and that not of yourselves: it is the gift of God:

Salvation means "deliverance from evil, danger, or trouble." It is God's gift, through Christ, to deliver men's souls. We all need a savior because all have sinned and fallen short of God's glory. Each of our souls needs to be delivered from the evil forces of darkness. How do we receive salvation? Salvation comes through love, the precious love of Jesus. Christ left His throne in glory, came down in the form of man, took on Himself sin, even though He knew no sin, and allowed Himself to be crucified on the cross, that through his blood, men can be free from sin, even have the forgiveness of sins. Men's souls can now be saved! It is not by works, lest any man should boast, but it is the precious gift of God!

God's Love

God loves you so much that He sent His only Son, Jesus Christ, into the world and allowed Him to be crucified. His death on the cross was the ultimate sacrifice made for our sins. He has bought us with His blood and paid the price of sin in full. The Lord is good, just, and merciful beyond our understanding. Who can fathom the depth of his love?

> For God so loved the world, that he gave his only begotten Son, that whosoever believeth in him should not perish, but have everlasting life. For God sent not his Son into the world to condemn the world; but that the world through him might be saved.

Dr. Marlene Brown

—John 3:16–17

The Father loveth the Son and hath given all things into his hand. He that believeth on the Son hath everlasting life: and he that believeth not the Son shall not see life, but the wrath of God abideth on him.

—John 3:35–36

The love of God for you is permanent and everlasting. He loves you to the very end. What we do, think, and say does not affect God's love. No problem is too big or too small for Him to solve. The Scripture says in John 13:1: "When Jesus knew that his hour has come that he should depart out of this world unto the Father, having loved his own which were in the world, he loved them unto the end." Because of this love He has for us, His precious wounds are healing people today. The Scripture says:

> But he was wounded for our transgressions; he was bruised for our iniquities: the chastisement of our peace was upon him, and with his stripes, we are healed.

—Isaiah 53:5

Who his own self bare our sins in his own body on the tree, that we, being dead to sins, should live unto righteousness.

—1 Peter 2:24

In whom we have redemption through His blood, the forgiveness of sins, according to the riches of His grace.

—Ephesians 1:7

Only one man loves us unconditionally right through to eternity, and that man's name is Jesus! The only man willing to give His life for us gave His life for us so that we can have eternal life through Him by believing He is indeed the Son of the living God. The love of God goes right through to eternity. Romans 8:35–39 declares:

Who shall separate us from the love of Christ? Shall tribulation, or distress, or persecution, or famine, or nakedness, or peril, or sword? As it is written, For thy sake, we are killed all the day long; we are accounted as sheep for the slaughter. Nay, in all these things, we are more than conquerors through Him that loved us. For I am persuaded that neither death, nor life, nor angels, nor principalities, nor powers, nor things present, nor things to come, Nor height, nor depth, nor any other creature, shall be able to separate us from the love of God, which is in Christ Jesus our Lord.

Remember: Christ and his promises remain the same yesterday, today, and forever (Heb. 13:8).

He Left His Throne in Glory

It never ceases to amaze me that a King would leave His throne in glory to die for a world His enemy destroyed. Christ's sole purpose for coming was to end the works of darkness so that He might destroy sin once and for all. 1 John 3:8 says: "For this purpose, the Son of God was manifested, that he might destroy the works of the devil." The Scripture also tells us that He has conquered death and the grave. He said, "O death, where is thy sting? O grave, where is thy victory?" (1 Cor. 15:55). In Revelation 1:18, Jesus says, "I am alive for evermore Amen, and have the keys of hell and of death."

He Came Down in The Form of a Man

It is a great mystery that the Son of the living God would choose to come down to earth in the form of man—it is indeed a great honor and mystery. He made himself a little lower than the angels to taste death for every man.

Forasmuch then as the children are partakers of flesh and blood, he also himself likewise took part of the same; that through death he might destroy him that had the power of death, that is, the devil; And deliver them who through fear of death were all their lifetime subject to bondage. For verily he took not on him the nature of angels, but he took on him the seed of Abraham.

—Hebrews 2:14–16

He Knew No Sin

The Father made Jesus become sin for us, even though Jesus knew no sin so that we can be made the righteousness of God in Him (2 Cor. 5:21). The Scripture says, "It pleased the Lord to bruise him; he hath put him to grief: when thou shalt make his soul an offering for sin, he shall see his seed, he shall prolong his days, and the pleasure of the Lord shall prosper in his hand" (Isa. 53:10). The Scripture says He poured out His soul unto death. On the cross, He said, "Father, forgive them for they know not what they do" (Luke 23:34). On the cross, we see the compassion and mercy of Jesus to those who did Him wrong. While suffering, He did not threaten His tormentors but committed Himself to the righteous God (1 Pet. 2:23).

He Allowed Himself to Be Crucified

> Therefore doth my Father love me, because I lay down my life, that I might take it again. No man taketh it from me, but I lay it down of myself. I have the power to lay it down, and I have the power to take it again. This commandment have I received of my Father.
>
> —John 10:17–18

I was witnessing to someone about Jesus, and he was describing to me the god that he worshiped: Buddha. He told me that he received whatever he asked his god Buddha for; then he turned to me and said, "The man Jesus was doing a lot of good things, and they killed him! Why did they do that?" I responded that they did

His Second Coming

not kill Him; He laid down His life. The man looked at me, puzzled. This is how Jesus explains it in His Word:

> Verily, verily, I say unto you, I am the door of the sheep. All that ever came before me were thieves and robbers, but the sheep did not hear them. I am the door: by me, if any man enters in, he shall be saved and shall go in and out and find pasture. The thief cometh not, but for to steal, kill, and destroy: I have come that they might have life and have it more abundantly. I am the good shepherd: the good shepherd giveth his life for the sheep. But he that is a hireling, and not the shepherd, whose own the sheep are not, seeth the wolf coming, and leaveth the sheep, and fleeth: and the wolf catcheth them, and scattereth the sheep. The hireling fleeth because he is a hireling and careth not for the sheep. I am the good shepherd, and know my sheep, and am known of mine.
>
> As the Father knoweth me, even so, know I the Father: and I lay down my life for the sheep. And other sheep I have, which are not of this fold: them also I must bring, and they shall hear my voice, and there shall be one fold, and one shepherd. Therefore doth my Father love me, because I lay down my life, that I might take it again. No man taketh it from me, but I lay it down of myself. I have the power to lay it down, and I have the power to take it again. This commandment have I received of my Father.
>
> —John 10:7–18

Jesus says, "Here I am, the entrance, the door through which sheep go in and out and find green pasture. I am He who brings salvation to those who follow My guidance. I am the way, the truth, and the life; no one can come to God except through Me. I am the good shepherd. A shepherd will give his life for his sheep because he wants to protect them and save them from the wicked wolf, but a hired servant will run when he sees the wolf coming. He will run because he is just a hired servant; the sheep do not belong to him. He will not sacrifice his life to protect the sheep, but the good shepherd will." Jesus demonstrated this to us when He laid down his life on Calvary's cross to save us from Satan, the wolf, and sin so that we can find peace through Him and have eternal life.

Let us consider our earthly Father and how he would love us if we had risked our lives to protect our earthly sheep. David is a perfect example. David was a man who walked with the integrity of heart and uprightness according to the statutes of God. David was also a shepherd boy who tended the sheep of his father. One day, while David was tending his flock of sheep, a lion, and a bear came to devour them, and he risked his life to protect his sheep. In 1 Samuel 17:34-36, David explains to Saul what took place:

> And David said unto Saul, Thy servant kept his father's sheep, and there came a lion, and a bear, and took a lamb out of the flock: And I went out after him, and smote him, and delivered it out of his mouth: and when he arose against me, I caught him by his beard, and smote him, and slew him. Thy servant slew both the lion and the bear.

Jesus, however, did not risk His life for His sheep; He gave His life for His sheep and died in our place so that we could be saved through Him.

Through His Blood, We Can Have Forgiveness of Sin

The Scripture declares:

> Blessed are they whose iniquities are forgiven and whose sins are covered.
>
> —Romans 4:7

His Second Coming

Come now, and let us reason together, saith the Lord: though your sins be as scarlet, they shall be as white as snow; though they are red like crimson, they shall be as wool.

—Isaiah 1:18

Dr. Marlene Brown

Chapter 20
What Is Faith?

So then faith cometh by hearing, and hearing by the word of God.

—*Romans 10:17*

The Bible declares that "faith is the substance of things hoped for, and the evidence of things not seen" (Heb. 11:1). The Greek word for *substance is hupostasis*. *Hupostasis* means "to have confidence in a substance, which actually exists, or in a real being." It also means "the substantial quality or nature of a person or thing." The Greek word for *hope is elpizo,* which means "to wait for salvation with joy and full confidence, and to trust in this hope."

So then, the Scripture says that we should have all confidence in believing in whatever substance or thing we are asking the Lord for and that we should wait for the reply or answer with great joy and confidence, believing that we will receive it. This joy and confidence come through listening and hearing God's spoken Word. The Bible says faith comes by hearing and hearing the Word of God (Rom. 10:17). Hearing the Word of God means we receive faith for our salvation in the blood of Christ. It is also through the grace of God upon us that we are saved through faith and not by ourselves. Salvation is not by works, lest any man should boast, but is the precious gift of God. Someone may say, well, what about our good works? The Bible says that we were created in Christ Jesus to perform good works, and God ordained us to walk in them. However, it is not by the works that we are saved; it is the precious gift of God (Eph. 8–10).

His Second Coming

So then, we see that our salvation is not based on something seen but rather on faith and hope in the Word of God and His promises. The Bible declares in Romans 8:24 that hope, which is seen, is not hope. For what a man sees, why does he yet hope for it? Our faith and hope are also based on Christ's rise from the dead over two thousand years ago. He is now seated on the right hand of God, and He promises to return for us and receive us unto Himself that where He is, there we will also be (1 Cor. 15:17). It is also based upon His promise that He has gone to prepare a place for us. This is the joyous hope we have as believers in the Holy Christ. We have this blessed hope in Him because His Words are truth (John. 17:17). His Words are spirit, and they are life, according to John 6:63. It is this faith that God wants us to live by. He said in His Word that without this kind of faith in Him and His Word, it is impossible to please Him. So, the Lord wants us to have this great faith in Him and in His Son. He wants us to wait for His Son with joy and confidence mixed with great expectation, believing that He will return to earth again and having complete knowledge that our faith is not useless or in vain. God wants us to have this faith in His Son. He clearly stated that whatever we ask of Him when we pray in His name, He will give it to us if we believe. So, He declared in His Word that "without faith, it is impossible to please him: for he that cometh to God must believe that he is" (Heb. 11:6). So, the question is: Who is God? Various names are given in the Bible to indicate one's character or peculiar quality. God expressed his attributes through faith in his name.

The Names of God

God has revealed Himself to Moses through a few of His names. Here are a few of His names that denote His attributes and deity as God.

The Bible says He is *Jehovah Jireh*, the God who sees. He sees all you are going through, knows all you are going through, and will provide. *Jehovah Jireh* sees and also provides. He will provide for you during your time of need, during your time of difficulty when you're having problems in this life. He wants you to have complete faith and confidence in Him and in His name as the great provider.

God is also known as *Jehovah Rapha*, which means He is the God that heals you. He is the great physician, the great healer. He restores both people and nations. God says in His Word in Exodus 15:26 that if we listen diligently to His voice, obey Him, do what is right in His sight, and listen to His commandments, He will not put any of the diseases upon us which He brought upon the Egyptians. "For he is the Lord that healeth thee." He is *Jehovah Rapha*, the God who heals.

He is *Jehovah Shalom*, which means "Jehovah is peace." This type of peace surpasses all understanding. He says in His Word that if we keep our minds on Him and allow His presence and anointing to saturate our minds during our times of trouble, He will keep us in perfect peace.

Another name that speaks of his deity is *El Olam*. This means "the enduring God." The Scripture declares that He is never weary and never grows faint. When you feel weak in heart and in body, then cry out to the almighty God, El Shaddai, who is strong in might, will strengthen you and uphold you with the right hand of His righteousness.

In Isaiah 40:25, 28–31, He says:

> To whom then will ye liken me, or shall I be equal? Saith the Holy One. Hast thou not known? Hast thou not heard that the ever-lasting God, the Lord, the Creator of the ends of the earth, fainteth not; neither is weary? There is no searching of his understanding. He giveth power to the faint, and them that have no might he increaseth strength. Even the youths shall faint and be weary, and the young men shall utterly fall: But they that wait upon the Lord shall renew their strength; they shall mount up with wings as

eagles; they shall run, and not be weary; and they shall walk, and not faint.

God said, do not fear the enemy! Only put our faith and confidence in Him, and He will see us through. He will strengthen us, He says; He will help us and uphold us with the right hand of His righteousness. I believe that the essential characteristic of God is love. The Scripture declares in 1 John 4:16–20 that God is love. So then, knowing that our Father in heaven is love itself, we can approach the mercy seat with great confidence to receive grace and abundance of favor from our heavenly Father. Only when we seek His face diligently will He give us our rewards. As He declares in His Word, He is a reward to those who diligently seek Him. So, the God of the universe says, "If you believe in Me, believe in My love for you, know My name, put your trust in Me, acknowledge Me, and seek My counsel, then I will direct your path and make the crooked path straight. Nothing shall be impossible for you with me because, with God, nothing is impossible." (See Hebrews 11:6.) The Scripture asks rhetorically, "Is anything too hard for the Lord?" (Gen. 18:14). This was the question God asked Abraham when He told him that Sarah, his wife, would give him a son in her old age.

Jeremiah 32:27 says,

> "I am the God of all flesh: is there anything too hard for me?" He also points out that His hand is not shortened, that it cannot be saved, or that His ear is so heavy that He cannot hear. So, the Lord of the universe wants us to approach His mercy seat believing that whatever we ask for in His name, He will give to us if we only believe in Him. As He pointed out, if we do not believe in Him, who is the supernatural God and His power, it will be impossible to please Him because we need to live by faith in the realm of the supernatural. Habakkuk 2:4 says, "The just shall live by his faith.

In Matthew 6:30–33, the Bible says:

Wherefore, if God so clothes the grass of the field, which today is, and tomorrow is cast into the oven, shall he not much more clothe you, O ye of little faith? Therefore take no thought, saying: What shall we eat? Or, What shall we drink? Or, Wherewithal shall we be clothed? (For after all these things do the Gentiles seek:) for your heavenly Father knoweth that ye have need of all these things. But seek ye first the kingdom of God, and his righteousness; and all these things shall be added unto you.

If we have faith in God, the Scripture tells us it will bring a good report to our lives. Faith will get good news (Heb. 11:2). My faith in God kept me through the delivery process with my second child, born dead, who came out not breathing for fifteen minutes. I just kept trusting and believing God that He would come through for me as I continued to pray and plead the blood of Jesus where the child lay. I even remember quoting this Scripture: "Call upon me in the day of trouble: I will deliver thee, and thou shalt glorify me" (Ps. 50:15).

So, I reminded the Lord of His Word, and sure enough, I heard a faint cry coming from the area where they had the baby.

The cry was softer than a cat's meow. However, that was good enough for me. They then brought the baby over, weighing 9 ½ lbs., with not much life in his body, but then, that was enough for me to know that my God had heard and answered my prayer. The baby is alive and well and is now twenty-one years old. Faith will indeed bring a good report in your life. This kind of faith also brings salvation through Jesus Christ.

Chapter 21
Doubts of Your Salvation

Trust in the Lord with all thine heart; and lean not unto thine own understanding. In all thy ways acknowledge him, and he shall direct thy paths.

—Proverbs 3:5-6

The Bible says that if you confess with your mouth the Lord Jesus, that God raised Him from the dead, and you believe with your heart, then you shall be saved. If you have prayed the prayer with all conviction and believe with your heart, you are saved indeed! The Bible says it is not by works that you are saved. The Scripture says in Ephesians 2:8–10:

> For by grace are ye saved through faith; and that not of yourselves: it is the gift of God: Not of works, lest any man should boast. For we are his workmanship, created in Christ Jesus unto good works, which God hath before ordained that we should walk in them.

Nevertheless, there will be times when the devil will come before you with your past before your eyes, saying to you, "You are not really saved!"

This is when you need faith to hold on to the Word of God. Rebuke the enemy, and he will flee from you (James 4:7). Jesus says that Satan is a liar and the father of lies (John 8:44). The Bible declares, "With the heart, man believeth unto righteousness; and with the mouth, confession is made to salvation" (Rom. 10:9–11). The Bible also declares, "Whosoever shall call upon the name of the Lord shall be saved" (Rom. 10:13). He did not say only those with a few sins, no! He did not say only those with sin that is not too terrible, or only murderers and homosexuals are excluded, no! He says: "*Whosoever.*"

Most of us will not be found guilty of killing each other; however, we are certainly guilty of using our tongues to murder each other. So, I thank God that He said, "Whosoever that calls upon me shall be saved!" This is the most beautiful offer given to man under heaven. He did not say you will be saved only if you have never committed abortions or mass abortions; He said in His Word, "Whoever you are, if you call upon me, you shall be saved." That statement makes me think of how awesome God is. The Lord did not say only if you have never done prostitution! He did not say only if you are of a certain skin color! He did not say that salvation was only for the Jews. And the list goes on. Yes, salvation is also available for Muslims and Hindus in faith. We see God's love spreading more profound, deeper and deeper, broader and more comprehensive.

Our God is a God of love. So, in His Word, He declares that it does not matter what state the enemy had us in before or what stronghold the enemy had on our life; His blood is pure, holy, and powerful enough to bring us out and wash us white as snow. So, the beautiful Lord says, "Whoever calls upon my name shall be saved"! To be "saved" means to be made whole in body, mind, soul, and spirit.

Now that we are saved, we must turn from our past life to righteousness. Now, we only do the things of God according to His Word. Remember what the Word of God says, "If any man is in Christ, he is a new creature: old things are passed away . . . all things have become new" (2 Cor. 5:17). This is the most beautiful miracle, or experience, a child of God can have: the experience of being born again. What happens is that once you receive Christ into your heart, His Holy Spirit enters within you and drives out all evil forces of darkness. The forces of darkness no longer control you; you are now

His Second Coming

controlled by the Holy Spirit of light in Christ. Once His spirit lives within you, you are sealed forever with eternal life. You will notice that your walk and your talk have changed, and how you look at life, and the world has completely changed. You now have thoughts and desires that are of Christ. The Bible says you are now called ambassadors for Jesus Christ and reconciled back to the Holy Father. The Word of God says, "For Christ has made himself sin so that we can be made the righteousness of God in him" (2 Cor. 5:20–21). However, you need to renew your mind with the Word of God daily to complete the transformation of your mind (Rom. 12:2). Read the Word of God and do what the Word of God says so that you can experience the complete transformation of life. Now that we have been made free from sin, the Scripture says we have become servants of righteousness.

The Scripture explains:

> Just as we have yielded the members of our bodies as servants to uncleanness and iniquity unto iniquity, this is how we need to surrender our members as servants of righteousness unto holiness." Many of us are ashamed of those things that we have done in the past, and the fruits of those things bring forth death. As the Bible says, the wages of sin is death, but the gift of God is eternal life through Jesus Christ, our Lord. But now, we are made free from sin and have become servants to God so that the fruits that we will be bringing forth are holiness, and the end of holiness is life eternal.
>
> —Romans 6:19-23

Dr. Marlene Brown

Chapter 22
Significance of the Blood

But now in Christ Jesus ye who sometimes were far off are made nigh by the blood of Christ.

— Ephesians 2:13

Blood is the life-giving fluid of the body. In the Old Testament, it is regarded as the seat of life, but since shed blood signifies death, the word is used for both life and death. The life of the body is found in the blood. Blood also makes atonement for the soul, meaning that the blood is used to cleanse the soul from sin. The significance of Jesus' blood is now clearly understood as it is blood without spot or blemish, which is used for the atonement of our soul to cleanse us from all sins (Lev. 17:11)

In the days of the Old Covenant, only the high priest entered the inner room each year, not without blood. The "inner room" is the place of the Holy of Holies. The high priest took the blood of goats and calves, which he offered to God for his sins first and then for the people's sins. The Holy Spirit did not disclose the way into the holiest place as long as the first tabernacle was present. The gifts and sacrifices offered during this ceremonial time could not make the conscience of the worshippers clean and clear, for the blood of animals, bulls, and goats couldn't take away sins (Hebrews 9:5-10).

But Christ being come a high priest of good things to come, by a greater and more perfect tabernacle, not made with hands, that is to say, not of this building; Neither by the blood of goats and calves, but *by his own blood be entered in once into the holy place, having obtained eternal*

His Second Coming

redemption for us. [So now we are sanctified through the offering of the body of Jesus Christ once and for all] For if the blood of bulls and of goats, and the ashes of a heifer sprinkling the unclean, sanctifieth to the purifying of the flesh: How much more shall the blood of Christ, who through the eternal Spirit offered himself without spot to God, purge your conscience from dead works to serve the living God?

—Hebrews 9:11-14

I now go to the cross of Jesus regularly, asking Christ, my high priest, to cleanse me of my sins through His blood and purge my conscience from dead works to serve the living God. For Christ was the one who offered the sacrifice, and He was the sacrifice itself. Not just superficially, but His blood purged your conscience, removing the defilement of sin from the very core of your being.

When Christ came into the world, He said:

Sacrifice and offering thou wouldest not, ***but a body hast thou prepared me***: In burnt offerings and sacrifices for sin thou hast had no pleasure. Then said I, Lo, I come (in the volume of the book it is written of me), to do thy will, O God. Above when he said, Sacrifice and offering and burnt offerings and offering for sin thou wouldest not neither hadst pleasure therein; which are offered by the law; Then said he, Lo, I come to do thy will, O God. ***He taketh away the first that he may establish the second by which will we are sanctified through the offering of the body of Jesus Christ once and for all.***

—Hebrews 10:5–10

The Word of God says that every priest stands daily, ministering and offering the same sacrifices year after year. This type of sacrifice can never take away sin once and for all, but after Jesus offered one sacrifice for sins forever, He sat down on God's right hand, perfecting those who are sanctified forever. And the Holy Ghost, the Bible says, is a witness to us. For the Lord said before in His Word:

> This is the covenant that I will make with them after those days, saith the Lord, I will put my laws into their hearts, and in their minds will I write them; And their sins and iniquities will I remember no more. Now where remission of these is, there is no more offering for sin.
>
> —Hebrews 10–18
>
> For Christ is not entered into the holy places made with hands: which are the figures of the true; ***but into heaven itself, now to appear in the presence of God for us:*** Nor yet that he should offer himself often, as the high priest entereth into the holy place every year with blood of others; For then must he often have suffered since the foundation of the world: ***but now once at the end of the world hath he appeared to put away sin by the sacrifice of himself*** So Christ was ***once offered to bear the sins of many***; and ***unto them that look for him shall he appear the second time*** without sin unto salvation.
>
> —Hebrews 9:24–26, 28

His Second Coming

Chapter 23
Cleansing Power of the Blood of Jesus

> *But if we walk in the light, as he is in the light, we have fellowship one with another, and the blood of Jesus Christ his Son cleanseth us from all sin.*
>
> —*1 John 1:7*

For one to believe in the cleansing power of the blood of Jesus Christ, one first needs to ask the question: "Was Jesus just a man, or just another prophet? Or was He the Son of the living God?" For the correct answer, we need to go directly to the Scriptures. The Bible tells us that Jesus came in the form of sinful flesh. He took on Himself the form of man. Why? So that He could destroy him who had the power of death, that is, the devil. The next question is: Why? The answer is that He could deliver us who had been kept in bondage through fear of death! So, the Bible says He took on Himself not the nature of angels but the seed of Abraham. The Bible says He wanted to be just like us, having the exact origin, being made as a man instead of as an angel (Phil. 2:7), so that He could become a merciful and faithful high priest in things pertaining to God to make reconciliation for the sins of the people. Since He suffered and was tempted as a man, He can likewise help us who are tempted (Heb. 2:14–18).

Jesus, being full of the Holy Spirit, operated as 100 percent man. In this fashion, He went to the cross to be crucified. Though Jesus was 100 percent man on earth, He was also 100 percent God and made this very clear to Mary, whose brother Lazarus had died before He raised Him from the dead.

Jesus said to her: I am the LIVING GOD: The resurrection, and the life: whoever trusts in me, even if he dies, he shall live." And everyone who lives because of faith in me will never really die. Do you believe this?"

"Yes, Lord!" she replied. "I believe you are the Christ, the Son of God. You are the one we hoped would come into the world" (John 11:24-27 CEV). Jesus made his deity known once more and said, "Very truly I tell you, **whoever hears my word** and believes him who sent me **has eternal life** and **will not be judged** but **has crossed over from death to life** (John 5:24 NIV).

(It is important to note here that Jesus becoming God's Son did not happen by God desiring a wife to have sexual relations, according to what many religions teach, but through the Father's perfect will).

Jesus became a Son of God by a decree that was made by God the Father spoken to Him from eternity past according to the Psalmist: I will proclaim the decree spoken to Me by the LORD: "You are My Son; today I have become Your Father" (Psalms 2:7).

The Scripture in another place says, "For to which of the angels did God ever say: "You are My Son; today I have become Your Father"? Or again: "I will be His Father, and He will be My Son"? (Hebrews 1:5) Jesus, being perfect God, had to become a perfect man, called by God to be the perfect High Priest to minister to the things about God. In the same way, Christ did not take on himself the glory of becoming a high priest. But God said to him, "You are my Son; today I have become your Father" (Hebrews 5:5).

Consequently, this great High Priest would also offer a gift and sacrifice to God like other high priests. This God-man would offer up himself as a living sacrifice as a gift to God for the harsh payment of the suffering of humanity. His soul would be made as an offering for sin. "He would see the fruit of his offering and be satisfied"

His Second Coming

(Isaiah 53:10-11, Masoretic Text). The blood of the Holy God-man would take away the sin of the world.

Jesus is the perfect lamb of God. As the God-man, His blood would be perfect to make atonement for sin. The Scripture declares that the next day, John saw Jesus coming unto him and said:

> Behold the Lamb of God, which taketh away the sin of the world. This is he of whom I said, After me cometh a man which is preferred before me: for he was before me. And I knew him not: but that he should be made manifest to Israel, therefore am I come baptizing with water. And John bare record, saying, I saw the Spirit descending from heaven like a dove, and it abode upon him. And I knew him not: but he that sent me to baptize with water, the same said unto me, Upon **whom thou shalt see the Spirit descending, and remaining on him, the same is he which baptizeth with the Holy Ghost**. And **I saw** and **bare record** that **this is the Son of God**. Again the next day after John stood, and two of his disciples; And looking upon Jesus as he walked, he saith, **Behold the Lamb of God**.
>
> —John 1:29–36

Before Jesus went to the cross to be crucified, He told His disciples that His body would be destroyed, but He would raise it on the third day. This He did, conquering both death and the grave. Today, Jesus is seated at the right hand of God, making intercession for us. This is very important for us to understand and to know the truth. The Bible says it is this truth that will set us free. This truth needs to be told! That if Jesus was just an ordinary man or a prophet who came to earth to show us how to live according to some faith, then His sacrificial death would not be able to save us from our sins. There would be no power in His shed blood to forgive us of our sins and to cleanse us from all unrighteousness (1 John 1:9). The Bible says the Holy Spirit bore witness that He was the Son of God with power when He was raised from the dead (Rom. 1:3–4).

The Holy Spirit Himself that lives within the bodies of the believers also bears witness that Jesus is exactly who He says He is, the Son of the living God! Jesus Himself said in His Word that if you do not believe in His Word, you should believe in the very works that He does because He does nothing of Himself, but whatever the Father told Him to do, He does (John 10:37-38). Then you will know that He came out of the very bosom of His Father to be the ultimate sacrifice for sin and the Savior of man's soul (John 1:18; 8:42).

Now, let us go deeper into the Word of God, and we will see why the cleansing power of Jesus can and does make us clean (whiter than snow). Remember, the words of Jesus are truth, spirits, and life. Jesus says in His Word:

> Come now, and let us reason together, saith the Lord: though your sins be as scarlet, they shall be as white as snow; though they be red like crimson, they shall be as wool.
>
> —Isaiah 1:18

Jesus is saying that His blood can wash you and make you clean. Remember, God told Moses that the blood cleanses the soul from sin. Blood is used as atonement for the soul (Leviticus 17:11). Jesus tells us in His Word that we have no life within us unless we eat His flesh and drink His blood. We are like walking dead. In our society today, we find many people who go around saying that they are good folks as they try to convince themselves that they have a right to

His Second Coming

enter into the kingdom of heaven. Jesus says, "Without my blood washing you and making you clean, you have no part of me. You are like a walking dead. All of your righteousness is as filthy rags before me" (see Isa. 64:6). You have no light within you: You have no life within you (John 8:12). Just as bread gives life to the body, so does the body of Christ, which is the true bread, the living bread give life to the world spiritually and give us life eternal. The Bible says that the blood of Christ has redeemed us. Through His blood, our sins can be forgiven (Eph. 1:7). He has purchased us and restored us to the Father by His blood. It is His blood and faith in the power of His blood that has given us a blessed assurance and peace of mind that our eternity is secure in Him

Hebrews 10:19-22 states:

> And so, dear brothers and sisters, we can boldly enter heaven's Most Holy Place because of the blood of Jesus. By his death, Jesus opened a new and life-giving way through the curtain into the Most Holy Place. And since we have a great High Priest who rules over God's house, let us go right into the presence of God with sincere hearts fully trusting him. For our guilty consciences have been sprinkled with Christ's blood to make us clean, and our bodies have been washed with pure water.

For this reason, God has given Christ the Messiah, a human body, not the body of angels, so that through his body, which is the veil or the curtain, a consecrated way is open for humanity. It is now possible for humanity to enter into the Most Holy place before God by the blood of Christ. This is the hope that Jesus Christ has given to us. Christ has given humanity a firm and secure anchor for the soul (Hebrews 6:19).

This blood, the Bible says, is without spot or blemish; it is holy. The Bible says this is a new and living way (Heb. 9:11). We can now come boldly before the throne of God to receive grace. This is now possible through the cleansing and atoning blood of Jesus Christ. For this reason, we need to give thanks unto the Father:

> . . .which had made us meet to be partakers of the inheritance of the saints in light: Who has delivered us from the power of darkness, and hath translated us into the kingdom of his dear Son: In whom we have redemption through his blood, even the forgiveness of sins. Who is the image of the invisible God, the firstborn of every creature: For by him were all things created, that are in heaven, and that are in earth, visible and invisible, whether they be thrones, or dominions, or principalities, or powers: all things were created by him, and for him: And he is before all things, and by him, all things consist. And he is the head of the body, the church: who is the beginning, the firstborn from the dead; that in all things he might have the preeminence.
>
> For it pleased the Father that in him should all fulness dwell; And, having made peace through the blood of his cross, by him to reconcile all things unto himself; by him, I say, whether they be things in earth or things in heaven.
>
> —Colossians 1:12–20

Unto Jesus Christ, "who is the faithful witness, and the first begotten of the dead, and the prince of the kings of the earth. Unto him that loved us, and washed us from our sins in his own blood: And hath made us kings and priests unto God and his Father; to him be glory and dominion forever and ever. Amen" (Rev. 1:5–6).

His Second Coming

Chapter 24
Direct Communication to Jesus, Our High Priest

The LORD hath sworn, and will not repent, Thou art a priest for ever after the order of Melchizedek.

—Psalm 110:4

It is indeed a wonderful privilege for us to come before the throne of the Most High God through the blood of His Son Jesus Christ, our great High Priest. We have such a High Priest that is set on the right hand of the throne of the Majesty in the heavens. Let us draw near with a true and humble heart.

> For it became him, for whom are all things, and by whom are all things, in bringing many sons unto glory, to make the captain of their salvation perfect through sufferings. Forasmuch then as the children are partakers of flesh and blood, he also himself likewise took part of the same; that through death he might destroy him that had the power of death, that is, the devil; And deliver them who through fear of death were all their lifetime subject to bondage. For verily he took not on him the nature of angels, but he took on him the seed of Abraham. Wherefore in all things it behooved him to be made like unto his brethren, that he might be a merciful and faithful high priest in things pertaining to God, to make reconciliation for the sins of the people For in that he himself hath suffered being tempted, he is able to succor [help] them that are tempted.

Dr. Marlene Brown

—Hebrews 2:10, 14–18

The Scripture revealed to us why Jesus was given a body. Jesus wanted to experience the same suffering that man experienced in the body. Jesus wants to identify with humans to be a merciful and faithful high priest in things concerning God for us. As a high priest, his job is to make reconciliation for the sins of the people. As the captain of our salvation, he also wants to experience suffering as a human so that he might destroy Satan through his death. Satan had the power of death. Another significant reason Jesus had to be made human was to fulfill the spoken words of Isaiah, who said that the Messiah would be a suffering servant.

The prophet Isaiah said:

> Surely he hath borne our griefs, and carried our sorrows: yet we did esteem him stricken, smitten of God, and afflicted. But he was wounded for our transgressions, he was bruised for our iniquities: the chastisement of our peace was upon him; and with his stripes we are healed.
>
> —Isaiah 53:4

The apostle Peter said: "He himself bore our sins" in his body on the cross so that we might die to sins and live for righteousness; "by his wounds, you have been healed" (1 Peter 2:24). Our great High Priest took the responsibility of the curse of sin unto himself (Galatians 4:13). He is like none other. He alone should be worshipped and adored as our great high priest. We have a High Priest whose blood is used to save us and whose body is used to heal us. We have a High Priest who makes intercession for us daily as He sits at the right hand of the Highest. This is excellent indeed. It is a much better covenant than the first covenant.

The Scriptures encourage us now to come direct to our high priest who is before the throne of grace:

His Second Coming

Seeing then that we have a great high priest passed into the heavens, Jesus, the Son of God, let us hold fast to our profession. For we have not a high priest which cannot be touched with the feeling of our infirmities; but was in all points tempted like as we are, yet without sin. ***Let us, therefore, come boldly unto the throne of grace***, that we may ***obtain mercy and find grace*** to help ***in time of need***.

—Hebrews 4:14–16

So now, brethren, we enter boldly into the holy of holies by the blood of Jesus when we pray. It is our new and living way that Christ has consecrated for us. Now we have a High Priest in the house of God; let us draw near with a true heart in full assurance of faith, having our hearts sprinkled with His blood to cleanse an evil conscience and our bodies washed with pure water to serve the living God.

Dr. Marlene Brown

Chapter 25
Significance of the Cross

For the preaching of the cross is to them that perish foolishness; but unto us which are saved it is the power of God.

—1 Corinthians 1:18

The cross is a symbol of Christianity; it signifies salvation. It also signifies life as well as death by crucifixion. No wonder Paul says we need to die to ourselves daily, and Jesus says we need to deny ourselves and take up our cross to follow Him (Luke 9:23).

To fully understand the great significance of the cross, one first needs to look into the world of crucifixion. What does crucifixion mean? What happens to someone when they are crucified? What are the characteristics of the type of people that got crucified? Only through the revelation of these facts and truths can we come to the profound reality and appreciation of what Jesus did for us when He went to the cross.

It is also important to note that before Jesus went to the cross, He revealed to His disciples what death He would suffer and how He would rise again on the third day (Matt. 20:18–19). He also clarified to them that no man took His life, but He laid it down Himself so that He could pick it up again: He has the power to lay it down and take it up again. Jesus said in His Word that He received this commandment from His Father; by doing this, He knew that His Father would love Him because He laid down His life to take it up again. He then made it very clear that He is the good shepherd, and the good shepherd is willing to lay down His life for His sheep. He

His Second Coming

pointed out that a hired servant would see the wolf coming and run because the sheep do not belong to Him. The good shepherd, however, will lay down His life to rescue His sheep. The good shepherd will also leave ninety-nine sheep to go out looking for the lost one (John 10:11–18). Jesus also spoke these words to the people concerning who He is and what death He would suffer: Then he said: "And I, if I be lifted up from the earth, will draw all men unto me" (John 12:32). He declared again in John 8:28–29: "When ye have lifted up the Son of man, then shall ye know that I am he and do nothing of myself; but as my Father taught me, I speak these things. And he that sent me is with me: the Father hath not left me alone; for I always do those things that please him." Jesus told Nicodemus that "as Moses lifted up the serpent in the wilderness, even so, must the Son of man be lifted up: That whosoever believeth in him should not perish, but have eternal life" (John 3:14–15).

The cross signifies life. It represents the love of God toward man. Man was hopeless in sin and in dire need of a Savior, so God had to send forth His Son, whom His love can redeem through the death of His Son on the cross. Jesus pointed out that when you lift Him up on that cross, He will begin to draw all men unto Him by His love for them, that through Him, they would have eternal life. He says no man has greater love than laying down his life for his friend.

Now we see that when Christ went to the cross, He went to fulfill a command from the eternal God, His Father. To fully appreciate the cross and the crucifixion of Christ, we need to understand the procedures that one goes through when one goes to the cross to be crucified. Who were the people that got crucified?

The Crucifixion, according to First-Century Authors

Written below are the gruesome details of crucifixion done by the Roman soldiers, as described by first-century authors.[2] The Greek

---

[2] "Crucifixion" found at http://www.biblestudytools.com/dictionaries/smiths-bible-dictionary/crucifixion.html (accessed January 19, 2010).

word for *crucify* is *stauroo*, which means "to drive down stakes." This is a Roman means of execution in which the victims, such as thieves, were nailed to a cross. First-century authors vividly describe to us the agony and disgrace of being crucified. They tell us that Jesus was laid down upon the implementation of torture:

> His arms were stretched along the cross-beams, and at the center of the open palms, the point of a huge iron nail was placed, which, by the blow of a mallet, was driven home into the wood. Then, through either foot separately, or possibly through both together, another huge nail tore its way through the quivering flesh as they were placed one over the other. [This can be confirmed by my vision of Christ on the cross. His arms were stretched along the crossbeams with His palms opened at the center. Both of His feet were together with one on top of the other, with His knees bent.] Whether the sufferer was also bound to the cross we do not know; but, to prevent the hands and feet from being torn away by the weight of the body, a wooden projection, strong enough to support at least in part, a human body [was placed], which soon became a weight of agony.

Then the "accursed tree" with its living human burden was slowly heaved up, and the end fixed firmly in a hole in the ground. The feet were but a little raised above the earth. The victim was in full reach of every hand that might choose to strike. Death by crucifixion seems to have included all that pain and death can have of the horrible and ghastly—dizziness, cramp, thirst, starvation, sleeplessness, traumatic fever, tetanus, publicity of shame, the long continuance of torment, horror of anticipation, mortification of untended wounds, all intensified just up to the point at which they can be endured at all, but all stopping just short of the point which would give the sufferer the relief of unconsciousness. The unnatural position made every movement painful; the lacerated veins and crushed tendons throbbed with incessant anguish; the wounds,

His Second Coming

inflamed by exposure, gradually gangrened; the arteries, especially of the head and stomach, became swollen and oppressed with surcharged blood; and while each variety of misery went on gradually increasing, there was added to them the intolerable pang of a burning and raging thirst. Such was the death to which Christ was doomed. Farrars states in "Life of Christ:" The crucified was watched, according to custom, by a party of four soldiers (John 19:23) with their centurion (Matthew 27:66) whose express office was to prevent the stealing of the body. The fracture of the legs was especially adopted by the Jews to hasten death (John 19:31). The sepulture [burial] was generally therefore forbidden, but in consequences of (Deuteronomy 21:22-23), an express natural exception was made in favor of the Jews (Matthew 27:58). This accursed and awful mode of punishment was happily abolished by Constantine.

The strength and cry that Jesus made showed that He did not die the ordinary death of those crucified; those men who commonly suffered long periods of complete agony and exhaustion usually went unconscious before dying. We read in the Bible that Jesus was not unconscious through His long period of suffering and agony because the Scriptures declare that He cried with a loud voice and then gave up the ghost (Matthew 27:50).

Dr. Marlene Brown

Chapter 26
The Cross Experience of Jesus

For he hath made him to be sin for us, who knew no sin; that we might be made the righteousness of God in him.

—*2 Corinthians 5:21*

Yes, Jesus went to the cross, the one that was just described. He did endure all that the crucifixion entails. However, there was just one problem: He was not found guilty in any way, shape, or form before He went to the cross or even during the process of the crucifixion. The Bible says as a lamb to the slaughter, He was carried off, and as a sheep, before the shearer is dumb, so He opened, not His mouth. Neither was there any guile or bitterness found in His mouth. The Scripture says in Philippians that He was obedient even unto the death of the cross.

Over four hundred years before Christ's birth, the prophet Isaiah prophesied of the cross and what the Messiah would go through. Here is what the prophet Isaiah saw:

> He is despised and rejected of men; a man of sorrows, and acquainted with grief: and we hid as it were our faces from him; he was despised, and we esteemed him not. Surely, he hath borne our griefs and carried our sorrows: yet we did esteem him stricken, smitten of God, and afflicted. But he was wounded for our transgressions and bruised for our iniquities: the chastisement of our peace was upon him, and with his stripes, we are healed. All we, as sheep, have gone astray; we have turned every one to his own way, and the Lord hath laid on him the iniquity of us all. He was

oppressed, and he was afflicted, yet he opened not his mouth: he is brought as a lamb to the slaughter, and as a sheep, before her shearers are dumb, so he openeth not his mouth. He was taken from prison and judgment: and who shall declare his generation? for he was cut off from the land of the living: for the transgression of my people was he stricken. And he made his grave with the wicked and the rich in his death; because he had done no violence, neither was any deceit in his mouth. Yet, it pleased the Lord to bruise him; he hath put him to grief: when thou shalt make his soul an offering for sin.

—Isaiah 53:3–10

King David also had an insight into the cross as he envisioned what the Messiah would go through. He gave details as to what Jesus was feeling while on the cross. This was before the birth of Christ and recorded in Psalm 22:13– 20:

They gaped upon me with their mouths like a ravening and a roaring lion. I am poured out like water, and all my bones are out of joint: my heart is like wax; it is melted in the midst of my bowels. My strength is dried up like a potsherd, and my tongue cleaveth to my jaws, and thou hast brought me into the dust of death. For dogs have compassed me: the assembly of the wicked have enclosed me: they pierced my hands and my feet. I may tell all my bones: they look and stare upon me. They part my garments among them and cast lots upon my vesture. But be not thou far from me, O Lord: O my strength, haste thee to help me. Deliver my soul from the sword; my darling from the power of the dog.

Let us view the fulfillment of the prophecy of Christ the Messiah as He went to the cross before Pontius Pilate, the governor, to receive His death sentence for the sins of the world.

The Scripture tells us that they took Jesus before the governor, and as He stood, the governor asked Him, "Are you King of the Jews?" He answered and said, "Thou sayest." But when the chief priest and elders accused him, He did not say a word. Then Pilate said to him, "Haven't you heard how many things they witness against you?" He answered him, not a word, so much that the governor greatly marveled. I believe that at this point, Jesus had already been strengthened through prayer in mind and spirit to go through the execution before Him, so trying to defend Himself would have been useless. The Bible says it was customary for the governor to release a prisoner to the people at that particular feast. So, when they were gathered together, Pilate asked them, "Whom do you want me to release unto you, Barabbas or Jesus, who is called Christ?" They answered, "Barabbas!" The Bible says that Pilate knew that they had delivered Jesus out of envy.

Personally, I find this statement to be remarkable. It reveals that Pilate knew the reason why they brought Jesus before him. He knew that the people were very envious of Him. This was so obvious! Why were they envious of Him, one might ask? Because He went about doing a lot of good! His only crime was being too good to society. He went around healing the sick, cleansing lepers, driving out demons, and making people whole in body, mind, and spirit. Jesus says in Matthew 7:6 that He testifies of the world that its deeds are evil, so the world hates Him! Sure enough, we see this with the scribes and Pharisees who did not like Him. He was too anointed; He was too good. The anointing of God was too powerful on Him.

It is important to note that this type of jealousy and envy existed not only in biblical times but also today among Christians. For this reason, Paul warns us not to let jealousy and envy, among other sins, "be once named among you as you become saints."

The Scripture says that the chief priest and elders persuaded the multitude to ask for Barabbas and destroy Jesus. At this point, someone might ask, "What is the chief priest's and elders' role?"

His Second Coming

Their role was to enter into the holy of holies (from which the other priests were excluded) and offer sacrifices for their own sins as well as the sins of the people. They also presided over the Supreme Council when convened for judicial deliberations. So, Pilate asked them, "What shall I do with this man Jesus?" and they answered and said: "Let him be crucified!" Pilate then asked the crowd, "What evil has he done?" But they cried out even more, the Bible says, saying: "Let him be crucified." When Pilate realized that he could not change their minds or prevail against them, he washed his hands with water and said, "See to it that I am innocent of this just person!" What the crowd said was most interesting. They cried out a blood-chilling response: "His blood be upon us and upon our children!" So, Pilate released Barabbas unto them, and when he was through scourging Jesus, he delivered him to be crucified. Scourging was the Roman method of flogging. They used a whip made of several strips of leather into which were embedded (near the ends) pieces of bone and lead. The Jews limited the number of stripes that the victim could receive (in practice, they would give thirty-nine stripes in case of a miscount). The Romans, however, did not place such limitations on the number of stripes, and victims of Roman floggings most times would not survive; sometimes, the victims died before execution. Now we see why Jesus fell under the cross. Being just a man, most of His strength was already drained from this type of flogging, with the pieces of bone and lead burning through His flesh.

They then took Jesus into the common hall and gathered around Him the entire band of soldiers, who stripped Him and put on Him a scarlet robe. They then plaited a crown of thorns, put it on His head, and put a reed in His right hand. The crown of thorns came from a prickly plant. The Greek word for *thorns* means "briers"; many are in the Holy Land. The robe and crown were parts of the attire they placed upon Jesus to mock Him. They then bowed before Him and mocked Him, saying, "Hail, King of the Jews!" And they spit upon Him, and took the reed, and smote Him on the head. And after they mocked Him, they took the robe off Him, put His own clothing on Him, and led Him away to crucify Him.

Dr. Marlene Brown

What horrible, horrible treatment Jesus went through for us! No wonder some religions teach that He did not go to the cross! What Christ went through for us was total shame and degradation. He was stripped of all his clothing before all the soldiers, then had a crown of thorns or briers placed on His head. He was then mocked and spit upon while people hit Him on the head. Not to mention the stripes still stinging his back from the flesh that had been ripped open by the flogging. This was definitely too much for Jesus Christ to bear as a man! No wonder when He went into the garden of Gethsemane to pray, He cried and said, "Father, if it is possible, let this cup pass from me!

Nevertheless, not my will, but thy will be done!" He said that He wished there was some other way to redeem man instead of going through what He would be going through. He had to become a sin! He had to taste sin! He had to experience being separated from the Father for the first time to become a sin! The holiness of who He is could not bear the thought of becoming defiled and filthy before the holy God, as God's eyes are too pure to look upon sin. But He knew that He had to drink from that particular cup. God designed it for Him to go through this process as a man to bear our sins! Nevertheless, He told His disciples that His soul was exceedingly sorrowful even unto death.

These were the horrible things that Jesus went through for us. He took on Himself all of the shame and disgrace of our past. No wonder He said in His Word that no condemnation to them take on His name and His identity; those who abide in Him and walk not after the flesh but the spirit. Jesus is telling us that He went through all different types of condemnation for us, and once you take onto yourself His name and identity, there is no more condemnation. He will never ever condemn you. He will meet you wherever you are in sin, wash you, and make you clean. No pain is too great that He cannot feel or sin too deep that He cannot bear it. The Bible says Christ has borne it all. For this reason, He is touched by the feelings of our pain and infirmities. The Scripture says that Christ had become sin itself, who knew no sin, so that we can be made the righteousness of God in Him, according to 2 Corinthians 5:21.

The scriptural account of Jesus's execution says that as the soldiers and Jesus made their way to Calvary, they found a man of Cyrene, Simon by name, whom they compelled to bear the cross. At this point, the weight was too much for Christ to bear. As I read this Scripture, a hymn came to my mind: "Must Jesus bear the cross alone, and all the world goes free? There is a cross for everyone, and there is a cross for me." Jesus also said in the Scriptures that if any man comes after Him, he should deny himself, take up his cross, and follow Him (Matt. 16:24). As Christians, we need to understand the kind of warfare we are constantly going through. The Word of God points out that our warfare is not with flesh and blood but against principalities and powers, rulers of the darkness of this world. It is all about the prince of this world entering into man's heart to condemn man and deceive him so that he will continue to live in sin. So then, the cross that we will have to carry as Christians is composed of the decisions that we make from day to day as we continue to live in the flesh but walk in the spirit. This means that our hearts and minds need to be steadfast on God's things, whether they are things on earth or things in heaven. The Word of God controls us. These decisions should reflect the fruits of the spirit in our lives and represent Christ, even if it costs us our lives. As Jesus pointed out in Revelation, we must be faithful unto death, and then He will give us the crown of life! He guarantees this promise.

The Bible declares:

> And when they have come unto a place called Golgotha, that is to say, a place of a skull, They gave him vinegar to drink mingled with gall: and when he had tasted thereof, he would not drink. And they crucified him, and parted his

garments, casting lots: that it might be fulfilled which was spoken by the prophet, They parted my garments among them, and upon my vesture did they cast lots. And sitting down they watched him there, and set up over his head his accusation written, "THIS IS JESUS THE KING OF THE JEWS."

—Matthew 27: 33–37

The Scripture continues to say He was crucified between two thieves, one on the right hand and one on the left. When the people passed by, they reviled Him, wagging their heads and saying, "Thou that destroyest the temple, and buildest it in three days, save thyself. If thou be the Son of God, come down from the cross" (Matt. 27:40). In their ignorance, they could not comprehend that Jesus was referring to His body. The Bible says our body is the temple of the Lord. Moreover, He did die and rise again on the third day. The Word of God continues:

Likewise also, the chief priests mocking him, with the scribes and elders, said, He saved others; himself he cannot save. If he be the King of Israel, let him now come down from the cross, and we will believe him. He trusted in God; let him deliver him now, if he has him: for he said, I am the Son of God. The thieves, who were crucified with him, cast the same in his teeth.

—Matthew 27:41–44

When I read this verse, I shake my head at these people because then I realize how simple men are in their thoughts and how simple men can be. The Bible points out that the natural man cannot understand the spiritual things of God because they are spiritually discerned. These people did not know that He was indeed the Son of the living God and that He could have called a host of angels to destroy the world and set Him free. However, the Scriptures must be fulfilled. And His purpose on earth must be completed. As He pointed out in the Scriptures, no man took His life from Him, but He laid it down so that He could pick it up again. The Scriptures continued by saying:

> Now from the sixth hour, there was darkness over all the land unto the ninth hour. And about the ninth hour, Jesus cried loudly, saying, Eli, Eli, lama sabachthani? That is to say, My God, my God, why hast thou forsaken me? When they heard that, some of them that stood there said, This man calleth Elias. And straightway, one of them ran, took a sponge, filled it with vinegar, put it on a reed, and gave him to drink. The rest said, Let be; let us see whether Elias will come to save him. Jesus, when he had cried again with a loud voice, yielded up the ghost. And, behold, the temple's veil was rent in twain from top to bottom; the earth did quake, and the rocks rent, giving us free access to the Father, to the precious throne of grace. And the graves were opened, and many bodies of the saints which slept arose, And came out of the graves after his resurrection, and went into the holy city, and appeared unto many.
>
> —Matthew 27:45–53

Wonderful Savior indeed! I believe that apart from the blood of Jesus that was shed to redeem man and the stripes on His body that have given us our healing, tearing the veil from top to bottom was the most beautiful thing we could ask for as believers. The tearing of the veil provides us the awesome privilege to go directly before the throne of God. The veil was the inner curtain that they used to separate the holy place from the holiest place. So, when this veil or curtain was torn in two, it signified that Christ had torn down the middle wall of partition between God and man. He now makes it possible for a man to come directly before God's throne and before His presence to receive His love, grace, forgiveness, and mercy without an earthly priest (Heb. 9:1–14, 10:14–22). Christ has now become man's High Priest, sitting at God's right hand, making intercession for us. He is the mediator between God and man. Now, we see the ultimate sacrifice that Jesus made for us. The Bible says He became poor so you and I can become rich. The cross was the only way the Father could redeem a man. The cross was the only way God could commune with a man once more as He did with Adam in the garden in the cool of the day before sin. The cross allowed man to regain this great relationship with the Father as it destroys sin in our lives and gives us the righteousness of God through Jesus Christ. It gives us back our rightful place on earth once more to rule, reign in righteousness and true holiness, and have dominion, thus allowing the kingdom of God to come on earth as in heaven. The cross gives us the right to become Sons of God; it gives us eternal life and an inheritance with the saints. This is the great significance of the cross.

Now we see why God has highly exalted Jesus according to Philippians 2:9–11, for He deserves such glory, honor, and praise. The Scripture says:

> God also has highly exalted him and given him a name above every name. That at the name of Jesus, every knee should bow, of things in heaven, and things in earth, and things under the earth; And that every tongue should confess that Jesus Christ is Lord, to the glory of God the Father.

Through the precious blood of the cross, people are still being saved, delivered, and set free, and the power of His stripes is still healing others today.

His Second Coming

Chapter 27
Born Dead for 15 Minutes—The Cross

And it shall come to pass, that whosoever shall call on the name of the Lord shall be saved.

—*Acts 2:21*

The wounds, and the stripes of Christ are still healing people today. I am living proof that the Word of God is true and faithful and that by His stripes, we are healed. Let me share with you my experience of the birth of my second child—how the stripes of Jesus healed him and made him whole. This story of my child's birth and the miracle God performed on him by the stripes of Jesus was also aired on "Something Good Tonight Hour of Healing." The airdate was 1/12/04, on Richard Roberts's television program worldwide and on Internet stations. After reading my story concerning the birth and recovery of my child, you will see that Jesus, the Son of God, is still in the healing business because of His great love and mercy towards us, His children.

On February 22, 2002, I gave birth to a beautiful baby boy named Brian, but my ordeal tested my faith. At the time of birth, the doctor had cut the umbilical cord around the baby's neck while the baby's body was still inside the womb without my knowledge. He must have thought the process would be easy because the baby's head was small. However, he was wrong because the baby took five minutes or more to come out fully. When he came out, he was huge. He weighed 9 lbs. 8 ounces and was neither breathing nor crying. The doctors began to work on him, but there was no response. I then heard several sirens in the hospital and someone speaking on the intercom, saying code pink! I then saw the room begin to fill up with doctors and nurses who were all trying desperately to save the baby.

During this time, I remained calm. I did not have one twitch of fear. While the doctor was still working on my body, I stretched my hand toward the area where they had the baby and tried to revive him. I was in intense prayer to my Lord Jesus. I began to say, "Lord, no, not like this. Please don't let the enemy do this to me." I remembered a specific Scripture that the Lord had given me while I was pregnant, and it went like this: "Call upon me in the day of trouble: I will answer thee, and thou shalt glorify me" (Ps. 50:15).

So, I began to pray this prayer and remind the Lord of His Word. I began to plead the blood of Jesus as well. After a good while of intense prayer with the Lord—fifteen minutes or more—I heard a faint cry from the baby. This was all I needed to hear. The cry was softer than a cat's meow. But for me, it was OK. The baby was going to be okay. He had an oxygen tube on his face when they brought him over to me. His body was huge, with hardly any life in his system. They then rushed him off to the intensive care unit. When the ordeal was over, they took me to my room. I then phoned the ICU to find out how my baby was doing. The nurse who answered the phone asked me whether I would like a visit from the doctor to explain what was going on with the baby. I immediately said, "Sure," thinking nothing of it.

After a few minutes, the doctor came to my room, introducing himself as a baby specialist. He told me that they had x-rayed the baby's chest and found that the baby only had one fully developed lung, and one side of his diaphragm was paralyzed. He then showed me the x-ray for me to have a look. And sure enough, I could see ribs on one side and fog on the other. I could also see one side of the diaphragm up and another side down. The specialist reassured me that it would be OK because, he explained, many people are living with one lung. My response was, "Really, well, let me tell you

His Second Coming

something: the Lord is going to heal him! I want to hear nothing of it because the Lord will heal him!" Of course, he thought I was crazy for saying that my son would be healed. When I returned to my maternity room, my family doctor came to visit, and this was his response: "I saw the baby; he is a very big baby, but there is not much life in his body for his size. He only has one lung functioning, but many people live with only one lung today. They would remove one lung, especially if you smoke and have lung cancer. Don't worry about it; you must be careful if he should catch a cold. It would be more difficult for him to breathe," he explained. I responded, "Really, well, let me tell you something. My God will heal him! I want to hear nothing of it because he will be healed." He looked at me as though I were crazy for saying that. I remember my husband asking one of the specialists if they could do an operation on his chest to fix it. And the response was he was too young and weak. There is nothing that we can do. They were also thinking of sending Brian to a sick kids' hospital in Toronto, Canada, because of the severity of his condition.

However, that hospital had no vacant beds. I believe the Lord's plan was to show His mercy and His power toward us to bring glory to His name. Almost every hour of the day, we would go in to have a visit with Brian. His face would seem brighter and brighter, and he looked stronger and stronger. Brian spent less than two weeks in the hospital, and the only treatment the doctors gave him during his stay was an oxygen tube. He received no form of medication from the doctors. While he was in the hospital, the doctors did two x-rays.

Reading from the X-Ray

Pediatric chest: This newborn patient is **intubated with the tip of the endotracheal tube** just above the carina and can be pulled back slightly. **Opacification in the right upper lung zone** may represent the thymus or right upper lobe collapse. Follow-up is recommended.

Brian's Second X-Ray

The second pediatric chest x-ray result read: Comparison with previous radiographs dated February 22, 2002. ***The endotracheal tube has been removed.*** The ***previously seen opacity*** projecting over the right upper lung zone is ***no longer evident.*** The volume of the ***right lung***, however, ***is still smaller than the left*** with elevation of the right hemidiaphragm.

These were the results of the two x-rays they did on Brian while he was in the hospital. As mentioned before, he spent ***less than two weeks*** in the hospital. The following week, we did the first follow-up x-ray of his chest. When we went to see the specialist for the result, the result was most excellent!

Brian's Follow-up with Specialist after 2 Weeks

Due to the improvement shown on Brian's second x-ray, the doctors released him from the hospital and admonished us to see a heart and lung specialist. The specialist admonished us to have another chest x-ray done to see how much swelling there was in his head.

Third X-Ray Reading

It read, "***Chest***: The heart and mediastinal structures ***are normal. The lungs clear.***" That was all written on the sheet. Brian's specialist addresses Brian as the miracle baby. He could not believe Brian was healed without any medication or operation. Needless to say, I was jumping and shouting and giving God the glory right in his office!

The Lord of the universe, Jesus, in His name, reached down and performed an operation that doctors could not do. To him be all honor and glory. Yes, by his stripes, Brian was healed!

Brian is also doing exceptionally well. He has been talking from ten months old and walking at one year. His

His Second Coming

vocabulary is extensive, and his words are clear. He is very handsome, strong, and healthy. To God be all the glory, honor, and praise.

Jesus went to the cross for you and for me. Greater love than this has no man than for one to lay down his life for his friends! He said in His Word that we are no longer servants but friends. "In this was manifested the love of God toward us, because that God sent his only begotten Son into the world, that we might live through him. Herein is love, not that we loved God, but that he loved us, and sent his Son *to be the* propitiation [substitute] for our sins" (1 John 4:9–10). The cross means life! It is our only hope. "For God so loved the world, that he gave his only begotten Son, that whosoever believeth in him should not perish, but have everlasting life" (John. 3:16).

Dr. Marlene Brown

Chapter 28
The Resurrection of Christ

O death, where is thy sting? O grave, where is thy victory?

—1 Corinthians 15:55

Jesus Christ is raised from the dead. Alleluia! The resurrection of Christ is the most crucial event that has ever taken place in the world. It is the heart of Christianity. Our hope in Christ is based on the fact that He has defeated death and hell. Christ has conquered the grave, and because He lives, those who trust Him shall also live.

Let us go through the event that took place on the day when Christ was raised. This is found in Luke 24. The Scripture declares that "upon the first day of the week, very early in the morning, they came unto the sepulcher, bringing the spices which they had prepared, and certain others with them" (Luke 24:1). The first day of the week signifies that it was a Sunday. By Jewish time, Sunday begins at sundown on Saturday. This allowed the women time to buy spices for the next day, which was Sunday.

> And they found the stone rolled away from the sepulcher. And they entered in and found not the body of the Lord Jesus. And it came to pass, as they were much perplexed thereabout, behold, two men stood by them in shining garments: And as they were afraid, and bowed down their faces to the earth, they said unto them, Why seek ye the living among the dead? He is not here, but is risen: remember how he spake unto you when he was yet in Galilee, Saying, The Son of man must be delivered into the

hands of sinful men, and be crucified, and the third day rise again. And they remembered His words And returned from the sepulcher, and told all these things unto the eleven, and to all the rest. It was Mary Magdalene and Joanna, and Mary the mother of James, and other women that were with them, which told these things unto the apostles. And their words seemed to them as idle tales, and they believed them not.

—Luke 24:2–11

Now we see that women did the first preaching of Christ's resurrection. The Bible also declares that the apostles took the message as idle tales. Not only did they not believe the women, but they also forgot the words spoken to them directly by Jesus Christ Himself, the Son of the living God. This makes me wonder, did they believe Christ when He mentioned to them that He would die and then rise again on the third day? Or were they saying to themselves, this is still happening among us today; the Lord is speaking, but many of us are just not listening or simply do not believe His message? So, we hear the Word, and then we quickly forget His Word.

The Bible continues to say:

Then arose Peter and ran unto the sepulcher; stooping down, he beheld the linen clothes laid by themselves and departed, wondering in himself at what was come to pass. And, behold, two of them went that same day to a village called Emmaus, which was from Jerusalem about threescore furlongs. And they talked together of all these things which had happened. And it came to pass that, while they communed together and reasoned, Jesus himself drew near and went with them. But their eyes were holden that they should not know him. And he said unto them, What manner of communications are these that ye have one to another, as ye walk, and are sad? And the one of them, whose name was Cleopas, answering said unto him, Art thou only a stranger in Jerusalem, and hast not known the things which are come to pass there in these days? And he said unto them, What things? And they said unto him, Concerning Jesus of Nazareth, which was a prophet mighty in deed and word before God and all the people: And how the chief priests and our rulers delivered him to be condemned to death, and have crucified him. But we trusted that it had been he which should have redeemed Israel: and beside all this, to day is the third day since these things were done.

—Luke 24:12–21

The Scripture says that they were expecting Jesus to be their redeemer. It seems as though all of their hopes had been dashed to pieces by this time. I believe to this very day that Israel is still looking for their redeemer. Their redeemer came, and they rejected Him; His name is Jesus, your Messiah. Zacharias prophesied and said in Luke 1:68–72:

Blessed be the Lord God of Israel; for he hath visited and redeemed his people, And hath raised up a horn of salvation for us in the house of his servant David; As he spake by the mouth of his holy prophets, which have been since the world began: That we should be saved from our enemies, and from the hand of all that hate us; To perform the mercy promised to our fathers, and to remember his holy covenant.

Before Jesus went to the cross, I believe He was grieved in His spirit over Jerusalem's people. He wanted to hug and embrace them to Himself, but this was impossible for Him because of their unbelief that He was the Christ, the Messiah, the Son of the living God. This brings to my mind a Scripture in Luke 13:34–35, in which Jesus spoke concerning Jerusalem. He said:

His Second Coming

> O Jerusalem, Jerusalem, which killest the prophets, and stonest them that are sent unto thee; how often would I have gathered thy children together, as a hen doth gather her brood under her wings, and ye would not! [This means they would not come to him.] Behold, your house is left unto you desolate: and verily I say unto you, Ye shall not see me until the time come when ye shall say, Blessed, is he that cometh in the name of the Lord.

The people of Jerusalem did not accept Jesus Christ as their Messiah.

The rejection of the Jews had consequences. For Jesus declared unto them that they would make this confession with their mouths and say, "Blessed is he who comes in the name of the Lord," then Christ will return to them once more to his people.

So, the Scripture describes what happened to the disciples as they walked on the road to Emmaus. Jesus appeared to them as just another traveler, and they conversed with Him. Luke 24:22–31 tells us that the men said to Jesus, "Certain women also of our company made us astonished, which were early at the sepulcher; And when they found not his body, they came, saying, that they had also seen a vision of angels, which said that he was alive. And certain of them who were with us went to the sepulcher and found it even so as the women had said: but they saw him not. Then he said unto them, O fools, and slow of heart to believe all that the prophets have spoken: Ought not Christ to have suffered these things, and to enter into his glory? And beginning at Moses and all the prophets, he expounded unto them in all the Scriptures, the things concerning himself. And they drew nigh unto the village, whither they went: and he made as though he would have gone further. But they constrained him, saying, Abide with us: for it is toward evening, and the day is far spent. And he went in to tarry with them. And it came to pass, as he sat at meat with them, he took bread, and blessed it, and brake, and gave to them. And their eyes were opened, and they knew him, and he vanished from their sight." The account continues:

> And they said one to another, Did not our heart burn within us, while he talked with us by the way, and while he opened to us the Scriptures? And they rose up the same hour, and returned to Jerusalem, and found the eleven gathered together, and them that were with them, Saying, The Lord is risen indeed, and hath appeared to Simon. And they told what things were done in the way, and how he was known of them in breaking of bread. And as they thus spake, Jesus himself stood in the midst of them, and saith unto them, Peace be unto you. But they were terrified and affrighted and supposed that they had seen a spirit. And he said unto them, Why are ye troubled? And why do thoughts arise in your hearts? Behold my hands and my feet, that it is I myself: handle me, and see; for a spirit hath not flesh and bones, as ya see me have.
>
> —Luke 24:32–39

The Bible says that when Jesus finished speaking, He showed them His hands and feet. "And while they yet believed not for joy, and wondered, he said unto them, Have ye here any meat? And they gave him a piece of broiled fish and a honeycomb. And he took it, and did eat before them" (Luke 24:23–43). I believe Jesus asked for meat to eat, not because He was hungry, but because of the present unbelief. He wanted to eliminate doubt or suspicion about whether He was a spirit.

So, to demonstrate to them that He was flesh and blood, He not only showed them His hands and feet but also asked for food to eat, thus erasing any doubt from their minds.

The Gospel of Luke continues to say:

His Second Coming

> And he said unto them, These are the words which I spake unto you, while I was yet with you, that all things must be fulfilled, which were written in the law of Moses, and in the prophets, and in the psalms, concerning me. Then opened he their understanding, that they might understand the Scriptures, And said unto them, Thus it is written, and thus it behooved Christ to suffer, and to rise from the dead the third day: And that repentance and remission of sins should be preached in his name among all nations, beginning at Jerusalem. And ye are witnesses of these things.
>
> —Luke 24:44-48

I am thrilled Jesus took the time to explain to the disciples what was written in the Psalms and the law of Moses concerning Him. I am delighted that He opened their understanding, erasing all doubt about who He really is. I can see the joy and happiness on their faces in the spirit to know that God had finally sent their Messiah. The Christ that was promised to them by their forefathers had finally arrived. Their Messiah had come! Their deliverer is here. I believe that from this day on, they were filled with renewed strength and power to take on the world. They were ready for whatever challenges life offered them, preaching in the mighty name of Jesus. They were now committed and ready to perish for the gospel of Christ. I believe that at this point, they were ready to go forward with everything they had to let people know that Jesus Christ is Lord! Now, they were ready to sell everything they had and give everything they had to preach the good news, drive out devils, heal the sick, and walk in the power and authority of His name.

The Scripture tells us that Jesus then told His disciples that He would send the promise of His Father upon them and that they should tarry or stay in the city of Jerusalem until they were endued with power from on high. He then led them out as far as Bethany lifted up His hands and blessed them. While Jesus blessed them, the most awesome event occurred: He was parted from them and carried up into heaven. And they worshiped Him, and returned to Jerusalem with great joy: And were continually in the temple, praising and blessing God. Amen. (See Luke 24:49–53.) Beautiful, beautiful Savior indeed! There is no one else to compare!

He is indeed gloriously wonderful. All nations should bow down before Him and worship Him. The Bible declares that God was manifested in the flesh as a man. He was given the name Jesus. There is no other man who can be compared to Him. As a man, He was perfect and spotless. He was a Lamb without blemish, the perfect Lamb of God who takes away the sin of this world.

In Revelation 1, we read of Jesus again being in the splendor He had had since before the world began.

John, one of Jesus's disciples, saw Jesus in His glory while he was on the Isle of Patmos for the Word of God and the testimony of Jesus. He was in the spirit on the Lord's day when he heard a voice, as of a trumpet, saying: "I am Alpha and Omega, the first and the last: and, What thou seest, write in a book, and send it unto the seven churches" (Rev. 1:11). John then turned to see the voice that spoke to him and saw seven golden candlesticks, and in the midst of them was Jesus.

> [He was] clothed with a garment down to the foot and girt about the paps with a golden girdle. His head and his hairs were white like wool, as white as snow; and his eyes were as a flame of fire; And his feet like unto fine brass, as if they burned in a furnace; and his voice as the sound of many waters. And he had in his right hand seven stars: and out of his mouth went a sharp two-edged sword: and his countenance was as the sun shineth in his strength. And when I saw him, I fell at his feet as dead. And he laid his right hand upon me, saying unto me, Fear not; I am the first and the last: I am he that liveth, and was dead; and, behold,

His Second Coming

I am alive for evermore, Amen; and have the keys of hell and of death.

—Revelation 1:13–18

John also saw four beasts and four and twenty elders fall down before the Lamb:

Having every one of them harps and golden vials full of odors are the prayers of saints. And they sang a new song, saying: Thou art worthy to take the book, and to open the seals thereof: for thou wast slain, and hast redeemed us to God by thy blood out of every kindred, and tongue, and people, and nation; And hast made us unto our God kings and priests: and we shall reign on the earth. And I beheld, and I heard the voice of many angels round about the throne and the beasts and the elders: and the number of them was ten thousand times ten thousand, and thousands of thousands: Saying with a loud voice, Worthy is the Lamb that was slain to receive power, riches, wisdom, strength, honor, glory, and blessing.

And every creature which is in heaven, and on the earth, and under the earth, and such as are in the sea, and all that are in them, heard I saying, Blessing, and honour, and glory, and power, be unto him that sitteth upon the throne, and unto the Lamb for ever and ever. And the four beasts said, Amen. And the four and twenty elders fell down and worshipped him that liveth for ever and ever. Amen.

—Revelation 5:8–14

Dr. Marlene Brown

Chapter 29
Doubts About Christ's Resurrection

Then he said to Thomas, "Put your finger here; see my hands. Reach out your hand and put it into my side. Stop doubting and believe.

—John 20:27

Our beautiful Lord Jesus is indeed Savior and Lord! He is indeed the God of the universe. King of kings and Lord of lords! There is none to compare. Before Him, there was no God formed, and after Him, there will be none. He said in His Word in Isaiah; He knows not of any. There will be none. He said in His Word in Isaiah; He knows not of any. As Jesus proclaimed in His Word, "I am the resurrection and the life: he that believeth in me, though he was dead, yet shall he live" (John 11:25).

Paul, an apostle of Jesus Christ, was called into question concerning his preaching of hope in Jesus Christ and His resurrection. When he was brought before the council, which consisted of the high priest Ananias (pronounced *An-a-ni'-as*), the Pharisees, and the Sadducees (pronounced *Sad'-du-cees*), he was condemned by both until he declared unto them that he was a Pharisee. The Pharisees believed in the resurrection of the dead, while the Sadducees believed that there was no resurrection of the dead, or angel, or spirit, but the Pharisees confessed both (Acts 23:1–8).

Paul now wrote a letter to the church reminding them of what the Scriptures say about Christ so that the faith would remain alive. He

His Second Coming

reminded them that the Scriptures said that Christ died for their sins and that He was buried and rose again on the third day, in accordance with the Scriptures. He also reminded them, "Christ was seen of Cephas, then of the twelve: After that, he was seen of above five hundred brethren at once; of whom the greater part remain unto this present, but some are fallen asleep." Then he mentioned that Christ was seen of James, then of all the apostles. Last of all, Paul says Christ was seen of him. He noted that he knew how he had persecuted the church of God but that this made him even more determined to bring souls to Christ. Paul told the church that he had seen Christ and so had many others, so they preached the resurrection so they would believe that Christ had been raised from the dead (1 Cor. 15:1–10).

Now, Paul is addressing the real issue of resurrection. He said:

> If Christ be preached that he rose from the dead, how say some among you that there is no resurrection of the dead? But if there be no resurrection of the dead, then is Christ not risen: And if Christ be not risen, then is our preaching vain, and your faith is also vain. Yea, and we are found false witness of God; because we have testified of God that he raised up Christ: whom he raised not up if so be that the dead rise not. For if the dead rise not, then is not Christ raised: And if Christ be not raised, your faith is vain; ye are yet in your sins. Then they also, which are fallen asleep in Christ, perished. If in this life only we have hope in Christ, we are of all men most miserable.
>
> —1 Corinthians 15:12–19

Not only do we have hope in Him in this world, but also in the world to come. In Him and through Him, we have eternal life. Since Christ first rose from the dead, those who die in Christ shall also rise from the dead; because He lives, they shall live also.

Dr. Marlene Brown

Our Christian faith is based on the principle that Jesus Christ rose from the dead. If this is not true, just as Paul declares, our preaching is in vain.

The birth of Christ was indeed a great miracle. This is quite a miracle when one thinks that a virgin could conceive and bring forth a Son without in-vitro fertilization or without artificial insemination. To believe that the Holy Spirit of the Living God overshadowed her and impregnated her with the Living Word that existed with the Father before the creation of time is remarkable. Then this Living Word became a human—this God became man—and was given the name Jesus because His purpose in being human was to save His people from their sins.

The miraculous story did not end there because this Jesus who was crucified on the cross to bear the sins of humanity and to destroy sin went into the grave, took the keys of hell and death from Satan, took the sting out of death for us, and conquered death! As Jesus rose, He declared, "O grave, where is thy victory? O death, where is thy sting?" Jesus destroyed hell, death, and the grave! This same Holy Spirit that produced His human birth entered back into His body and brought Him to life again! This is the most spectacular miracle that the world has ever known! It is so spectacular that many do believe in His birth but not His death and resurrection. This is a work of the living God so that through His resurrection, men will believe and know that He is Christ, the anointed one: the Son of God who came to take away the world's sin. This is the principle that the Christian faith is based on! This same Jesus then ascended on high. He is gone to prepare a place for us, His children, where we will be where He is there. He said that in His Father's house, there are many mansions; if it were not so, He would have made it known to us. He will return to earth again to receive only those who put their faith and trust in Him, who have made Him Lord of their lives and Savior of their souls, just as He promised, to bring them to the marriage supper, a special occasion for the saints. Yes, the Scripture declares

His Second Coming

in Revelation, "Blessed are they which are called unto the marriage supper of the Lamb" (Rev. 19:9).

No other religion offers such blessed hope! No other religion offers such firm, sure promises! And because He lives, we will live also. Our faith is not based on doubts but on a solid foundation! Our belief is not based upon one in the grave with no power to get out, but rather one that has defeated the grave and is alive in heaven today.

The Scripture says, just as in Adam, all die; even so, in Christ shall all be made alive.

> But every man in his own order: Christ the first fruits; afterward they that are Christ's at his coming. Then cometh the end, when he shall have delivered up the kingdom to God, even the Father; when he shall have put down all rule and all authority and power. For he [Christ] must reign till he hath put all enemies under his feet. The last enemy that shall be destroyed is death.
>
> —1 Corinthians 15:23–26

Paul is making it clear to us and the church in Corinth that there will be a resurrection of the dead when we die. He said, speaking of the resurrection, for this reason, we stand in jeopardy or danger every hour. We are in constant danger from the enemy. The Scripture says that the enemy walks around like a roaring lion seeking whom he may devour. Paul said that for this reason, he dies daily in the flesh. He also said that if the dead are not raised, we should eat and drink, for tomorrow, we die. Paul viewed the communication of those people who declared that there is no resurrection from the dead as evil, so he warns us that we should not be deceived by these religions (1 Cor. 15:27–33).

Now, Paul is encouraging the church that we should awaken to righteousness and not sin. For even though we have been born again, not many know what the will of God is, and not many know the knowledge of God. Because of this lack of knowledge of God, many will ask: "How are the dead raised? And with what body do they come?" "Thou fool," Paul says. He points out that "that which thou sowest is not quickened, except it dies" (1 Cor. 15:35–36). This means that whenever you plant a seed in the ground, it is of no use to you unless it dies. The seed must die to germinate and bring forth much fruit or wheat. He continued to say that whatever you sow, you sow to receive not what you did sow, but you sow to receive wheat or some other grain. "God giveth it a body as it hath pleased him, and to every seed his own body" (1 Cor. 15:38). Just as in the case of flesh:

> All flesh is not the same flesh: but there is one kind of flesh of men, another flesh of beasts, another of fishes, and another of birds. There are also celestial bodies, and bodies that are terrestrial: but the glory of the celestial is one, and the glory of the terrestrial is another So also is the resurrection of the dead. It is sown in corruption; it is raised in incorruption: It is sown in dishonor; it is raised in glory: it is sown in weakness; it is raised in power: It is sown a natural body; it is raised a spiritual body. There is a natural body, and there is a spiritual body. And so it is written: The first man Adam was made a living soul; the last Adam was made a quickening spirit. The first man is of the earth, earthy: the second man is the Lord from heaven. As is the earthy, such are they also that are earthy: and as is the heavenly, such are they also that are heavenly. And as we have borne the image of the earthy, we shall also bear the image of the heavenly. Now, this I say, brethren, that flesh and blood cannot inherit the kingdom of God; neither doth corruption inherit incorruption.
>
> —1 Corinthians 15:39-40,42-45,47-50

His Second Coming

Therefore, my beloved brethren, be ye steadfast, unmoveable, always abounding in the work of the Lord, forasmuch as ye know that your labor is not in vain in the Lord.

—1 Corinthians 15:58

Dr. Marlene Brown

Chapter 30
Gone to Prepare a Place for You

For a day in thy courts is better than a thousand. I had rather be a doorkeeper in the house of my God, than to dwell in the tents of wickedness.

—Psalm 84:10

How happy are the saints to know that Jesus is faithful to His promises. In John 14:1, He tells us that we should not let our hearts be troubled. I have often noted that when Jesus speaks, His Words are the same. "Fear not, be not dismayed," he said in Joshua 1:9. His Words are always filled with comfort and good cheer.

The King of the universe promised us that He would prepare a place for us. What an excellent assurance that He has given to us! He said that there are many mansions in His Father's house; Jesus also pointed out that the way to His Father's mansion is only through Him. The Greek word for the mansion is *mone*, translated as "staying, abiding, or dwelling place." Jesus continued by saying that He would have told us if it were not. Christ also said that if He goes, He will come again and receive us unto Himself, that where He is there, we will also be. (Here, Jesus pointed out clearly that He is from above and has the power and authority to take us to His Father's home. So, Jesus pointed out clearly here that He is the way to heaven, He is the truth, and not only is He truth, but He is life itself.) He continues by saying that no man comes to the Father except one who goes through Him. (See John 14:2–6.)

His Second Coming

The place that the Son of the Most High God had gone to prepare was seen by one of the apostles, John. John was on the isle of Patmos, in the spirit on the Lord's day, for the testimony of Jesus and the Word of God, when he saw a new heaven and a new earth as well as the place that the Lord had gone to prepare.

John says in Revelation 21:

> And I, John saw the holy city, new Jerusalem, coming down from God out of heaven, prepared as a bride adorned for her husband. And I heard a great voice out of heaven saying, Behold, the tabernacle of God is with men, and he will dwell with them, and they shall be his people, and God himself shall be with them, and be their God.
>
> And God shall wipe away all tears from their eyes; and there shall be no more death, neither sorrow, nor crying, neither shall there be any more pain: for the former things are passed away.
>
> —Revelation 21:2–4

Wow! The Scripture says no more death or crying or pain. This is heaven, indeed! As people of God, we need to overcome the enemy in this world to be in this place.

The Scripture continues to say:

> And he that sat upon the throne said, Behold, I make all things new. And he said unto me, Write: for these words are true and faithful. And he said unto me, It is done. I am Alpha and Omega, the beginning and the end. I will give unto him that is athirst of the fountain of the water of life freely. He that overcometh shall inherit all things, and I will be his God, and he shall be my son. But the fearful, and unbelieving, and the abominable, and murderers, and whoremongers, and sorcerers, and idolaters, and all liars,

shall have their part in the lake which burneth with fire and brimstone: which is the second death.

—Revelation 21:5–8

I have often wondered why the "fearful" will be partakers of the same death as the murderers and sorcerers and those who do abominable deeds. Many people in the world today are Christians, yet they still have fear in their lives. They have a fear of their past, fear of their present situation, and fear of their future. Some are even fearful of evil spirits. I then found the answer in the Word of God: "God has not given us a spirit of fear but of power, love, and of a sound mind." The Lord of the universe knows that fear derives from an evil spirit, and He has not given us that type of spirit. He has given us a spirit of love. Perfect love, He says, will cast out all fear. He went on to say that greater is the spirit within us than he in the world (1 John 4:4). So then if the spirit within us is much greater, why would we be fearful of anything or anyone? He said in His Word that He had given us power over all the enemy's power, so He called us to be conquerors. He said we are more than conquerors through Christ, who loves us. We need to understand these Scriptures as head knowledge and believe for His Word to take root within our lives. We often quote the Scriptures, but if we do not exercise the words and believe in the power of the word, we will never be victorious Christians. The enemy will still try to attack our minds with fear. But when we believe in the truth, then this truth will reveal the power that is within us through Jesus Christ, and it is this truth that will set us free.

Let us continue in Revelation 21:9. The Scripture says one of the seven angels who had the seven vials full of the seven last plagues came unto John and talked with him, saying, "Come hither, I will shew thee the bride, the Lamb's wife." One may be wondering, "Who is the Lamb?" The Lamb is Jesus. As John said in John 1:29, "Behold, the Lamb of God who takes away the sin of the world." John the Revelator tells us that one of the seven angels came and

His Second Coming

took him away in the spirit to a great and high mountain and showed him that great city, the holy Jerusalem, descending out of heaven from God, having the glory of God. John said that her light was like a stone most precious, even like a jasper stone, clear as crystal.

The city, John said, had a wall great and high. It also had twelve gates, and at the gates, twelve angels and names are written thereon, which are the names of the twelve tribes of the children of Israel: On the east three gates; on the north three gates; on the south three gates; and the west three gates. And the wall of the city had twelve foundations and the names of the twelve apostles of the Lamb on them.

> And he that talked with me had a golden reed to measure the city, and the gates thereof, and the wall thereof. And the city lieth foursquare and the length is as large as the breadth: He measured the city with the reed, twelve thousand furlongs. The length and the breadth and the height of it are equal.
>
> And he measured the wall thereof, an hundred and forty and four cubits, according to the measure of a man, that is, of the angel. And the building of the wall of it was of jasper: and the city was pure gold, like unto clear glass. And the foundations of the wall of the city were garnished with all manner of precious stones. The first foundation was jasper; the second, sapphire; the third, a chalcedony; the fourth, an emerald; The fifth, sardonyx; the sixth, sardius; the seventh, chrysolite; the eighth, beryl; the ninth, a topaz; the tenth, a chrysoprasus; the eleventh, a jacinth; the twelfth, an amethyst. And the twelve gates were twelve pearls; every several gates was of one pearl: and the city's street was pure gold, as it were transparent glass. And I saw no temple therein: for the Lord God Almighty and the Lamb are the temple of it. And the city did not need of the sun, neither of the moons, to shine in it: for the glory of God did

lighten it, and the Lamb is the light thereof. And the nations of them which are saved shall walk in the light of it: and the kings of the earth do bring their glory and honor into it. And the gates of it shall not be shut at all by day: for there shall be no night there. And they shall bring the glory and honor of the nations into it. And there shall in no wise enter anything that defileth, neither whatsoever worketh abomination nor maketh a lie: but they which are written in the Lamb's book of life.

—Revelation 21:15–27

Wow, such a beautiful city indeed! The Scripture says the streets were paved with gold that looked like transparent glass. The Bible also declares that there is no night there or anything that defiles or is an abomination! I know I will be there. As the Scripture says, hold fast unto that which you have and let no man take thy crown. No wonder Paul the apostle said in His Word, to live is to live for Christ and to die; you will gain Him. The Word of God is true and faithful.

Nothing on the face of this earth should be of more value or interest to you than living for Christ. I am so anxiously waiting for His return. Are you?

His Second Coming

Chapter 31
Signs of the End of the World

And this gospel of the kingdom shall be preached in all the world for a witness unto all nations; and then shall the end come.

—*Matthew 24:14*

Everyone knows that we are in the last and final—days no matter how daft you are or whether you believe in a God or not! We can see the turmoil that the world is in. Here is what Jesus has to say about it.

In Luke chapter 12, Jesus spoke to the people concerning discerning the times that we are now living in. He said that when you see the cloud rise from the west, you immediately know there will be a shower, and a shower comes, and when you see the south wind blow, you know that heat is on the way, and we do get heat. Now, He is asking the question by saying, why are we being such hypocrites? We can study the face of the sky and the earth, yet we cannot discern or tell how close it is to the end of the world (Luke 12:54–56).

In Matthew 24, we read about Jesus teaching His disciples the various signs they should look for toward His coming and the end of the world. When Jesus came out from the temple and His disciples came to Him to show Him the various buildings of the temple, He said unto them, "See ye, not all these things? Verily I say unto you, There shall not be left here one stone upon another, that shall not be thrown down. And as he sat upon the Mount of Olives, the disciples came unto him privately, saying, Tell us, when shall these things be? and what shall be the sign of thy coming and the end of the world?"

(Matt. 24:1–3). The Mount of Olives is a long north-south ridge that lies just east of Jerusalem. The Scripture says that the disciples had two basic questions on their minds. First, they wanted to know when the temple would be destroyed as Jesus said it would be, and, secondly, what the sign of His coming would be, which would coincide with the end of the world. The first part of the question is answered in Luke 21:20–24, and the Scripture says when you see Jerusalem surrounded with armies, then know that the destruction of Jerusalem is near. Jesus continued to say that there would be distress in the land and wrath upon the people of Jerusalem. He also mentioned that they will fall by the sword and be taken away as prisoners into all the nations.

Jerusalem will be trodden down by the Gentiles until the times of the Gentiles are fulfilled.

The second part of the question is answered in Matthew 24:3–10.

The Scripture says Jesus answered and said unto them:

> Take heed that no man deceives you. Many shall come in my name, saying I am Christ, and deceive many. And ye shall hear of wars and rumors of wars: see that ye be not troubled: for all these things must come to pass, but the end is not yet. For nation shall rise against nation, and kingdom against kingdom: and there shall be famines, and pestilences, and earthquakes, in divers places. All these are the beginning of sorrows. Then shall they deliver you up to be afflicted, and shall kill you: and ye shall be hated of all nations for my name's sake. And then shall many be offended, and shall betray one another, and shall hate one another.

The Lord Jesus says there shall be great persecution for His name. This makes me really wonder how many of us are ready to suffer persecution in the name of Christ. The name of Christ does not only mean eternal life, but it also means persecution. For this

His Second Coming

reason, Jesus said in His Word that if you love Me, then pick up your cross and follow Me. As He suffered persecution in this world, so will you suffer as well because the servant is not greater than his master. The Scriptures remind me of those Christians in Northern Sudan who are tortured, murdered, or enslaved for the name of Christ. The Bible says great is their reward in heaven.

Jesus continued saying, "Many false prophets shall rise and deceive many. And because iniquity shall abound, the love of many shall wax cold. But he that shall endure unto the end shall be saved. This gospel of the kingdom shall be preached in all the world for a witness unto all nations; and then shall the end come" (Matt. 24:10–14). Jesus declares that the world's end will come when the gospel is being preached worldwide as a witness to all nations. There will be no excuse for not being saved.

The Scripture continued to say in Matthew 24:15: "When ye, therefore, shall see the abomination of desolation, spoken of by Daniel the prophet, stand in the holy place, (whoso readeth, let him understand:)." This abomination of desolation is found in Daniel 9:24, as well as in Daniel 10:3. Jesus pointed out that those days are going to be the days of vengeance. He said:

> Let them which be in Judaea flee into the mountains: Let him which is on the housetop not come down to take anything out of his house: Neither let him which is in the field return back to take his clothes. And woe unto them that are with child, and to them that give suck in those days! But pray ye that your flight be not in the winter, neither on the Sabbath day: For then shall be great tribulation, such as was not since the beginning of the world to this time, no, nor ever shall be. And except those days should be shortened, there should no flesh be saved: but for the elect's sake those days shall be shortened. Then if any man shall say unto you, Lo, here is Christ, or there; believe it not. For there shall arise false Christs, and false prophets, and shall

shew great signs and wonders; insomuch that, if it were possible, they shall deceive the very elect.

—Matthew 24:16-24

Jesus continued to say: Behold, I have told you before. Wherefore if they shall say unto you, Behold, he is in the desert; go not forth: behold, he is in the secret chambers; believe it not. As the lightning cometh out of the east, and shineth even unto the west, so shall also the coming of the Son of man be. For wheresoever the carcass is, there will be the eagles gathered together. Immediately after the tribulation of those days shall the sun be darkened, and the moon shall not give her light, and the stars shall fall from heaven, and the powers of the heavens shall be shaken: And then shall appear the sign of the Son of man in heaven: and then shall all the tribes of the earth mourn, and they shall see the Son of man coming in the clouds of heaven with power and great glory. And he shall send his angels with a great sound of a trumpet, and they shall gather together his elect from the four winds, from one end of heaven to the other.

—Matthew 24:25–31

Jesus also gave a parable of the fig tree. Jesus said when you see that the branch of the fig tree is tender, and it brings forth her leaves, then you know that summer is near. Jesus is saying it is the same when we see all these things; we should know that the world's end is near, even at the door.

> Verily I say unto you, This generation shall not pass till all these things be fulfilled. Heaven and earth shall pass away, but my words shall not pass away. But of that day and hour knoweth no man, no, not the angels of heaven, but my Father only. But as the days of Noah were, so shall also the coming of the Son of man be. For as in the days that were

His Second Coming

before the flood they were eating and drinking, marrying and giving in marriage, until the day that Noah entered into the ark, And knew not until the flood came, and took them all away; so shall also the coming of the Son of man be. Then shall two be in the field; the one shall be taken, and the other left. Two women shall be grinding at the mill; one shall be taken, and the other left. Watch, therefore: for ye know not what hour your Lord doth come.

But know this: if the goodman of the house had known in what watch the thief would come, he would have watched and would not have suffered his house to be broken up. Therefore be ye also ready: for in such an hour as ye think not the Son of man cometh. Who then is a faithful and wise servant, whom his lord hath made ruler over his household, to give them meat in due season? Blessed is that servant, whom his lord when he cometh shall find so doing. Verily I say unto you, that he shall make him ruler over all his goods.

But if that evil servant, shall say in his heart, My lord delayeth his coming; And shall begin to smite his fellow servants, and to eat and drink with the drunken; The lord of that servant shall come in a day when he looketh not for him, and in an hour that he is not aware of, And shall cut him asunder, and appoint him his portion with the hypocrites: there shall be weeping and gnashing of teeth.

—Matthew 24:34–51

So then let us be ready and waiting, for the Son of man comes at a time when you think not! May we all be found worthy in Jesus's name. Amen.

Dr. Marlene Brown

Chapter 32
The Self-Righteous

If we say that we have not sinned, we make him a liar, and his word is not in us.

—*1 John 1:10*

Someone may say today, "I am a good person; I have never done wrong in all my life!" The Bible has to say this about the self-righteous:

We are all unclean things: He also said all our righteousness is as filthy rags (Isa. 64:6). This means that our good works before God cannot make us righteous. For this reason, God sent His Son so that we can be made the righteousness of God in Him and through Him. Second Corinthians 5:21 says, "For he [God] hath made him [Jesus] to be sin for us, who knew no sin; that we might be made the righteousness of God in him." We will never be good enough or righteous by our good merits or by keeping the law: our righteousness can come only through Jesus Christ, who became our sin and gave us His righteousness. While we were yet sinners, Christ died for the ungodly. Therefore, just as sin entered the world through one man, Adam, and death through sin, so that all have sinned, the free gift of righteousness came through one man, Christ Jesus our Lord. (See Romans 5:12–15.) So, then, we see that only by the grace of God, through righteousness in Christ, can we receive eternal life!

Righteousness outside of Christ profits nothing. Neither can we be made righteous by our race, creed, or color or by being a Jew or Gentile. The Bible says we are all under sin, and none is righteous, no, not one. Man falls short of God's standards. "For all have sinned and fall short of the glory of God" (Rom. 3:23). The Bible declares the body's life is in the blood. The blood makes atonement for the soul; it is the only thing that can cleanse the soul from all sin (Lev. 17:11). The blood of Jesus is used for the atonement of the soul to cleanse the soul from sin. The blood of Jesus is pure, without spots or blemishes.

One cannot become saved because of race, color, or creed. Neither can you be saved because you are a Jew or a Gentile. The Bible says we are all born in sin and shaped in iniquity. There needs to be a sacrifice for your sins. And almost all things are purged with blood by the law; without shedding blood, there can be no remission of sin (Heb. 9:22). One of God's attributes is showing mercy. In heaven, there are cherubims of glory overshadowing the mercy seat. God gave Moses this insight when he told Moses to build a Tabernacle. Therefore, Moses made the "Ark of the Covenant," a sanctuary for God to dwell amongst his people. Moses received God's instructions for the Ark's design (Exodus 25:1-40).

In the tabernacle was the golden censer, and the ark of the covenant overlaid roundabout with gold. It also has the golden pot with manna, Aaron's rod that budded, and the covenant tables; over it, the cherubims of glory shadowing the mercy seat (Hebrews 9:5). Now there were the priest and high priest that carry out their priestly duty before God. Only the priest could enter the first area of the Tabernacle. However, in the second area behind the veil, only the high priest could enter each year, and not without blood: This was the holiest of all. And almost all things are by the law purged with blood, and without shedding of blood is no remission.

Subsequently, the high priest enters the holiest place within the Tabernacle, with the blood of calves and goats and the ashes of a heifer to sprinkle the unclean so that the flesh can be purified and sanctified before God.

> So then, if the blood of bulls and of goats, and the ashes of
> a heifer sprinkling the unclean, sanctifieth to the purifying

of the flesh: How much more shall the blood of Christ, who through the eternal Spirit offered himself without spot to God, purge your conscience from dead works to serve the living God? And for this cause, he is the mediator of the New Testament, that by means of death, for the redemption of the transgressions that were under the First Testament, they which are called might receive the promise of eternal inheritance. —Hebrews 9:6-15

Therefore, Jesus has become the only mediator between God and man. He has made a new and living way through his blood. Through the Holy Spirit, he offered himself up to God to allow his blood to cleanse your conscience from dead works and free you from the guilt of sin so that you can be guiltless before the Holy God. A corrupted man cannot pay God a ransom for his soul. Only the perfect and Holy God-man can.

The Scripture says:

But he was wounded for our transgressions; he was bruised for our iniquities: the chastisement of our peace was upon him, and with his stripes, we are healed. All we, as sheep, have gone astray; we have turned every one to his own way, and the Lord hath laid on him the iniquity of us all. He was oppressed, and he was afflicted, yet he opened not his mouth: he is brought as a lamb to the slaughter, and as a sheep, before her shearers are dumb, so he openeth not his mouth. He was taken from prison and from judgment: and who shall declare his generation? for he was cut off out of the land of the living: for the transgression of my people was he stricken.

And he made his grave with the wicked and the rich in his death; because he had done no violence, neither was any deceit in his mouth. Yet it pleased the Lord to bruise him; he hath put him to grief: when ***thou shalt make his soul an offering for sin***, he shall see his seed, he shall prolong

His Second Coming

his days, and the pleasure of the Lord shall prosper in his hand. He shall see of his soul's travail and be satisfied: ***by his knowledge shall my righteous servant justify many; for he shall bear their iniquities. Therefore will I divide him a portion with the great, and he shall divide*** the spoil with the strong; because he hath poured out his soul unto death: and he was numbered with the transgressors; ***and he bares the sin of many, and made intercession for the transgressors.***

—Isaiah 53:5–12

Now we are born of His seed—no longer of a corruptible seed from the sin of one man, which is Adam, but now of the incorruptible seed of Christ. Jesus Christ had given Himself for us as an offering and as a sacrifice for sin to God for a sweet-smelling savor (Eph. 5:2). As the Scripture declares:

For God so loved the world, that he gave his only begotten Son, that whosoever believeth in him should not perish, but have everlasting life. For God sent not his Son into the world to condemn the world; but that the world through him might be saved.

—John 3:16–17

The Lord is calling unto all those who consider themselves to be self-righteous to seek Him now. The Scripture declares in Isaiah 55:6–9 said that we should:

Seek the Lord while he may be found, call ye upon him while he is near: Let the wicked forsake his way, and the unrighteous man his thoughts: and let him return unto the Lord, and he will have mercy upon him; and to our God, for he will abundantly pardon. For my thoughts are not your thoughts, neither are your ways my ways, saith the Lord. For as the heavens are higher than the earth, so are my ways higher than your ways, and my thoughts than your thoughts.

When you receive the righteousness of His Son, then Christ's thoughts become your thoughts, and the mind of Christ becomes yours. First Corinthians 2:16 says we have the mind of Christ. The spirit of God now dwells within us—the same Spirit that raised up Jesus from the dead. The Scripture says in Romans 8:2 that it is the Spirit of life that is in Christ Jesus that will make you free from the law of sin and death. And in Romans 8:9, the Scripture says, "If any man has not the Spirit of Christ, he is none of his."

His Second Coming

Chapter 33
The Importance of Baptism

He who has believed [in Me] and has been baptized will be saved [from the penalty of God's wrath and judgment]; but he who has not believed will be condemned.

—John 16:16 AMP

Once a believer is saved (that is, has accepted Jesus Christ as their Lord and Savior), it is extremely important for the believer to be baptized. The word *baptize* is from the Greek word *baptizo* pronounced *bap-tid'-zo*. This means "to be baptized or to be cleansed of your sins or past life by being dipped in water." This is a purification rite. When men confess their sins, they become bound to a spiritual change. They received God's pardon for their past sins as they made way for the Messiah.

The first baptism that we read of in the Bible was John's baptism. John was a prophet sent from God. John was filled with the Holy Ghost from his mother's womb (Luke 1:15). He went in the spirit and power of Elijah. The Word of God says John was to turn the hearts of the fathers to the children and the disobedient to the wisdom of the just, to make ready a people prepared for the Lord (Luke 1:17). John baptized in the wilderness and preached the baptism of repentance for the remission of sin. The Bible tells us that John baptized Jesus when He came. John had always preached that there would be coming one mightier than he: John answered all of them: "I baptize you with water, but One more powerful than I will come, the straps of whose sandals I am not worthy to untie. He will baptize you with the Holy Spirit and with fire (Luke 3:16).

So, the Bible declares that John bore a record of Jesus and that He would be the one to baptize with the Holy Ghost. John declared:

> I saw the Spirit descending from heaven like a dove, and it abode upon him. And I knew him not: but he that sent me to baptize with water, the same said unto me, Upon whom thou shalt see the Spirit descending, and remaining on him, the same is he which baptizeth with the Holy Ghost.
>
> —John 1:32–33

It is important to note, however, that this particular Scripture in John points out to us that the process of baptism came directly from God, first to John, then to Jesus, and then to His disciples.

Now, we need to go deeper into the Word of God concerning water baptism and see the relevance or significance of being baptized.

In John 3:2–7, we read of a man called Nicodemus, who was a member of the Pharisees and a ruler of the Jews. He came to Jesus by night and said to Him:

> Rabbi, we know that thou art a teacher comes from God: for no man can do these miracles that thou doest, except God be with him. Jesus answered and said unto him, Verily, verily, I say unto thee: Except a man be born again, he cannot see the kingdom of God. Nicodemus saith unto him, How can a man be born when he is old? Can he enter into his mother's womb the second time and be born? Jesus answered, Verily, verily, I say unto thee, Except a man be born of water and of the Spirit, he cannot enter into the kingdom of God. That which is born of the flesh is flesh, and that which is born of the Spirit is spirit. Marvel not that I said unto thee, Ye must be born again.

His Second Coming

Jesus was explaining to Nicodemus that being born of the water and the spirit is a spiritual rebirth and that this is a very significant criterion needed for one to see the kingdom of God and to be able to enter it. As we go further into the Scripture, we read of how we are born again when we enter into this spiritual process called baptism by water as well as baptism by the Holy Spirit.

Jesus pointed out in His Word that except a man is born of the water and of the Spirit, he cannot enter into the kingdom of God. These are important criteria for us to meet. However, the question remains: "What does seeing the kingdom mean? And how do we enter?"

The Greek word for *see* is *eido*, which means "to perceive with the eyes; to ascertain or discern what must be done." So, Jesus was saying to Nicodemus that without this spiritual rebirth, he could not perceive with the spiritual eyes or discern the kingdom of God. He could see the works that Jesus was doing, yet he was spiritually blind to the will and plan of God.

Jesus then pointed out to Nicodemus that we need to first see the kingdom of God by the water and spirit, and then we can enter into the kingdom of God. It is important to note that the kingdom of God is within you, according to Luke 17:21, and that our bodies are the temple of the living God.

So, then the question is, "How do we enter into the kingdom of God?" The Greek word for *enter* is *eiserchomai*, which means "to come into existence or to come into life." So, when we read Matthew 18:1–3, Jesus told His disciples that you cannot enter into the kingdom of God unless you are converted and become like a little child. So, it is through humility that we enter in, not false humility. However, true humility comes through genuine repentance for sins and spiritual washing by the water and by the Word. Then, this new man begins to see the kingdom and enters therein.

So, the Word of God is saying when you become born again through that spiritual rebirth and are baptized, you can see the work that His kingdom on earth needs. We begin to see the things that are necessary to have His kingdom established as we enter through humility. It is only through humility that these things can be established. We now see how important and significant it is for a believer in Christ to be baptized.

However, it is important to note that spiritual rebirth does not stop at baptism. Once we receive this spiritual rebirth, our minds need to be renewed by the Word of God so that our new identity can now be seen in Him. The Bible says, let your light so shine before men that they see your good works and glorify God in heaven. "And be not conformed to this world: but be ye transformed by the renewing of your mind, that ye may prove what that good, and acceptable, and perfect, will of God is" (Rom. 12:2). "That ye put off concerning the former conversation the old man, which is corrupt according to the deceitful lusts; And be renewed in the spirit of your mind; And that ye put on the new man, which after God is created in righteousness and true holiness (Eph. 4:22–24).

His Second Coming

Chapter 34
The Holy Spirit, or the Comforter

The grace of the Lord Jesus Christ, and the love of God, and the communion of the Holy Ghost, be with you all. Amen.

—2 Corinthians 14:14

Many of us believe and also teach that the Holy Ghost is simply for speaking in different languages or tongues as described in Acts 2:1–8. It is important for every believer to experience the power of speaking in other tongues as the Spirit gives utterance, as there is great strength and power in the speaking of tongues. For example, when one comes under attack by the enemy, whether in everyday life or in a vision/dream, the power of speaking in tongues unto God and the anointing that flows from it defeats the enemy. It draws upon a supernatural strength that does not exist in the natural as the power of the Holy Ghost is unleashed to defeat the enemy in the spiritual realm.

However, there is another reason why we need to be filled up with the Holy Spirit: He empowers us for service.

The Holy Spirit releases to us a deep revelation of the Word of God, which does not come through theology and cannot be learned in a seminary but is revealed to us through His Holy anointing.

The Holy Spirit or the Comforter (*Parakletos*) is the one that came to be with the apostles in place of Christ (after Christ went up to be with the Father), and that led the disciples to a deeper knowledge of the gospel truth. The Comforter also gave them the divine strength they needed to undergo trials and persecutions on behalf of the divine kingdom of God.

Dr. Marlene Brown

The Bible tells us that the Holy Spirit reveals to us the deep things of God. As the Scripture says in 1 Corinthians 2:9–11:

> As it is written, Eye hath not seen, nor ear heard, neither have entered into the heart of man, the things which God hath prepared for them that love him. But God hath revealed them unto us by his Spirit: for the Spirit searcheth all things, yea, and the deep things of God. For what man knoweth the things of a man, save the spirit of man which is in him? Even so, the things of God knoweth no man, but the Spirit of God.

The Holy Ghost, which is the intercessor, has promised to be with us by Christ, and His purpose is to comfort and teach believers the way of Christ and also to make believers more powerful and effective witnesses of the gospel of Christ as the kingdom of God is not in words but in power.

We first read of the Holy Ghost descending from heaven when Jesus was being baptized and praying. We read that the heavens were opened, and "the Holy Ghost descended in a bodily shape like a dove upon him, and a voice came from heaven, which said, Thou art my beloved Son; in thee, I am well pleased" (Luke 3:22). Jesus then became filled up by the Holy Ghost and was taken into the wilderness by the Spirit. He fasted for forty days without food and was tempted by the devil for forty days. During His temptation or His trial of testing, the devil did not have the power to overcome Him because the Holy Spirit had already empowered Him to serve the Most High God. The Bible says the devil tempted Him, saying:

> If thou be the Son of God, command this stone that it be made bread. And Jesus answered him, saying: It is written, That man shall not live by bread alone, but by every Word of God: And the devil taking him up into a high mountain, shewed unto him all the kingdoms of the world in a moment of time. And the devil said unto him, All this

His Second Coming

power will I give thee, and the glory of them: for that is delivered unto me; and to whomsoever I will I give it. If thou therefore wilt worship me, all shall be thine.

—Luke 4:3–7

Jesus knew why He had come to earth; the Bible says His purpose was to destroy Him that had the power of death, that is the devil (1 John 3:8).

Jesus knew He had come to destroy the devil and His power, so then, it was not necessary for Him to sell Himself short by falling down to worship His adversary. Jesus also told His disciples that He had given them power over all the powers of the enemy. Even though the world was delivered into Satan's hands, Jesus had made him powerless by destroying principalities and powers and making an open mockery of them by going to the cross.

Jesus said to him, "It is said, Thou shalt not tempt the Lord thy God" (Luke 4:12). Jesus was full of the Word of God. When the devil realized that he could not entice Jesus with the things of this world; the Bible says that he left Jesus only for a season (Luke 4:13).

Now, it is here that we see the ministry of Jesus began. When He returned to Galilee, full of the Holy Spirit, He began to teach in the synagogues and was recognized and glorified by all. The Bible says He came to Nazareth, where He had been brought up, and, according to what they are accustomed to, He went to the synagogue on the Sabbath day and stood up to read.

> And there was delivered unto him the book of the prophet Esaias. And when he had opened the book, he found the place where it was written, The Spirit of the Lord is upon me, because he hath anointed me to preach the gospel to the poor; he hath sent me to heal the brokenhearted, to preach deliverance to the captives, and recovering of sight to the blind, to set at liberty them that are bruised, To preach

the acceptable year of the Lord. And he closed the book, and he gave it again to the minister, and sat down. And the eyes of all them that were in the synagogue were fastened on him. And he began to say unto them, This day in this Scripture fulfilled in your ears. And all bare him witness, and wondered at the gracious words which proceeded out of his mouth. And they said: Is not this Joseph's son?

—Luke 4:17–22

Once Jesus had received the Holy Ghost and was filled with great power and anointing, we see He began to do the work of His Father. He had been equipped for ministry. He taught in the synagogues and, healed the sick, raised the dead, and cast out devils. The function of the Holy Spirit is to equip you and empower you to do the work of God.

The Scripture says Jesus then left Galilee, went into a city called Capernaum, a city of Galilee, and began teaching them on the Sabbath days. The people were all astonished at His doctrine and the power of His Word. The Bible tells us that the first demonstration of Jesus's power was seen in the synagogue. A man, who had an unclean devil, cried out with a loud voice:

> Saying, Let us alone; what have we to do with thee, thou Jesus of Nazareth? art thou come to destroy us? I know thee who thou art; the Holy One of God. And Jesus rebuked him, saying, Hold thy peace, and come out of him. And when the devil had thrown him in the midst, he came out of him, and hurt him not. And they were all amazed, and spake among themselves, saying, What a word is this! for with authority and power he commandeth the unclean spirits, and they come out. And the fame of him went out into every place of the country round about.
>
> —Luke 4:37–39

We also see Him rebuking a fever from Peter's mother-in-law.

His Second Coming

In Luke 11:13, the Bible tells us that the Holy Spirit is a good gift from our heavenly Father, and He will give the Spirit to them that ask Him. We also read in John 1:33–14 that Jesus, the Son of the living God, is the one who baptizes with the Holy Ghost. So, John said he saw and bore record of Him that He was the Son of God. We now know that the baptism of the Holy Ghost is from Jesus.

This baptism of the Holy Spirit is extremely important for believers to have, as Jesus says He (the Holy Spirit) teaches us all things. This He explained in John 14:26: "But the Comforter, which is the Holy Ghost, whom the Father will send in my name, he shall teach you all things, and bring all things to your remembrance, whatsoever I have said unto you." In John 15:26, Jesus said, "When the Comforter comes, whom I will send unto you from the Father, even the Spirit of truth, which proceedeth from the Father, he shall testify of me." Christ pointed out to His disciples that not only would the Holy Ghost be His witness, but they also (which means His disciples) because they have been with Him from the beginning. So now we see why we need this baptism of the Holy Spirit as believers in Christ, as the Holy Spirit will teach us all things. In John 16:8–15, Jesus told His disciples that He needed to go away in order to send the precious Comforter. Jesus says if He does not depart, the Comforter will not come. Jesus also explains that when the Comforter comes, He will reprove the world of sin, righteousness, and judgment. Another word for *reprove* is *convict*. The Comforter will bring to light sin and expose sin for what it is. He will also speak of the coming judgment of God, and also His righteousness.

> Of sin, because they believe not on me; Of righteousness, because I go to my Father, and ye see me no more; Of judgment, because the prince of this world is judged. I have many things to say to you, but ye cannot bear them now. Howbeit when he, the Spirit of truth, is come, he will guide you into all truth: for he shall not speak of himself; but whatsoever he shall hear, that shall he speak: and he will shew you things to come.

Dr. Marlene Brown

—John 16:9–13

The Bible says the Holy Spirit will show you things to come! This He did when He revealed the many prophetic visions and dreams to me, and also showed me personal things in my life that needed to be done, for the kingdom or otherwise.

Jesus says, "He shall glorify me: for he shall receive of mine, and shall shew it unto you. All things that the Father hath are mine: therefore said I, that he shall take of mine, and shall shew it unto you" (John 16:14–15). I am so happy that Jesus pointed out that the Holy Spirit would not speak of Himself, but whatever Jesus says or wants us to see, He will reveal this to us, and in so doing, Jesus will be glorified.

His Second Coming

Chapter 35
Receiving The Holy Spirit

I indeed baptize you with water unto repentance. but he that cometh after me is mightier than I, whose shoes I am not worthy to bear: he shall baptize you with the Holy Ghost, and with fire.

—*Matthew 3:11*

Acts 2:1–7, 13–18 describes to us what the apostles' experiences were as they received the baptism of the Holy Spirit.

The Scripture says:

And when the day of Pentecost was fully come, they were all with one accord in one place. And suddenly there came a sound from heaven as of a rushing mighty wind, and it filled all the house where they were sitting. And there appeared unto them cloven tongues like as of fire, and it sat upon each of them. And they were all filled with the Holy Ghost, and began to speak with other tongues, as the Spirit gave them utterance. And there were dwelling at Jerusalem Jews, devout men, out of every nation under heaven. Now when this was noised abroad, the multitude came together, and were confounded, because that every man heard them speak in his own language. And they were all amazed and marvelled, saying one to another, Behold, are not all these which speak Galilaeans? Others mocking said, These men are full of new wine. But Peter, standing up with the eleven, lifted up his voice, and said unto them, Ye men of Judaea, and all ye that dwell at Jerusalem, be this known unto you, and hearken to my words: For these are not drunken, as ye suppose, seeing it is but the third hour of the day. But this is that which was spoken by the prophet Joel; And it shall come to pass in the last days, saith God, I will pour out of my Spirit upon all flesh: and your sons and your daughters shall prophesy, and your young men shall see visions, and your old men shall dream dreams: And on my servants and on my handmaidens I will pour out in those days of my Spirit; and they shall prophesy.

I have personally experienced being filled with the baptism of the Holy Ghost. For me, the experience began with a dream before He became a reality in my life. I believe the good Lord Jesus wanted me to experience Him in my dream first to get rid of all preconceived ideas and fears that I may have had concerning His baptism. Here is the prophetic vision.

Prophetic Promise of Receiving the Holy Ghost

The fifth heavenly vision or dream that I, Marlene, saw.

It took place on December 24, 2000.

I woke up at 11:56 p.m.

I dreamed that I was at a group church meeting. We were having this meeting in an open space outside. The area was very dark. The pastor then said to a group of us, "All those who want to receive the Holy Ghost should join hands." He then started to read a particular Scripture. My hands were in the air, ready to receive the Holy Ghost. Suddenly, I saw a young man appear in the sky. I began to point at him, trying to get the attention of a girl who was standing beside me. I wanted her to see this man in the sky because I could not speak. I believe it was an angel in the appearance of a man.

I then heard a spirit within me say, "Keep your focus on him!" So, I kept watching him. Suddenly, I heard myself saying, "The Lord says, and the Lord says, and the Lord says!" This was coming from the bottom of my belly, and I could not stop it. In the dream, I said to myself, "But I am prophesying! How is it that I am not saying anything more than 'the Lord says'?" A powerful force then hit me. Suddenly, I found myself speaking in a different language, in a different tongue. I began to listen to myself rolling my tongue and speaking in tongues. I then woke up from my sleep. Bless the Lord! The Lord is worthy of all praise! Glory and Honor to His Holy name! Amen.

With this dream, I believe the Lord wanted me to have the experience first in my dream before I experienced the real thing, especially with the prophecy and the speaking in tongues coming from the bottom of my belly. So, on January 28, 2001, I experienced the real thing. The experience was most beautiful. I experienced the power of the mighty God. It is a great honor to share this experience with you.

Experience of the Baptism of the Holy Spirit

On January 28, 2001, a friend invited me to a particular church. It was a very cold Sunday morning. The preacher was preaching a very powerful sermon that Sunday morning. The title was "The Woman with the Issue of Blood." He then combined this topic with the Scripture that says, "Press on towards the mark of the highest calling, which is in Christ Jesus." The preacher was preaching under the anointing of the Holy Ghost. At one point, he began to crawl on his stomach while he was preaching, demonstrating the woman with the issue of blood, crawling to touch the hem of Jesus's garment so that she could be made whole. Another time, he knelt down on his knees at the altar, crying out, "I exalt you, Lord, I exalt you, Lord!" I tell you; the anointing was all over this preacher.

While he was preaching, I felt the presence of the Lord. I just kept crying, crying, crying while he was preaching. I kept seeing myself fighting like the woman with the issue of blood; however, in my case, it was to press on for the baptism of the Holy Ghost. So, after the preaching, there was an altar call. I immediately ran to the alter. Later, I was told I was the first one at the altar. I knew that I needed to press on at the altar to receive this baptism of the Holy Spirit.

As I stood there praying at the altar with a few others, I felt someone hit me on my back. I looked around, and a girl was jumping in the spirit. It took me out of my spiritual thinking of wanting to press toward receiving the baptism of the Holy Spirit and put me back in the flesh, breaking all the anointing within and the feeling that I had to pray. This girl was really hitting me hard in my back! Of course, the devil planned to distract me to prevent me from receiving the baptism of the Holy Ghost. However, I was not alone. The good Lord had sent a young lady who came my way and held me. This lady kept encouraging me to pray. The dialogue went like this: "Come on, pray!" she said. I began to pray when the feeling went. I stopped. "I can't!" I spoke. She repeated, "Come on, pray." Then I began to focus on the Lord, just like in the dream when the spirit told me to focus, and then He vanished. So, I stopped and said to her, "Nothing is there!" She then asked me, "What is it you want to press on for?" "The baptism of the Holy Ghost!" I responded. Her comment was, "You don't want this thing!"

I believe that was all she needed to say because I began to focus on Jesus, the vision of Him visiting me in the sky with an angel. I heard myself shouting, "Jesus! Hallelujah! Jesus!" Then I heard myself saying some strange words. The young lady had her arms around me, and her words were very encouraging. She was saying, "Come on, that's it! Come on, that's it!" I then found myself stiffening up and saying words a bit more fluently. I felt the hands of the pastor on my head, and I knew he was listening. I felt the mike at my mouth, and he said to the congregation, "Someone has just received the baptism of the Holy Ghost!"

I felt my body begin to walk away from everyone at the altar. Then, I found myself dancing in the spirit; it felt like I was in slow motion. I collided with someone who was getting in the spirit, too. I

His Second Coming

remember turning away from her and walking like I was in the air. I felt a great power in my being. My back was bent, and I walked with my fingers pointing as if I was rebuking the enemy. In my head, all thought process went! My head was filled with the Spirit as if I had become different. I began to listen to myself speaking in a new language, as though I had no control over my mouth and what was being said. I believe this confirms the Scripture that flesh and blood cannot enter God's kingdom. One needs to be born of the water and by His Spirit.

After listening to myself for a while, I crumpled to the ground, and my feet kicked sideways. I was not yelling or screaming, just my feet kicking sideways. It was like a robot put in motion, fallen over, but still kicking because the power within the robot was left on.

When the kicking had subsided, I lay quietly on the floor in a fetal position, totally amazed at the experience and, at the same time, feeling drained in my body. I then felt the hand of the preacher on my head, and he said to me, "God chooses you!" This remark reminded me of when the angel told Mary that God highly favored her. As I was still weak in my body, the only response I could make was nodding of my head. I have to say this, however, that a million dollars could not have given me those words of satisfaction to complete that day! But those words did! In the fetal position that I was in, I felt a great pain in my belly bottom. So, I quietly lay still with my feet in a fetal position, curled up because of the cramp I felt in my belly button and the pain. In fact, the pain came from the same area where I gave birth to my son, Brandon. At that time, my son was several months old. The pain, however, felt as though it ruptured a sore area in my womb that needed healing from the birth of my son. The young lady told me that it is called a re-birth. I guess this explains the pain. She mentioned that the Bible says that rivers of living water will flow out of your belly. Her explanation helped as I was fairly new in my faith.

The next day, I woke up, and I felt a great sense of peace that came over me. I could not understand this peace. I turned to my husband and said to him, "I feel great peace as if nothing in the world could upset me." At that particular time, I did not remember the Scripture that describes the peace of God. Jesus describes this peace as the peace that surpasses all understanding (John 14:27; Philippians 4:7). He said in His Word that this is the peace that He gave to us—that we should not let our hearts be troubled or afraid.

So, with this dream of the Holy Ghost, the Lord allowed me to experience His power in the dream and the birth of the Holy Spirit before I experienced it in reality.

To God belongs all the glory, all honor, and praise for allowing me to taste the baptism of the Holy Ghost. He is a faithful God with plenty of goodness and so true to His Word. He is truly the same God, yesterday, today, and forever!

Jesus also pointed out that we would become witnesses of Him. In Romans 1:8, He told us that we would receive power, after that the Holy Ghost would come upon us, and we would be witnesses of Him to the very uttermost part of the earth. Yes, I must declare that I have been a witness. First, I have witnessed Him in my community, then in Africa and India, also proclaiming His coming at a church in Jerusalem, in the Caribbean and the States, pretty soon to the uttermost parts of the earth.

This Holy Spirit we receive is not like the Spirit of the world. This Spirit is of God. This Spirit He has given us so that we might know the things that God gives us freely. This Holy Spirit does not teach with words that man teaches but the words that God teaches. "Comparing spiritual things with spiritual..." (1 Cor. 2:13). The Bible says, "The natural man receiveth not the things of the Spirit of God: for they are foolishness unto him: neither can he know them because they are spiritually discerned" (1 Cor. 2:12–14).

His Second Coming

Many churches today teach that the Holy Spirit has ended with the disciples and no longer manifests in such power. These people are "having a form of godliness, but denying the power thereof; from such, turn away" (2 Tim. 3:5). These people are causing the body of Christ to become weakened. Many people are being led astray by the lies of these pastors, causing the body of Christ to be weakened. Instead of the entire body of Christ being empowered to tear down the works of darkness, we have people among us who are spiritually weak. They are weak because they lack the anointing that comes from the Holy Ghost. The Bible says the anointing breaks the yoke of bondage within our lives and sets captives free (Isa. 10:27).

Dr. Marlene Brown

Chapter 36
Who Am I in Christ?

But ye are a chosen generation, a royal priesthood, an holy nation, a peculiar people; that ye should shew forth the praises of him who hath called you out of darkness into his marvellous light;

—1 John 2:9

The Bible says you are now called ambassadors for Christ and reconciled to the Father. The Word of God says, "For Christ has made himself sin so that we can be made the righteousness of God in him" (2 Cor. 5:21). We are now new people; we have been born again. We have been born of a new spirit of Christ Jesus our Lord. In 1 Peter 2:9, we are called a chosen generation. Peter says not only are we chosen, but also, we are a royal priesthood. He said we are a holy nation, and most of all, we are "a peculiar people; that ye should shew forth the praises of him who hath called you out of darkness into his marvelous light" (1 Pet. 2:9). The Bible says that we are more than conquerors through Christ who loves us (Rom. 8:38). This statement means that whatever the prince of darkness of this world comes to tempt us with, we can overcome!

Satan will try to remind us about our past life! He will try to convince us that we are not saved. We have to out-truth this demon of lies because the Bible says he is the father of lies (John 8:44). There is no truth in him. He has been a liar from the beginning when he deceived Eve into eating the tree of the knowledge of good and evil. This is why we need to read the Word of God daily to understand who we are in Christ. We have to feed upon the Word for our spiritual food. The Bible says we are now born with the incorruptible seed of the Word of God. We are no longer born of the corruptible seed of Adam (1 Pet. 1:23). The Bible also declares that the Word of God is truth; it is also spirit and life (John 17:17; 6:63). Once we hold on to the Word of the living God and do according to what is written in it, we will have good success; we will be more than conquerors in all that we say and do. Sin will have no more dominion over us. The Bible declares that the spirit within us is greater than he in the world (1 John 4:4).

Jesus is indeed wonderful! He is the fresh Bread of Life. He is the sweet bread. Greater love than this has no man. Christ loves us right until the end. Not only did Christ die for us, but He also gave us a new identity in Him. He has given us power and authority in His name and through His name. He says in His Word that He has given us power over all the enemy's powers. Jesus continues to say in Luke 10:19–20, "Behold, I give unto you the power to tread on serpents and scorpions, and over all the power of the enemy: and nothing shall by any means hurt you. Notwithstanding in this rejoice not, that the spirits are subject unto you; but rejoice because your names are written in heaven." I am happy that my name is written in the Lamb's Book of Life. I am also very happy to know that the spirits are subjected to us as Christians.

Can one imagine the torture and turmoil that we would be going through without this power and knowledge that we have the power to defeat the enemy and that the enemy is made subject to us? Without this power and authority, Jesus gives us, our lives would be in constant torment, suffering, oppression, and depression of the mind and body. But thank God for the love and mercy of Jesus, who has given us His name and the power and authority of His name for us to use against the enemy.

This is the mighty power and authority that we have within us, first as children of God, then sons of God. The Scripture declares that it is the same spirit that raised up Jesus from the dead that dwells within us (Rom. 8:11). The everlasting love that Christ has for us has given us victory in this life. Christ has loved us with everlasting love, and it is by loving kindness that He has drawn us. The Scripture goes on to say in Romans 8:35–39:

> Who shall separate us from the love of Christ? Shall tribulation, or distress, or persecution, or famine, or nakedness, or peril, or sword? As it is written, For thy sake we are killed all the daylong; we are accounted as sheep for the slaughter. Nay, in all these things we are more than conquerors through him that loved us. For I am persuaded, that neither death, nor life, nor angels, nor principalities, nor powers, nor things present, nor things to come, Nor height, nor depth, nor any other creature, shall be able to separate us from the love of God, which is in Christ Jesus our Lord.

This is the confidence that we have in Him and the great love that He has for us. Not only do we have confidence in His love, His power, and the new identity that He has given us, but we also have great confidence in the knowledge that whenever we pray, He hears us. As the Scripture declares in 1 John 5:14-15, "This is the confidence that we have in him, that if we ask.

He heareth us according to his will: And if we know that he hears us, whatsoever we ask, we know that we have the petitions that we desired of him." And another Scripture says, "Whatsoever ye shall ask in my name, that will I do, that the Father may be glorified in the Son. If ye shall ask anything in my name, I will do it" 'John 14:13-14). How can we fail when we have such promises and confidence in Christ? All we need is belief. We need to believe His Word so that He, God, can deliver whatever He promised. The Scripture declares that God is not a man and that He should lie! The Scripture also states that all things are possible to those who believe.

However, the Lord wants you to know that when you come to Him, you should know He is God and will reward those who diligently seek Him. We are totally new people in Christ. We have great power and authority and now sit in heavenly places.

His Second Coming

It is essential for a believer to read the Word of God continuously once that believer is saved. It is only through His Word that a believer grows strong and confident and becomes able to use the great power and authority he has been given to put the devil where He rightfully belongs— under our feet. When we feed upon the Word of God daily, we learn how to trust the Lord in all that we do and allow Him to direct and chart the course of our lives. When we know who we are in Christ, it is hard for the enemy to come and deceive us. The enemy is the great deceiver! The Bible says he is the father of lies. He will work on a believer's mind in every way possible to feed them lies whether they are a new believer or not. This is when the Scripture warns us not to give any place to the devil. The Scripture also advises us to resist the devil, and he will flee from us!

As the righteousness of God, the enemy will try to condemn us in all that we do. He will also try to condemn us if we do something that is not pleasing in the sight of the Lord. This is when the Scripture becomes critically important to know. As long as we live on this earth, we must understand that we will never be perfect. We must work towards holiness because the Bible says, you must be holy because I am holy. However, to be perfect, there is only one that is perfect: Jesus Christ our Lord. When we make a mistake through anger or frustration, it is essential to note that the Lord will always forgive us and cleanse us from all unrighteousness. In Isaiah 1:18, the Lord says, "Come now and let us reason together . . . though your sins be as scarlet, they shall be as white as snow; though they are as red like crimson, they shall be as wool. This is the precious promise of God to you today. Whether you are saved or unsaved, this is His precious promise to you today.

For those of us who are saved, the Bible declares, "There is therefore now no condemnation to them which are in Christ Jesus, who walk not after the flesh, but after the Spirit" (Rom. 8:1). When we were in the world, we talked after the flesh, the sinful nature. We walked according to lust, envy, witchcraft, idolatry, pride, and boastfulness; some of us were prostitutes, some had abortions—you name it. The world would condemn us for these acts of sin. Christ also condemns these acts of sin. The Bible says, "Righteousness exalts a nation: but sin is a reproach to any people" (Prov. 14:34). Because of these acts, we would be enemies of God, but now we are reconciled to the Father through His Son Jesus Christ.

Now that we are saved, we no longer walk in the flesh or go after the things of the flesh; we now walk after the spirit, looking toward things that are above. The human body is a triune being We are made up of body, soul, and spirit. As Christians, if we have not learned to keep the flesh under subjection, the enemy will try to tempt us, and if we heed to temptation and fall into sin, then we need to repent and turn away from the ways of the flesh and begin to walk after the Spirit once more.

If we do so, then there will be no condemnation. The Scripture says, "If we confess our sins, he is faithful and just to forgive us our sins, and to cleanse us from all unrighteousness" (1 John 1:9). All we need to do is to go to the foot of the cross, surrender ourselves there, and His blood will wash away all sin, making us pure and holy once more. These are the beautiful promises of becoming the righteousness of God in Christ.

Many people still believe they can buy their way into heaven or find their way through their good works. Can good works make you righteous? The Bible is saying there is none righteous, no not one. The Bible says because of one man, sin entered into the world, and death by sin; and so automatically death is passed upon all men because all have sinned; so is the free gift of God, which is the righteousness of God through Christ Jesus our Lord. The Scripture declared that one man disobeyed God, which is Adam, and Adam's offense caused sin. This sin came upon all men, in that all have sinned. So is the grace of God, which is given by one man, Jesus Christ our Lord, causing many to be made righteous (Rom. 5:12, 16–17). The Bible declares that the law of the spirit of life in Christ

Jesus hath freed me from sin and death (Rom. 8:2). The Bible says the wages of sin is death. But the gift of God is eternal life through Jesus Christ our Lord (Rom. 6:23).

There is a spirit of death in the bloodline of Adam. All of humanity is wrapped up in his lineage. The lineage of Adam reveals to man a sinful nature. Therefore, the law of God could not make sinful nature perfect. The sinful nature causes the law to be powerless.

Nevertheless, there is a spirit of life in Christ Jesus that brings life to all those that are within him. God sent His own Son in the likeness of sinful flesh and for sin, to condemn sin in the flesh so that we can become the righteousness of God through Him. Roman 8:8 Says, "They that are in the flesh cannot please God." In Romans 8:14, the Bible declares, "For as many as are led by the Spirit of God, they are the sons of God."

As the righteousness of God through Christ, we no longer receive the spirit of bondage again to fear. We now have the spirit of adoption, "whereby we cry, Abba, Father" (Rom. 8:15). I am so glad that the Lord did not give us this spirit of fear because wherever there is fear, it brings with it torment. Your mind is no longer in control. This fear grips our hearts and soul. It cripples us. We become tormented. We are not free in our minds to think. We are not free in our bodies to do what we usually do because we are gripped with fear. And this fear brings with it bondage. It keeps us in shackles.

So then, we know that this spirit is not of God. The Bible says that where the Spirit of the Lord is, there is liberty.

So then, the Lord is saying, "Cry unto me whenever this spirit of fear comes upon you." The Lord wants you to cry out to Him and say, "Abba, Father, please help me, Daddy, and release these chains now! Release me from this bondage and torment." The spirit of fear is of the world. The Bible says we have not received the spirit of the world, but the spirit, which is of God—freedom.

As the righteousness of God, we now depend upon the Holy Ghost to teach us all things. We now compare the spiritual thoughts of a man with the Word of God (1 Cor. 2:13). So, then we as Christians need to understand the language of the Holy Ghost and be at a settled point in our minds to hear His voice.

We are no longer walking in the flesh but after the spirit. The Bible says in 1 Corinthians 2:14 that the natural man cannot understand the spiritual things of God, "for they are foolishness unto him: neither can he know them, because they are spiritually discerned."

We are now new people in Christ. Second Corinthians 5:17 says, "Therefore if any man be in Christ, he is a new creature: old things are passed; behold, all things have become new." We are now new beings in Christ. We no longer look back at our past, filled with the lust of the flesh and things of this world. We are now ambassadors for Christ. Our minds have now been changed; we are pressing toward the mark of the high calling in Christ Jesus, walking by faith, not sight. These are His Words, and He wants us to believe in Him and His Words. Not only does Christ want us to believe, but He also wants us to accept our new position within Him.

Our New Positions in Christ

1. We are now brand-new persons within Him (2 Cor. 5:17).
2. We are now the righteousness of God in Him (2 Cor. 5:21).
3. We no longer walk after the flesh but after the Spirit (Rom. 8:1, 4)
4. We now walk by faith and not by sight (2 Cor. 5:7).
5. We now listen to the teachings of the Holy Ghost, not men's wisdom (1 Cor. 23).

6. We are now pressing forward toward the mark of the high calling in Christ (Phil. 3:14).
7. We are now ambassadors for Christ (2 Cor. 5:20).
8. We have been bought with a price (1 Cor. 6:20).

When we know our full position in Him and who we are in Him, our lives will become victorious. We can take on the challenge of the enemy at any time of day and let the devil know that we are fully aware of who we are in Christ. Satan's mental plans and attacks will not work anymore because we know who we are within Christ—we are His children (Eph. 1:5). We are now heirs with God and joint-heirs with Christ, and that position he will never have!

Dr. Marlene Brown

Chapter 37
How to Walk in Love Daily Through Christ

Owe no man any thing, but to love one another: for he that loveth another hath fulfilled the law.

—Romans 13:8

I truly believe that the church lacks the Anointing of God because of a lack of love. Many Christians today are heartless and selfish. Their motor is, "What is yours is mine, and what is mine is mine." But the church that Christ died for should be a church of love. As the Bible states, this is the second greatest commandment: We love another. The Bible also declares:

> Herein is love, not that we loved God, but that he loved us and sent his Son to be the propitiation for our sins. Beloved, if God so loved us, we ought also to love one another.
>
> —1 John 4:10–11

So many of us love with our tongues while our hearts are far from one another, especially if we are from a different race, culture, or creed. But the Scripture says we should love not in tongue or word, but in deed and truth. The Scripture says that if our heart condemns us, God is greater than our heart, and He knows everything. However, if our heart condemns us, we have confidence in God (1 John 3:18–21).

In Matthew 25:31–46, Jesus speaks of His return to earth and how He will treat those who immensely love His people. He also explains what will become of those who have not practiced love in

His Second Coming

their hearts. Jesus says when He returns in His glory, along with the glory of His holy angels, He will be sitting upon the throne of His glory. Then He shall gather all nations together and separate them, one from another, as a shepherd divides His sheep from the goats; and He shall set the sheep on His right hand, but the goats on the left. Then He shall say to those on His right hand, "Come, you blessed of my Father, inherit the kingdom prepared for you from the foundation of the world." Why?

> For I was an hungered, and ye gave me meat: I was thirsty, and ye gave me drink: I was a stranger, and ye took me in: Naked, and ye clothed me: I was sick, and ye visited me: I was in prison, and ye came unto me.
>
> —Matthew 25:35–36

One must note that one cannot work well to go to heaven. The only way to heaven is through the blood of Christ. His blood will cleanse us from all unrighteousness and bring us salvation. However, after we become saved, believers need to do good work. As we become His workmanship created in Christ Jesus to do good works, which God has ordained for us to walk in, we will inherit the kingdom prepared for us.

Jesus also mentioned in Revelation that He would come quickly, and His reward is with Him, to pay every man according to His works. So, we see here that good works in the name of Christ will give us rewards in heaven.

The Scripture continues to say that the righteous will answer and say, "Lord, when was it that we saw you hungry and fed you? Or thirsty and gave you drink? Or when was it we saw thee a stranger and took you in? Or naked and clothed thee: Or in prison, or sick and came to look for you?" (Matt. 25:37–39, author's paraphrase). But remember Jesus said in His Word, "A new commandment I give unto you: That ye love one another; as I have loved you, that ye also love one another. By this shall all men know that ye are my disciples if ye have love one to another" (John 13:34–35)

So, Jesus is saying if we show love to the least of our brethren, we show it unto Him. However, if we do not show love, He will say unto you on the left hand, "Depart from me, ye cursed, into everlasting fire, prepared for the devil and his angels. For I was hungered, and ye gave me no meat: I was thirsty, and ye gave me no drink: I was a stranger, and ye took me not in naked, and ye clothed me not: sick, and in prison, and ye visited me not. Then shall they also answer him, saying, Lord, when saw we thee an hungered, or athirst, or a stranger, or naked, or sick, or in prison, and did not minister unto thee? Then shall he answer them, saying, Verily I say unto you, In asmuch as ye did it not to one of the least of these, ye did it not to me. And these shall go away into everlasting punishment: but the righteous into life eternal" (Matt. 25:41–46). Scripture asks, "But whoso hath this world's good, and seeth his brother have a need, and shutteth up his bowels of compassion from him, how dwelleth the love of God in him?" (1 John 3:17). If we say we love God, we need to show love for one another. As Jesus says in His Word, "Why call ye me Lord, Lord, and do not the things that I say?" (Luke 6:46). He declares in His Word that whosoever comes to Him and does the things that are required is very wise.

> He is like a man which built an house, and digged deep, and laid the foundation on a rock: and when the flood arose, the stream beat vehemently upon that house, and could not shake it: for it was founded upon a rock. But he that heareth, and doeth not, is like a man that without a foundation built an house upon the earth; against which the stream did beat vehemently, and immediately it fell, and the ruin of that house was great.
>
> —Luke 6:48–49

The critical question is, "What if I give of myself and commit myself to feed the poor and needy as my ministry, but my heart is still hard towards others? I find it hard to walk in forgiveness and love. However, I love to work in ministry. Will I receive a reward from God as a Christian?"

Listen to what the Bible has to say to this believer:

> Though I speak with the tongues of men and of angels and have not charity, I am become as sounding brass or a tinkling cymbal.

Many rejoice in the gifts but not in love

> The Scripture says: And though I have the gift of prophecy, and understand all mysteries, and all knowledge, and bestow all my goods to feed the poor, and though I give my body to be burned, and have not charity, it profiteth me nothing. Charity suffereth long, and is kind; and envieth not; charity vaunteth, not itself, is not puffed up.
>
> —1 Corinthians 13:1–4

The next question is, "What will become of our work for Christ, though we lack love?" The answer is found in 1 Corinthians 3:13–15. The Scripture says, "Every man's work shall be made manifest: for the day shall declare it, because it shall be revealed by fire; and the fire shall try every man's work of what sort it is. If any man's work abides, he shall receive a reward. If any man's work is burned, he shall suffer loss, but he shall be saved."

So then, as saints of God, we need to be followers of God as dear children of God and walk in love, even as Christ has loved us and offered Himself to God as an offering and a sacrifice to God, as a sweet-smelling savor. The Bible declares that the fruit of the Spirit is in all goodness, righteousness, and truth, proving what is acceptable to the Lord. Colossians 1:9–10 tells us that we need to be "filled with the knowledge of his will in all wisdom and spiritual understanding; That ye might walk worthy of the Lord unto all pleasing, being fruitful in every good work, and increasing in the knowledge of God." In Isaiah 1:17, the Scripture says, we need to "do well; seek judgment, relieve the oppressed, judge the fatherless, plead for the widow." Micah 6:8 says, "What doth the Lord require of thee, but to do justly, and to love mercy, and to walk humbly with thy God?" By doing this, we will be walking through the perfect will of God for our lives.

Chapter 38
The Power of Humility

But made himself of no reputation, and took upon him the form of a servant, and was made in the likeness of men.

—*Philippians 2:7*

It is so crucial for the body of Christ to have humility. Humility in Greek is *tapeinophrosune* which is pronounced *tap-i-nof-ros-oo'nay*. This means humbleness of mind or lowliness of mind. The Bible says the younger ones should submit themselves to the elders. The body of Christ needs to be clothed with humility because God resists the proud but gives grace to the humble.

The Word of God says we should humble ourselves under the mighty hand of God, and He will exalt us in due time. The Word of God also declares that we should cast our burden upon Him because He cares for us (1 Pet. 5–7). It means whatever the situation the enemy may bring in our path or use to prevent us from being humble, we should take it to the Lord instead of being puffed up.

Many elders, however, are not walking in the spirit, so they will abuse their power and authority over those who are submissive and cause strife in the body of Christ. We should never forget that humility and the fear of the Lord are riches, honor, and life (Prov. 22:4). The fear of the Lord is also instruction in wisdom (Prov. 15:33). This means if we need instruction as to the pathway to take in this life, and if we fear the Lord, He will charter our course. If we acknowledge Him in all of our ways, He shall direct our path.

Our Lord is stringent on humility. For this reason (a lack of humility), He cast Satan (Lucifer) down from heaven. Satan had a lack of humility in his heart. Isaiah 14:11–14 describes his downfall:

> Thy pomp is brought down to the grave, and the noise of thy harps: the worm is spread under thee, and the worms cover thee. How art thou fallen from heaven, O Lucifer, son of the morning! how art thou cut down to the ground, which didst weaken the nations! For thou hast said in thine heart, I will ascend into heaven; I will exalt my throne above the stars of God: I will also sit upon the mount of the congregation, in the sides of the north: I will ascend above the heights of the clouds; I will be like the Most High.

Lucifer's statement in his heart shows his stupidity in who he thinks God is. If God were the one who created him, why would God not know the evil that Satan was plotting against Him? Truly, God knew the evil strategy that Satan was devising against Him, so He immediately cast him down to the pit of hell to show him that He was God. He is the Alpha and the Omega, the first and the last, and there will be no other God besides Him or indeed will be after Him. The Scripture says that those who see Satan will narrowly look at him and say, "Is this the man that made the earth to tremble, that did shake kingdoms; That made the world as a wilderness, and destroyed the cities thereof; that opened not the house of his prisoners?" (Isa. 14:16–17). Satan said it in his heart, in secret, but God exposed him publicly; because He is God, He knows the evil that one devises in their heart. The Scriptures says in Luke 8:17, "For nothing is secret, that shall not be made manifest; neither anything hid, that shall not be known and come abroad."

The Lord loves humility and a humble heart. The Bible says He gives grace to the humble. The Bible also declares, "A man's pride shall bring him low: but honor shall uphold the humble in spirit" (Prov. 29:23).

His Second Coming

We now see why Satan could not remain in heaven with his pride and his strategy to overthrow the Most High. God recognized those that are humble and rewarded them for their humility. His presence is among those with a contrite heart and a broken spirit, signifying humility before Him. For He said in His Word in Isaiah 57:15:

> For thus saith the high and lofty One that inhabiteth eternity, whose name is Holy; I dwell in the high and holy place, with him also that is of a contrite and humble spirit, to revive the spirit of the humble, and to revive the heart of the contrite ones.

Once our spirit becomes boastful, then the Most Holy will not be found among us. Satan found this out the hard way. Jesus said He looked on and saw Satan fall like lightning from heaven (Luke 10:18). Someone may ask the question, How would one know whether they are being too proud or boastful? The Scripture says that we should let this mind be in us, which was also in Christ Jesus. He was also in the form of God but did not think that it was unfair to be equal to God. He made Himself to be of no reputation—no great person or person of significance, but became a servant and was made in the form of a man. The Bible says when He found Himself in the form of a man, He humbled Himself and became obedient unto death, even obedient to death on the cross. (See Philippians 2:5–8.) The Bible says God looked and saw the great humility of His Son, and God highly exalted Him and gave Him a name that is above every other name, that at the very name of "Jesus," every knee should bow, of things in heaven, and things in earth, and things under the earth. I believe that men should revere and respect the powerful name Jesus and bow at the very mention of His name!

The Bible also declares that every tongue should confess that Jesus Christ is Lord, to the glory of God the Father. The more humble we are as children of men, the more God will exalt us in due season if we faint not. The Bible says that we cannot enter heaven's kingdom if we do not humble ourselves as little children. I remember a passage in Matthew 18 when Jesus's disciples came to Him and asked Him who was the greatest in the kingdom of heaven. Jesus called a little child to Him, placed the child in the middle of them, and said, "Verily I say unto you, Except ye be converted, and become as little children, ye shall not enter into the kingdom of heaven. Whosoever, therefore, shall humble himself as this little child, the same is greatest in the kingdom of heaven" (Matt. 18:3–4).

Here, we see Jesus teaching His disciples about the power of humility.

His Second Coming

Chapter 39
The Power of Forgiveness

Then came Peter to him, and said, Lord, how oft shall my brother sin against me, and I forgive him? till seven times? Jesus saith unto him, I say not unto thee, Until seven times: but, Until seventy times seven.

—Matthew 18:21-22

How hard is it for us as Christians to forgive others? Our parents, brothers or sisters, or neighbors or coworkers may have done us wrong. We find the pain so great we believe we will never be able to forgive those who have done us wrong. However, Jesus said in His Word, just as your heavenly Father forgives you of your trespass and sin that you have committed against Him, so you need to forgive others who have trespassed against you or those who caused you hurt. So, we pray, "Our Father, forgive us our trespasses as we forgive those that trespass against us!"

From the beginning of time, people have experienced others doing them wrong. It speaks of the heart of men. The Bible says the heart is desperately wicked, and no one knows it. As long as we remain on the face of the earth, we will encounter people or family who cause us pain to some extent. Or we will cause pain to others without knowing the damage that we do emotionally, spiritually, or physically. Sometimes, people get carried away with their beliefs, believing that they share the same beliefs or ideas, then the truth is revealed, and they are hurt. It breathes bitterness and an unforgiving spirit. Let us view the life and testimony of Joseph and his family and see the evil done to him while remembering that Joseph could find it in his heart to forgive the evil his brothers did to him. He also mentioned to them that the evil meant for him had been turned around by God and used to work for good so that he could deliver his people. Joseph was seventeen years old when he began to have dreams. He was beloved by his father, who made him a colorful coat, but hated by his brothers. He was also a great dreamer. Whenever Joseph had his dreams, he would disclose them to his brothers, who would hate him even more. One of Joseph's dreams speaks of Joseph reigning over his brothers, mother, and father, who would bow down to him (Gen. 37:10). The brothers hated Joseph even more for having such a dream. One day, Joseph's father sent him out to look for his brothers feeding his flocks in Shechem to see whether or not things were going well with them and the flock. So, Joseph went to look for his brothers. When he reached Shechem, however, he did not see his brothers. He saw a man who told him they had departed to Dothan, and there he found them. When his brothers saw him at a distance, they conspired against him to kill him. They said one to another, "Here the dreamer comes. Let us kill him, throw him into some pit, and then say some wild beast has killed him—then we will see what will become of his dreams. Reuben, one of his brothers, heard it and said, 'Let us not kill him and shed blood, but cast him into the pit in the wilderness'" (Gen. 37:18–22, author's paraphrase). Reuben intended to deliver Joseph and take him back to his father. So, the brothers came to Joseph, stripped him of the coat with many colors, and put him into an empty pit without food and water. I can't imagine how terrified Joseph must have felt when he noticed the evil intention that his own brothers did to him his flesh and blood.

Judah, one of Joseph's brothers, said to his other brothers, "Do not slay Joseph because he is our flesh and blood, but sell him to the Ishmaelites." So, they sold Joseph for twenty pieces of silver (Gen. 37:26, 28). I wonder what was going through Joseph's mind when he saw his flesh and blood sell him as an enslaved person. Most of us have not had such a dreadful experience happen to us; if we did, our hearts would be filled at this point with great hatred and revenge for our brothers. To think that the ones we trusted the most, our flesh and blood, would devise such evil against us.

The Bible says Reuben was not there when he returned to the pit for Joseph. So, he tore his clothes and went back to his brothers to inform them. They took Joseph's coat, killed a kid goat, dipped Joseph's colorful coat in the blood, brought it to their father, and said, "We have found this coat, but we have no idea whether it belongs to Joseph." Joseph's father, however, knew it was Joseph's coat and said an evil beast had devoured Joseph. He rented his clothes and began to mourn for Joseph for many days. Joseph's brothers and sisters tried to comfort their father, but he would not be comforted. He said he would die mourning for Joseph. Now, I wondered what was going through the brothers' minds.

Why would they do such an evil act towards Joseph and the father? What went through their minds as they saw their father mourning for Joseph? Not only were they heartless toward Joseph, but also, they were heartless toward their father. Sometimes, the one to really do us wrong comes from within our family, but we need to find that spiritual courage and strength to forgive the person that did us wrong! The Bible said that the Midianites then sold Joseph in Egypt to Potiphar, an officer of Pharaoh's and captain of the guard (Gen. 37: 1–36).

When Joseph was in Egypt, the Lord was with Joseph, and he was very prosperous. His master made him overseer over his house, and the Lord blessed the Egyptian's house for Joseph's sake. One day, Potiphar's wife came in and asked Joseph to lie with her, but Joseph refused. He told her that his master had given him authority over everything in the house and placed all things in his hands, except her, because she was his wife, so he could not do such a wicked act and sin against God. She did not take no for an answer; however, she kept asking and asking him to lie to her. One day, when Joseph went into the house to do his business, and none of the men were inside the house, she came to him, held him by his clothes, and said lie with me, so he left his garment in her hand and ran. When Potiphar's wife saw that Joseph's clothing was left in her hand, she called the men of the house and said to them, "Look . . . He brought a Hebrew unto us to mock us; he came in to lie with me, and I lifted up my voice and cried out, and he left his garment with me and fled!" When her husband came home, she told him the same story, and he was very angry and imprisoned Joseph. The Lord was with Joseph, though, and showed him mercy, giving him favor in the sight of the prison keeper. So, the prison keeper gave Joseph all the prisoners to take care of, without wondering about his work, because Joseph did prosper because the Lord was with him. (See Genesis 39:1–23.)

As the Scripture says, if God be for you, who can be against you? I know that so many of us would be grieved and mad with the world by now for going through such an evil experience. But I believe that Joseph trusted in his God. If we as Christians could only learn to put our trust in God and to know and believe that He will deliver us from whatever pitfalls, then we would deal with every situation with confidence in Christ without having bitterness within our hearts.

When Joseph was in prison, he was placed in a dungeon. They hastily brought him up from the dungeon, let him shave himself, changed his raiment, and took him to Pharaoh. Pharaoh said to Joseph, I have dreamed a dream, and none can interpret it, and I have heard of you that you can understand a dream to interpret it.

Pharaoh had a dream that the magicians or wise men could not interpret. So, he told Joseph about his dream, and Joseph gave him the interpretation. He said that he went to bed again and dreamed the second time and woke up and realized again it was a dream.

Joseph then interpreted Pharaoh's dream by telling him what God was about to do on the earth; he showed it to Pharaoh. He revealed the meaning of the dreams, which were seven years of plenty and seven years of famine, and that the famine would be grievous in the land of Egypt, and the famine would consume the land. Joseph explained to Pharaoh that the dream was doubled unto him twice

His Second Coming

because God had already established the plan and would shortly bring it to pass. (See Genesis 41:1–32.) Joseph had not only interpreted Pharaoh's dream, but he also gave Pharaoh, the king, great wisdom. Joseph advised Pharaoh to look for a very discreet and wise man and set him over the land of Egypt. He also advised Pharaoh to appoint officers over the land and take up fifth part of the land of Egypt in the seven plenteous years. They should also gather food and store up against the seven years of famine, which shall be in the land of Egypt so that the lands do not perish during the time of famine. What Joseph suggested to Pharaoh sounded good to him and in the eyes of all his servants. So, Pharaoh turned to his servants and said, "Can we find a man like this, a man in whom the spirit of God dwells? So, Pharaoh turned to Joseph and said: "God has shown you these things, and there is none so discreet and wise as you! You shall rule over my house! And according to your word shall all people be ruled; only in my throne will I be greater than you!" Pharaoh said to Joseph, "See, I have made you ruler over the land of Egypt!" How many of us know that when the hand of God is upon you, you will become wiser than your enemies? The Bible says you will even become wiser than those that are ruling over you. I do wonder what was going through Joseph's mind when he heard the king's remark. Making him, Joseph, ruler over all of Egypt! Here he is, sold by his brothers, thrown into a dungeon, and now, ruler over all of Egypt! No wonder the Scripture says if God is for you, who can be against you?

The Bible says Pharaoh took off his ring from his hand and put it upon Joseph's hand arrayed him in fine linen with a gold chain around his neck! He also made him ride in his second chariot, and the people cried before him and bowed down on their knees. The Bible says Joseph was only thirty years old when he stood before Pharaoh, king of Egypt. (See Genesis 41:33–46.) It means Joseph spent thirteen years in his affliction before being truly delivered! Many of us would have given up hope. Joseph held on to his faith and trusted that his God would deliver him from all of his trouble, which God did. He was delivered from the dungeon and entered right into the palace. He both lived and ruled in the palace. The Bible says that when the famine broke out, people from all over the country came to Egypt to buy corn, and Joseph opened all the storehouses to sell to the people as he was in charge.

Have you ever wondered what it is like to know that God's hand is upon you? It is when you know that no weapon formed against you shall prosper! It is when you have not just head knowledge but experience with the Highest God! Joseph said God had made him forget all his toil, labor, and his father's house, and God had also made him fruitful in the land of his affliction. (See Genesis 41:51–53.) It is a blessing to be sold as a slave by your brothers and then rise up with such power and authority because the hand of the living God is upon your life. We serve a mighty God indeed. He is an incredible living God who hears and answers prayer, looks down on the affliction of His people, and delivers them out of all their trouble. It is the reason why David speaks out in Psalm 1 by saying:

> Blessed is the man that walketh not in the counsel of the ungodly, nor standeth in the way of sinners, nor sitteth in the seat of the scornful. But his delight is in the law of the Lord, and in his law, he does meditate day and night. And he shall be like a tree planted by the rivers of water, that bringeth forth his fruit in his season; his leaf also shall not wither; and whatsoever he doeth shall prosper.
>
> —Psalm 1:1–3

I believe Joseph was the first to experience his fruit coming forth in its season. Joseph took thirteen years before he reached his promise. The Lord had promised Joseph to bless him, but Joseph had to experience the pit; he had to experience what hard life was like; he had to go through the flood, the rain, and the fire before he could reach his promise. He could not be fruitful until his season was established. God has a desired plan and season for all of us, but we have to learn to endure whatever hardship the enemy has for us. We have to learn to walk through our period of longsuffering because the God of the universe, our Father, promised never to leave us comfortless.

When I read the Psalm of David, it revealed to me his heart and his desires. It makes me wonder about Joseph's heart and desires toward his brethren when enslaved. Was he thinking, like David, that God is his refuge and strength, a very present help in times of trouble? I believe that Joseph trusted God totally and was confident that his dream given to him by God would come true, no matter what occurred to him. The Lord, his God, would deliver him of all of his trouble. The Bible says those who trust in the Lord shall never be ashamed. Joseph lived to see the salvation of the living God.

When Jacob, his father, **also called Israel**, saw that there was no corn in Egypt, the Bible says that Joseph's father said to his children, "Why are you looking at each other? I heard that there is corn in Egypt; go down there and buy for us that we can live and not die!" So, Jacob sent his ten children to Egypt, except Benjamin, in case something terrible happened there. At that time, Joseph was the governor of the land. It was the responsibility of Joseph to sell to all the people of the land. So, his brothers came and bowed themselves down before him with their faces to the earth, but Joseph acted as though he had no idea who they were.

Joseph talked roughly to his brothers and said, "Where are you from?" They said to him, "From the land of Canaan to buy food." The Bible says Joseph knew who they were, but they did not discover who he was. Immediately, Joseph remembered the dreams that he had of them. Ha, ha, one would say, Joseph, here is sweet revenge! Did Joseph try to let his brothers payback for what they did to him? Let us see how far Joseph went to get back at his brothers. Joseph said to them, "You are spies. You have come to spy out the land!" And they cried out, saying, "No, my lord, we are here to buy food! We are all one man's sons; we are truthful and good men, and we are no spies!" Joseph insisted, "No, you are spies and have come to see the land's nakedness!" Now try to picture this—his brothers all on their faces begging for their lives, trying to convince their own brothers that they are not spies; they are all one man's sons!

The Bible says if you make the Lord your strength and your refuge, a thousand shall fall at your side, and ten thousand at your right hand, but it shall not befall thee. Only with your eyes shall you behold and see the reward of the wicked.

Joseph let them quiver for a while for their lives. The questioning continued.

So, his brothers said to him, "We, your servant, are of twelve brothers, the son of one man in the land of Canaan, and the youngest is at home with our father, but one of them is not at home." Listen to Joseph's response: "That is why I said before that you are spies!" Then he said to them, "Now, I am going to prove you! Upon Pharaoh's life, you shall not leave here unless your little brother is brought here! Send one of you to get your brother, and the rest stay in prison to prove your word is truth." He put them all in a cell for three days.

So, on the third day, Joseph said to them, "You have to do this to live because I fear God; let one of your brothers remain in prison and bring your youngest brother back to me, and carry corn for the famine of your house." The Bible says the fear of God is the beginning of wisdom. Joseph could have dealt with his brothers more harshly than he did. All he did was to question them roughly, and he held them in prison for a couple of days; however, he feared God, so he did not take sweet revenge on them as some of us would have. The Bible declares that judgment belongs to God.

The Bible says the brothers began to feel bad about what they did to Joseph. Their consciences began to bother them, so they began to speak to each other, saying, "We are truly guilty of what we did to our brother! We saw the anguish of his soul when he begged us, and we would not hear! This is the reason why we have this trouble that

His Second Coming

comes upon us!" Reuben answered, "Didn't I tell you not to sin against the child? See now; his blood is upon us!"

As they spoke, they did not know that Joseph understood what they were saying because he used an interpreter whenever Joseph spoke to them. When Joseph heard what they said, he went away and wept! Then he came back to them and talked with them for a while.

I truly believe it was important for Joseph to hear his brothers' confession and guilt for doing such evil toward him. By weeping over what they did to him and hearing their confession, it brought healing to his soul. So many of us are still waiting to hear a confession from the one that hurt us; maybe that person is dead or will not give any admission, no matter what! So, we must learn to let go and let God heal that wound. Let go of the pain; let go of the ill-treatment. Let go of the wrong that was done to you; let go of the sexual molestation; give it to Jesus! Let God take full control. Let Him take control of the pain and the hurt; just give it all to Him. He understands; He knows! Just give it all to Jesus. Let Him love you with that everlasting love only He knows how to give. Please give it to the Father of fathers. Please share it with the great physician.

The Bible says Jesus has been through it all, so He understands what we are going through. The feelings of our infirmity touch him. He understands what we have been through, so He is able to help us. Since He understands the hurt and the pain, cry unto Him, and He will answer you; He will take away your pain or grief. Take your anguish and pain to the foot of the cross and allow Christ to heal you. Jesus wants to give you beauty for ashes: He wants to give you the oil of joy for mourning, the garment of praise for the spirit of heaviness; that you might be called trees of righteousness, the planting of the Lord, that he might be glorified (Isaiah 61:3). You will rise feeling refreshed and having a renewed spirit and life.

So, Joseph took Simeon away from them and bound him up before their eyes. He then commanded them to fill their sacks with corn, restore every man's money back to his sack, and give them food while they were returning to their father's house. They then lade their horses with corn and left.

Now, we see the kindness of Joseph's heart. He not only gave them what they came to buy, but he also gave them provisions to keep them on their way back home and restore to them even the money they would use to pay for the goods.

The Bible says that when the brothers found out that their money was still in their sacks, their hearts failed them, and they were terrified. So, they began to wonder what God did to them. When the brothers reached home, they told their father what had happened to them. Joseph's father, however, was heartbroken about hearing that Simeon had been left behind. The sons told their father that Joseph required Benjamin as proof of their identity before Simeon could be released. Jacob then declared to his sons that he could not release Benjamin because if any evil befell him, he would go down in the grave, grieving for him. (See Genesis 42:1–38.)

The famine was great in the land, so when they had eaten up all the food, Joseph's father asked them to go back to the land of Egypt to buy more food. Judah, however, reminded the father that they could not go unless they took Benjamin with them as promised. The father then agreed to let Benjamin go and said to them, "Take of the best fruits in the land in your vessels." Fruits! I am happy to know that at least they had fruits to eat from their land. Fruits, however, are certainly not food. One can be fasting on fruits and still die of hunger. He said to them, "Also, take double the money with you; maybe it was an oversight the first time." He also prayed that God would give them mercy before the man and that the man would release Benjamin and their brother.

So, the men did what their father told them and went back down to Egypt and stood before Joseph.

His Second Coming

When Joseph saw Benjamin with them, he said to the ruler of the house, "Bring these men to my house and slay and cook and make ready because these men shall dine with me at noon!"

Oh, Joseph! How much he longed to be with his family! Although his brothers caused him great pain, one could see that the love was still there. The forgiving heart was still there because they were family. All the riches and wealth in the world could not change that fact. Joseph strongly loved his family, but Christ has a stronger love for us! Think of us being partakers of the inheritance of the family of God by the blood of the Lamb. No matter how much we hurt our heavenly Father, He is always there to welcome us home and make us feel welcome. The Bible says there is great rejoicing in heaven when a sinner comes home; the angels in heaven rejoice! Such a heart of love only comes from the Father Himself.

So, the man did what Joseph told him to do: bring his brothers to his house. The brothers, however, were afraid because they thought it was the money they found in their sacks, and now their lives were at stake. So, when they came into Joseph's house, they met the steward there and told him there was a mistake with the money and that they found the money in their sacks to pay Joseph. The stewards told them that all was well because he had their money and that their God and the God of their fathers had given them treasures in their sacks. He then brought out Simeon to them. The men washed and made themselves ready to meet Joseph at noon.

When Joseph came home, they brought him their present and bowed themselves to him to the earth. Then Joseph asked them about their welfare and concerning their father, "Is your father well?" he asked. "The old man you spoke of: is he yet alive?" They answered and said, "Your servant, our father is well and in good health and alive." Joseph lifted his head, saw his younger brother, his mother's son, and said, "Is this your younger brother of which you spoke?" He said to Benjamin, "God be gracious unto you, my son!" Joseph then walked out fast because his bowels yearned for his brothers, and so he looked for a place to weep and quickly went into his chamber and wept there. He then washed his face, went out, refrained, and said set the bread ready. So, they ate and were full (Gen. 43:1–34).

Joseph could no longer refrain from his brothers, so he cried out and said, "Let every man leave me except my brother!" My brother! Joseph said it! My brother! Can one imagine what must have been going through the minds of his brothers to hear those words? My brother! He then began to weep so loud that the Egyptians and the house of Pharaoh heard it. I believe that Joseph's crying was really loud! I believe he could not refrain because of all the pent-up feelings of missing his father and his family and finally seeing his brothers before him. He then said to his brothers, "I am Joseph; is my father still alive?" His brothers could not answer him because they feared his presence. So, Joseph told them, "Come near me, I beg you!" So, they came near to him, and he said to them again, "I am Joseph, your brother whom you sold into Egypt! Don't be grieved or angry with yourselves that you sold me here, for God sent me before you to preserve life. For two years, the famine has been in the land, and there will not be any harvest in the next five years, so God sent me before you to preserve prosperity in the earth and serve all of your lives with great deliverance! So, it is not you who sent me here, but God! He has also made me a father to Pharaoh and ruler throughout all the land of Egypt. So, make haste and go to my father and let him know that God has made his son Joseph lord over all the land of Egypt. Tell him to come to me and linger not and that he should bring his household, his children, and his children's children!"

So, he ordered his brothers to tell his father about his fame in Egypt and kissed his brothers, and they did according to what they were told. Pharaoh commanded them not to regard their stuff because all the land of Egypt belonged to them.

How happy his brothers must have been to hear and see the heart of Joseph! It is the heart that God is expecting from us, His people. For this reason, the Scripture says, "Forgive us our trespasses as we forgive those who trespass against us!" It all begins with trust. How much do we trust the Father that He will deliver us from the hands of our enemies? If we truly trust the Father, we will quickly forgive.

Joseph's father had a hard time believing at first that Joseph was still alive, but when he saw the wagon that Joseph sent, he said, "That is enough! Joseph, my son is still alive." So, God spoke to Israel in a vision of the night and said to him, "Jacob, Jacob!" Jacob answered and said, "Here am I." And God said to him, "I am God! The God of thy fathers, do not be afraid to go down to Egypt, because I will go down with you there, and will make of you a great nation and bring you out again, and Joseph will put his hand upon thy eyes!" So, they came to the land of Goshen, and there Israel died. (See Genesis 46:1–5.)

Before Israel died, however, he met with Joseph and Joseph's sons. When Israel died, Joseph's brothers feared that Joseph would take revenge on them, seeing that their father was no longer around. So, they sent a messenger before them to Joseph that said, "Your father commanded before he died that you should forgive the trespass of your brothers and their sins, for what they did to you was evil! Now, I beg you to forgive the servants of the God of your father." So, Joseph wept when they spoke to him. His brothers also wept and said to him, "Now we are thy servants!" Joseph's response was: "Don't be afraid. Am I in the place of God? As for you, you thought evil against me, but God meant it for good, to bring to pass as how it is this very day so that many people can be alive! So do not be afraid; I will nourish your little ones." So, he comforted them and spoke kindly to them. (See Genesis 47:1–31; 50:1–26.)

God will take our disappointments, headaches, and pains and use them as testimonies within our lives. Whatever evil the enemy brings across our paths, our God will use it for good. You may not know how, you may not know when, but He will deliver you out of your bondage and set you free— both physical and spiritual bondage. He will fight the battle for you and set you free. Just stand still and see the salvation of the living God. As His Word says, "Is my hand too short where it cannot save? Is there anything too hard for God?" So that in the ages to come, we might know the exceeding riches of His grace toward us. So, in Him, we should put our trust. In Joseph's life, we see the Father's heart, the Father's love, and the Father's mercy toward us. As Christians, this is the heart the Father expects from us: a heart of love and mercy.

In Colossians 3:12–14, the Scripture says, "Put on therefore, as the elect of God, holy and beloved, bowels of mercies, kindness, humbleness of mind, meekness, longsuffering; Forbearing one another and forgiving one another, if any man quarrels any: even as Christ forgave you, so also do ye. And above all these things put on charity, which is the bond of perfectness." Ephesians 4:31–32 commands us to "let all bitterness, and wrath, and anger, and clamor, and evil speaking, be put away from you, with all malice: And be ye kind one to another, tenderhearted, forgiving one another, even as God for Christ's sake hath forgiven you."

In Matthew, Peter was asking Jesus how many times a person should be forgiven. So, Peter asked Jesus, "Should it be seven times, Lord?" Jesus answered and said to him, "I will not tell you seven times, but seventy times seven" (Matt. 18:21–22). Seventy times seven is actually four hundred and ninety times as often as necessary.

I will tell you that the Bible says the flesh of man is very weak; it will fail you. So, we need to walk in the Spirit so that we will not fulfill the lusts of the flesh. The flesh always screams to be heard and always wants to be correct but by dying to ourselves daily, we will eventually learn how to kill the flesh and become alive to the life of the Holy Spirit. The Holy Spirit will then release His anointing of strength in the inner man for Christ to dwell in our hearts richly by faith. We will then become rooted and grounded in love and will be able to comprehend with all the saints the love that Jesus Christ has for us and the love that we need to pass on to others. As the Word of God says, "Forgive one another even as God, for Christ's sake, has forgiven you" (Eph. 4:32).

Dr. Marlene Brown

Chapter 40
Are You an Addict Today?

The Spirit of the Lord is upon me, because he hath anointed me to preach the gospel to the poor; he hath sent me to heal the brokenhearted, to preach deliverance to the captives, and recovering of sight to the blind, to set at liberty them that are bruised;

—Luke 4:18

Addicted to drugs, alcohol, sex, or any other addiction not listed here: are you weak, poor, or lonely? Do you need a friend? Well, let me introduce to you someone who cares and will deliver.

All of the symptoms listed here are called bondage of the mind. It is the dwelling place of Satan. This is where he has total control. However, I know of one that is much stronger than the powers of Satan. His name is called Jesus. When He shows up, His anointing breaks all bondage of the enemy. He will set the captives free. If you are held captive behind your prison wall today, let the King of kings walk into your life. He will come in and sup with you and make an abode with you, and your life will never be the same again. There is none like Him, guaranteed.

If you are sitting in darkness—the darkness of your mind—from depression or oppression from the enemy, He said He is the light of this world, and those who follow Him will never be in darkness. He said in Isaiah 54:14 that He will establish you in righteousness, and you shall be far from oppression because you shall not fear; and from terror, because it shall not come near you. If you feel lonely and need a friend, the Bible says Jesus is a friend that sticks closer

His Second Coming

than a brother. If you are in the hospital bed today and feeling very weak, He said His strength is perfect in times of weakness if only you learn to trust Him and believe in His Word. Not only will He set you free from all of your bondage and sin, but He will also give you a brand-new life. Yes, my friend, a brand-new lease on life. A much better life than what you had before. In His Word, He said, "I came that you might have life and have this life abundantly!" He said, "I know the plans that I have for you to prosper you and not to harm you!"

Oh yes, my friends, I know He cares. Your grief touches him. He does care when your days are weary and your nights are dreary. The Bible describes Him as a man of sorrows and very much acquainted with grief. The Bible says the feelings of our infirmities touch him.

Whatever you might be going through this day, Jesus Christ cares. He wants to come in and take away all of your pain. He knows, and He understands. When no one else does, He knows and understands. Just trust Him today and release your burden at His feet.

I know that, at times, we feel so far gone it feels impossible to pray because of the pressure. Just simply say, "Jesus, my pressure is heavy, and my burden is heavy. I need deliverance, Lord. I need rest. I need peace of mind! Please release my burden this day, I pray, in Jesus's name. I give it all to you now. Amen."

My friends, He will release you of this addiction. He will release you of whatever bondage holds you in sin because He promised that He would. For His Word says, "Come unto me, all ye that labor and are heavily laden, and I will give you rest. Take my yoke upon you, and learn of me; for I am meek and lowly in heart: and ye shall find rest unto your souls. For my yoke is easy, and my burden is light!" (Matt. 11:28–30). Just cast your burden upon the Lord, for He cares for you, the Word of God says. Christ will not leave you comfortless.

Dr. Marlene Brown

Let us review and go deeper into the Greek meaning of what Jesus Himself is offering to you. He says to come to Him, the Son of the living God, if you are laboring and are heavily laden, and He will give you rest. The Greek word for *labor* is *kopiao*, which means "to be weary or tired with grief." The Greek word for *laden* is *phortizo*, which is pronounced as *fortidzo*. It means to place a heavy burden upon or to be loaded with a burden. So, Jesus says that if you are weary and tired of grief, He will give you rest and peace of mind. If you are walking around with a heavy burden, a load you do not want to carry—one that you would rather have lifted from your body, mind, soul, or spirit—then come to Him. He will release this burden from you; He will give you that peace of mind that you so desire because He is peace itself. He is the blessed Prince of Peace. He will help you recover and be refreshed. You will be strengthened and refreshed within Him. The next verse says, "Take my yoke upon you and learn of me: For I am meek and lowly in heart." The Greek word for *yoke* is *zugos*; which means a yoke that is put on draught cattle. However, it is also used metaphorically as any burden or bondage, like in slavery. The word *learn* in Greek is *manthano*, which means "to increase one's knowledge; to hear or to be informed; to learn by use and practice; to be in the habit of practicing." Then He went on to say, "For I am meek." The Greek word for *meek* is *praos*, which is pronounced *prahos*.

It means "gentle and mild." *Lowly* in Greek is *tapeinos*, which means "of low degree, very humble in heart." So, Jesus is saying here that you should put down your heavy burden, leave it at His feet, and take His yoke, which is much lighter. Try to increase your knowledge about Him. Try to be informed as much as possible, whether through church or Bible study, research through the internet, or on your own. Learn of Him. Learn of His ways, His character, His love, His mercy, His great goodness, and His power to save. Keep practicing what He says, for He is very meek, of low degree, and humble in heart. He will meet you where you are in life. You cannot be too far in sin where He will not come into your heart and eat with you. He is very humble in heart. He said in His Word,

His Second Coming

though your sins be as red as crimson, He will make them as white as snow. If only you will be willing and obedient to let Him in.

As Christians, we often fall by the way because of trials and tribulations. We were not strong enough in the Word of God to overcome these obstacles, so the enemy came in, took control of our lives, and snatched us away from Christ. Don't give up! Come back to the Master! The Bible says He is faithful and just to forgive you of your sins and to cleanse you from all unrighteousness. I find this the most beautiful thing about my Lord— His faithfulness. He never fails. He is always there to meet you at the midnight hour. He said in His Word, "Call upon me, and I will answer thee and show thee great and mighty things, which thou knowest not!" All He needs from you is a broken and contrite spirit. He said in His Word that a broken heart and a contrite spirit He would not despise. He encourages us to call upon Him in the days of our trouble, and He will answer us and deliver us, and we shall give Him the glory for doing so.

Living in this life, we will always be faced with tribulations and troubles. As long as the enemy remains loose on the face of this earth, he will try to have us entangled in some form of bondage. We must hang on to Jesus with our body, mind, soul, and spirit. Jesus is the only name given to men under heaven, whereby men can be saved, delivered, and set free. As the Bible declares, whomever the Son sets free is indeed free! Christ is the only one who can free us from all our troubles. He is the everlasting God and the precious Prince of Peace. The Word of God says, "Many are the afflictions of the righteous: but the Lord delivereth him out of them all" (Ps. 34:19). If you are a Christian or not, there will be afflictions in this life.

However, our confidence is that our Lord will deliver us of all of them. The beautiful thing is His Words are not just empty promises; His promises are yea and amen, which means it is already done! If His Word says it, then He will do it!

When you allow His spiritual Words to dwell within you richly, His Spirit, which is life, will bring life to your dead situation or life to your dead body! Or whatever the case may be! He said in His Word, "My word will not return unto me void or empty; but it will accomplish that which I please, and it will prosper into the thing in which where do I send it" (Isa. 55:11). He said His Word is Spirit and life (John 6:63). When we use His Word in prayer, something good will happen! The Bible says that all good and perfect gifts are from above. So, if we direct His Word toward our lives here on earth, then His Word will rise up before Him in prayer; He will send His Word to accomplish something good for us, and the gates and the powers of hell cannot prevail against it.

So let us come boldly before His throne of grace, in whatever situation or sin that we find ourselves, gently lay our burdens at His feet, and pick up His yoke, as His yoke is His glory and His anointing, which is very light. He will give you renewed strength and peace of mind. No matter what time of day or night you call upon Him, He will be there! As He declares in His Word, "Hast thou not known? Hast thou not heard that the everlasting God, the Lord, the Creator of the ends of the earth, fainteth not, neither is weary? There is no searching of his understanding. He giveth power to the faint; and to them that have no might he increaseth strength. Even the youths shall faint and be weary, and the young men shall utterly fall!" (Isa. 40:28–30). The Most High God, Jesus Christ, is His name, is telling you that there is none like Him! "But they that wait upon the Lord shall renew their strength; they shall mount up with wings as eagles; they shall run, and not be weary; and they shall walk, and not faint" (Isa. 40:31).

This is the reason He is encouraging us to call upon Him. So, let us trust Him today and come home to Him. Cast your burden upon Him, for He cares for you. Let Him take you into His arms. As you learn of Him and His ways, you will see that no one else is like Him. He is a God of great, abundant love and tender mercies. Jesus is a

His Second Coming

God that cares and understands; He is touched by the feelings of your infirmities, one that hears and answers prayer.

"I will bring you into the bosom of the Father," Jesus says. "I will bring you health. I came to bring you life and for you to have this life in great abundance. I am the one that will bring you peace because I am peace."

Jesus said in His Word that He will give us peace, not like what the world gives. The peace that He will give you is His peace. It is the type of peace that passes all understanding. During your trouble, you will find this peace. He is the Prince of Peace, so let not your heart be troubled, neither let it be afraid. Come to Him just as you are, without money or price, and He will give you rest. You will find rest for your soul: His yoke is easy, and His burden is light.

Remember that the Lord loves you with everlasting love and draws you to Him with lovingkindness. Remember, He said in His Word that while others may forget you, yet He will not forget you. "Behold, I have graven thee upon the palms of my hands" (Isa. 49:16). So, because of His promises, let us trust Him today because we serve a God who is love. We serve a God who is merciful, who will never leave us or forsake us, and who is able to deliver us of all of our troubles.

So, if you are seeking a friend today, He is a friend that sticks closer than a brother. If you are seeking strength, He is the almighty God. If you are in need of a father, He is the Father of fathers. The Bible calls Him the Everlasting Father. He is the Prince of Peace if you are searching for peace of mind. If your life needs counseling, the Bible calls Him the Wonderful Counselor. So, turn to Him today, and as the Word of God says, "Come taste and see that the Lord is good and his mercy endures forever!" (See Psalm 34:8.)

Dr. Marlene Brown

Chapter 41
How We Should View Preachers

Let the elders that rule well be counted worthy of double honour, especially they who labour in the word and doctrine.

—*1 Timothy 5:17*

Preachers are blessed people indeed! They are the ones that God chose to spread the gospel to the nations. Preachers are people who have been sold out for Christ. The Bible declares, "How beautiful are the feet of them that preach the gospel of peace, and bring glad tidings of good things!" (Rom. 10:15). Many of us would not have been saved today if it were not for the preaching of some preacher. For this reason, the Bible says we need to esteem them very highly in love for their work's sake and to know those who labor among you and are over you in the Lord. (See 1 Thessalonians 5:12–13.) These people watch over your soul. Most of these preachers are anointed by God to break the yoke of bondage on your lives so you can be free. The Scripture points out in Luke 4:18–19:

> The spirit of the Lord is upon me because he hath anointed me to preach the gospel to the poor; he hath sent me to heal the brokenhearted, to preach deliverance to the captives, and recovering of sight to the blind, to set at liberty them that are bruised, To preach the acceptable year of the Lord.

As Jesus was anointed to preach the gospel, preachers ought to be anointed. Preachers should be anointed to preach the gospel. They should also be anointed to set those who have been bound at liberty. The Bible declares that the anointing breaks the yoke of bondage. The yoke will be destroyed because of the anointing. However, not all preachers have this type of anointing, which is rather sad. Not many have discovered how to enter into the secret place of the Most High to obtain this type of anointing. It does not come cheap or easy. It comes through fasting, deep, intense prayer with Jesus, and spending time with Him. Sometimes, we find preachers who can preach the Scriptures, but their congregation is weak, sick, and in need of help. This is because the yoke has not been broken due to lack of anointing.

In our society today, we need not only preachers but also anointed preachers who understand their call to the body of Christ will not allow the size of their ministry to dictate how they should preach the gospel but will allow the Word of God to take its full course. As Paul pointed out, it should not be by men's wisdom but by teaching by the Holy Spirit so that the cross of Christ does not lose its effectiveness. We need men who boldly say, like Paul, "Woe unto me if I preach not the gospel." We need men who say, "I have nothing to glory of in myself if I preach the gospel because I must do so."

The Bible says that the gospel must be preached to all nations for the end to come. For this to happen or to be fulfilled, however, the preachers must be sent. How can the people be saved unless they hear about the name of Jesus? And how will they hear unless a preacher has been sent?

The corruption that is within our society, as well as in our churches today, has caused people to be less trusting. Many are primarily concerned about pastors using the 10 percent of the tithe for themselves rather than to further the gospel of Christ. While this concern may be valid, it should not be the reason why we fail to tithe. The Bible pointed out that the tenth part of a person's increase belongs to God. That part is holy. Then, the Lord promised to pour you out a blessing that you will not have enough room to contain when you bring all your tithes and offerings into His house. It is extremely important for the work of the gospel. Souls can be saved only through the preaching of the gospel. People need to hear the gospel being preached to them. In this way, they will develop faith in the Word of God. The Bible says, "Faith cometh by hearing and hearing by the Word of God" (Rom. 10:17). Our tithes and offerings allow the continuation of the gospel to go forth. We as children of God should not focus on pastors and preachers concerning how they live but rather on whether the great commission that Jesus gave is being fulfilled; that is, to go into the entire world and preach the gospel to every creature. This is the only way the end will come when the gospel is preached throughout the world. The Bible says, "He that believeth and is baptized shall be saved, but he that believeth not shall be damned" (Mark 16:16). The Bible also declares, "The Lord ordained that they which preach the gospel should live of the gospel" (1 Cor. 9:14).

We as Christians need to be aware that whatever we do for the Lord or for the work of the Lord, our reward will be in heaven. For this reason, the Bible says, "Let us not be weary in well doing: for in due season we shall reap if we faint not" (Gal. 6:9).

In our world today, we have strong, powerful, and truthful men who preach the gospel of Christ and men who preach a different gospel. The Scripture says, "If there come any unto you, and bring not this doctrine, receive him not into your house, neither bid him God speed: For he that biddeth him God speed is partaker of his evil deeds" (2 John 1:6–11).

The Bible tells us that in the last days, perilous times will come, and many will come, saying that they are Christ and will deceive many. The Bible warns us that there will be some that were Christians but left the faith. For this reason, the Bible says we need to try the spirits. We go about testing the spirits by the unction from the Holy Ghost, who knows all things. (See 1 John 2:19–20.) The Scripture tells us that these people or preachers are false apostles,

His Second Coming

deceitful workers, transforming themselves into the apostles of Christ, having a form of godliness but denying the power thereof.

The Bible declares, do not marvel at such a one because "Satan himself is transformed as an angel of light. Therefore, it is no great thing if his ministers also be transformed as the ministers of righteousness, whose end shall be according to their works" (2 Cor. 11:14–15).

> These things have I written unto you concerning them that seduce you. But the anointing which ye have received of him abideth in you, and ye need not that any man teaches you: but as the same anointing teacheth you of all things, and is truth, and is no lie, and even as it hath taught you, ye shall abide in him. And now, little children, abide in him; that, when he shall appear, we may have confidence and not be ashamed before him at his coming. If ye know that he is righteous, ye know that everyone that doeth righteousness is born of him.
>
> —1 John 2:26–29

So then, let us all walk in love and, at the same time, be aware of the preachers and teachers that we have around us. "Beware lest any man spoils you through philosophy and vain deceit, after the tradition of men, after the rudiments of the world, and not after Christ. For in him dwelleth all the fulness of the Godhead bodily. And ye are complete in him, which is the head of all principality and power" (Col. 2:9–10). As Mark 13:22 declares, "For false Christs and false prophets shall rise, and shall shew signs and wonders, to seduce, if it were possible, even the elect."

Dr. Marlene Brown

Chapter 42
Religion Versus Salvation

For if you are trying to make yourselves right with God by keeping the law, you have been cut off from Christ! You have fallen away from God's grace.

—*Galatians 5:4 NLT*

I thank God that the Christian pathway is not about a religion but salvation. This means having a personal relationship with Jesus Christ Himself. As Jesus pointed out in His Word: "I am the way, the truth, and the life, no man cometh unto the Father, but by me" (John 14:6). "I am the door: by me, if any man enter in, he shall be saved" (John 10:9)

I am so happy that Jesus has become our great High Priest. We now have a High Priest, one that is touched with the feelings of our infirmities. This is a much better covenant than what they had before in the days of Moses. In the days of Moses, the religious leaders were accustomed to having only the high priest enter into the holy of holies to offer up sacrifices before God for their sins and the sins of the people. Now, we can enter into that holy place, going boldly before the throne of God through the blood of Jesus. Through the power of His blood, He has redeemed us from sin and shame and has given us to God as a "sweetsmelling savor," according to Ephesians 5:2.

In the world today, there are many different types of religions. Everyone has a different concept as to what will make him or her enter into heaven. The interesting point that they are saying is that everyone worships the same God, no matter what religion. Well, I

His Second Coming

am here to remind them that either they are making Jesus a liar in His Word or His message is truth. Jesus says there is no other way to the Father except through Him. Jesus said in His Word that the Father sent Him. He said in His Word that He came to do the work of His Father. Before He was crucified, His last prayer to the Father was: "I have finished the work which thou gavest me to do, and they have believed that I came out from thee" (John 17:4, 8). On the cross, Jesus cried, "It is finished" John 19:30), which means He came to offer Himself to God as a sacrifice for sin, to save man's soul. He did this by offering Himself so that His blood, which is without spot or wrinkle, can be made an atonement for our sins. So then, I am here to remind you of the Scriptures and to let the world know that it is not about religion but salvation. Religion is all man-made. It is full of theoretical application. It is full of rules and regulations. When you come to Christ, there is no rule or regulation to follow as in a ritual. Jesus is saying it is already finished. He already did all the work that you need to do. Now you only need to follow Him. The new commandment that He gave us is for us to love one another, even as Christ has loved us and has offered Himself for us to God. This is how we ought to love one another. "Greater love hath no man than this," he said, "than a man lay down his life for his friends" (John 15:13).

I believe the big question is this: Do you have an anchor for your soul? We do have an anchor that keeps our soul steadfast and sure while the billows roll in our lives. The anchor is fastened to that rock, which is Christ. Grounded firm and deep in our Savior's love. The solid rock that we stand on is Jesus. He is the Alpha and the Omega, the first and the last. He is the beginning and the end. It is He who was dead and is now alive and lives forevermore. He has conquered death, hell, and the grave. The grave could not hold His body down because of the Holy Spirit that was within Him. God raised Him up, having loosed the pains of death because it was not possible for Him to be held by it.

Dr. Marlene Brown

This same Spirit that raised Jesus from the dead is living within us, according to Romans 8:11. Once you have made Jesus the Lord and Savior of your soul, you too can have this same Spirit that raised up Jesus from the dead. This very same Spirit can now dwell within you. He too will quicken your mortal bodies, the Bible says. The Bible says there is no other name given among men whereby you can be saved but by the name of Jesus. (See Acts 4:12.) The Bible says, "At the name of Jesus every knee shall bow, of things in heaven, and things in earth, and things under the earth; And that every tongue should confess that Jesus Christ is Lord, to the glory of God the Father" (Phil. 2:10). God has highly exalted Him and has given Him a name above every other name. Not the name of any other religion will be able to save you—only the name of Jesus. He is the King of kings and Lord of lords. The whole heavens declare His glory. The Bible says He was with the Father before the whole world began. He made all things for Him, and without Him was not anything made, declares John 1:3. He came from the bosom of the Father to free us from the curse of sin, according to John 1:18. Now, sin no longer has dominion over us; because the curse of sin is broken, we now have perfect liberty. This is because the spotless Lamb of God is risen and is alive forevermore. Yes, He is alive! My eyes have seen His glory! Because He lives, you and I shall live also, if we invite Him to come into our hearts, live within, and dwell with us. Invite Him in to cleanse you from all unrighteousness, wash you in His blood, and cleanse you from your sins. As the Bible pointed out, without the shedding of blood, there can be no forgiveness of sins.

Greater love than this has no man than for one to lay down his life for his friends. He said in His Word before He was crucified that He is the Good Shepherd, and the Good Shepherd lays down His life for His sheep. This He did on that day at Calvary's cross. He laid down His life for us.

So, the Bible says, "Let us therefore come boldly unto the throne of grace" (Heb. 4:16). Do not be scared to call upon Jesus on your

His Second Coming

own. You can reach Him on your own. You do not need a man or an earthly priest to call upon Him for you. Christ has broken that type of religion and tradition. He came and gave us a better covenant, a new covenant, the Bible says. The Bible says we now have a High Priest who can be touched by the feelings of our infirmities. He was in all points tempted just as we were, yet without sin. So, the Scripture encourages us to come boldly before His throne and let our requests be made known unto Him because He is now making intercession for us to the Father as He sits at the right hand of the Father. The Bible told us that we should come boldly, not in fear so that we will receive mercy and find grace to help us in times of need. (See Hebrews 4:15–16)

Dr. Marlene Brown

Chapter 43
Prepare to Meet Thy God

And, behold, I come quickly; and my reward is with me, to give every man according as his work shall be.

—Revelation 22:12

The tomb where the Lord Jesus was laid is empty! He has risen! He was seen by over five hundred brethren, including Peter and the other disciples. My eyes have also seen Him on earth and in heaven. He is indeed the King of kings and Lord of all! He is the great Alpha and Omega. He is the one who inhabits eternity.

He told His disciples that He would be going away. He said:

> Yet a little while I am with you. Ye shall seek me whither I go; ye cannot come. In my Father's house are many mansions: if it were not so, I would have told you. I go to prepare a place for you, And I will pray to the Father, and he shall give you another Comforter, that he may abide with you forever; Even the Spirit of truth; whom the world cannot receive, because it seeth him not.
>
> —John 13:33; 14:2, 16–17

Yes, the Word of Jesus Christ is indeed truth and life. There is no shadow of turning in His Words or His ways. We can depend on Him according to His Words. Jesus has promised us that He will return again, but are you ready to meet Him? The God of the universe sent forth His Son to us so that through His Son, we would not be condemned but have everlasting life. All He is asking of you is your heart. He wants to cleanse you from all your unrighteousness; He wants to forgive you of your sins and to remember them no more. He said He would throw your sins in the sea of forgetfulness and remember them no more. This is the greatest hope that mankind could ask for. Tell me, what more could Jesus do? What more could He have offered you, for you to receive this eternal life? It is pretty useless for us to depend upon the laws of the land to get us into heaven or even to depend upon the law of Moses for us to live by. The Bible declares, "For what the law could not do, in that it was weak through the flesh, God sending his own Son in the likeness of sinful flesh, and for sin, condemned sin in the flesh" (Rom. 8:3)

A man could not keep the law of Moses and be perfect in keeping it—because of the old Adamic nature and our sinful nature. This is why Christ had to come to destroy sin and set us free so that through His blood and spirit, we can now serve the Father in the beauty of holiness and righteousness. For this reason, the Bible says that if Christ is in you, your spirit is alive because of righteousness. Is Christ within you today? Are you dead to sin? Are you ready to meet the Lord? Are you ready to meet the King of kings? For the law of the spirit of life, which is in Christ Jesus our Lord, has made us free from the law of sin and death.

Jesus tries to encourage us to be on the watch for His great return. He said that we should watch, for we do not know the day or the hour when the Son of man shall make His appearance. Will His coming surprise us as a thief in the night? Or will we be on the watch? The Bible says that He shall appear for those who look for Him the second time. Are you looking for Him?

Paul reminded us that we do not know the time or season of Christ's return, but we should watch for His return. "Wherefore comfort yourselves together, and edify one another, even as also ye do now we exhort you, brethren, warn them that are unruly, comfort the feebleminded, support the weak, be patient toward all men. See that none render evil for evil unto any man; but ever follow that which is good, both among yourselves and to all men. Rejoice evermore" (1 Thess. 5:11, 14–16).

John wrote, "My little children, these things write I unto you, that ye sin not. And if any man sin, we have an advocate with the Father, Jesus Christ the righteous: And he is the propitiation for our sins: and not for ours only, but also for the sins of the whole world And now, little children, abide in him; that, when he shall appear, we may have confidence, and not be ashamed before him at his coming" (1 John 2:1–2, 28).

May the God of peace keep your hearts and minds through Christ Jesus, our Savior and Lord. Amen!

His Second Coming

Chapter 44
Letter of Encouragement to Be on the Watch!

For yourselves know perfectly that the day of the Lord so cometh as a thief in the night.

—*1 Thessalonians 5:2*

It gives me great joy to share these visions/dreams with you. I truly hope and pray that you have been blessed and that whether you are saved or not saved, the revelation from my visions/dreams will help to renew your commitment or to draw you closer to the Lord. It is just a few more days before the church's Rapture. Will you be ready to meet Him? The Lord said in His Word that He would return for a church without spot or wrinkle. This means that our spiritual garments should be clean, and our vessel, the temple of the living God, should be filled with fresh oil to meet Him.

Jesus is saying, however, that when He returns for His church, His bride, He hopes to find her not sleeping or being taken up by the cares of this world but on the watch for Him.

Essentially, let me share with you a vision that I received on Friday, June 1, 2001, as I heard the audible voice of God.

In this vision, I heard the audible voice of God speaking to me to deliver a warning message to an individual. The person is a very close family member that lives in a different country. I woke up between 2:30 and 3:00 a.m.

Dr. Marlene Brown

I dreamed that I was dreaming. I began to have a second dream called a vision in this dream. In this vision, the living God spoke to me, and these were His Words:

She said that she is getting her clothes ready for church on Sunday . . . Tell her that, tell her that make sure her inside is ready! Make sure her soul is ready when I come to visit her, or else!

In this vision, her name was given to me.

I woke up from my second dream but still sleeping in the first one. So, I began to tell people in this first dream about the warning that I had just received for this individual.

As I woke up from both dreams, my body was too "drunk" for me to get up. I was not drunk because of sleep, but as if I were under heavy anesthesia. I was conscious enough with my eyes open to know that I had gotten a warning to deliver to this person, but I could not move!

A few minutes after my body became alive, I could call this individual and deliver the message at 4:00 a.m.

As I delivered the message and began to encourage her in the Lord, her response to me was, "So, the Bible is *real*!" Many Christians need to ask ourselves: "Do we believe the gospel?" My friend, the gospel is real! The Scripture says many will not enter into his rest because of unbelief (Hebrews 3:19).

Jesus Christ is alive, and His eyes are watching your every move. Oh yes, He knows what we do in private as Christians or not! So many Christians are focusing on the outward appearance and not the heart, not holiness! The Word of God is still true, that without holiness, no man shall see the Lord, says Hebrews 12:14. I know the word is not being preached as it should; as a result, even pastors and leaders are now living in sin due to a lack of true holiness. However, the Word of God still holds true irrespective of man's belief. As God

His Second Coming

will not reduce His holiness to please us, we have to kill the flesh to please Him.

I am not talking about receiving His righteousness as this was freely given to us through Christ Jesus our Lord, according to Romans 3:21. First Thessalonians 4:3–4, 7, 9 says:

> For this is the will of God, even your sanctification, that you should abstain from fornication: That every one of you should know how to posses his vessel in sanctification and honour. For God had not called us unto uncleanness, but unto holiness. But as touching brotherly love ye need not that I write unto you: for ye yourselves are taught of God to love one another.

In Matthew chapter 25, Jesus tells the parable of the ten virgins. He said the kingdom of heaven could be likened to the ten virgins who took their lamps and went out to meet the bridegroom. Five of these virgins were wise, and five were foolish. The foolish ones took their lamps but no additional oil to keep them burning. The wise took not only their lamps but oil as well. While the bridegroom delayed his coming, they slept. At midnight, there was a cry, "Behold, the bridegroom comes, go out to meet him!" Then, all those virgins rose up and trimmed their lamps. The foolish virgins realized that their oil was finished, and their lamps had gone out, so they said to the wise ones, "We need some of your oil!" The wise virgins answered and said to them, "Not so, should there not be enough for us and you included. Why not go out to those that sell oil and buy for yourselves?" So, while they went out to buy, the bridegroom came; they that were ready went in with him to the marriage, and the door was shut. "Afterward came also the other virgins, saying, Lord, Lord, open to us. But he answered and said, Verily I say unto you, I know you not. Watch, therefore, for ye know neither the day nor the hour wherein the Son of man cometh" (Matt. 25:11-13). We as Christians need to have that flame on the inside of us keep burning, waiting for the coming of the Lord. We need to

Dr. Marlene Brown

continue to have the anointing oil of the Holy Spirit on the inside of us keep flowing, Remember, the Bible said it is the anointing that breaks the yoke of the enemy. Without this anointing oil flowing on the inside of us, we will be weakened and become distracted by the lust of the flesh and the cares of life.

And what I say unto you I say unto all, Watch.

—Mark 13:37

Part III
Prophetic Heavenly Visions of Christ with Interpretations

Dr. Marlene Brown

Chapter 45
Prophetic Vision of God's Heart for Young People

And he said, Hear now my words: If there be a prophet among you, I the LORD will make myself known unto him in a vision, and will speak unto him in a dream.

—*Numbers 12:6*

On the 16th of March 2001, I had the two most beautiful dreams. I received one dream in the early morning and the other in the afternoon.

Prophetic Dream for Young People

A dream that I, Marlene, saw on March 16, 2001.

The time was between 2:30 and 3:00 a.m. when I woke up.

I dreamed that I was in a different world. I say different because the place looked strange. I saw a little girl about the age of thirteen years. She was hearing directly from God and was prophesying. How do I know that it was from God? There was a great rumbling sound from the heavens whenever she spoke.

This little girl was prophesying many things. There is a portion of one of her prophecies, which I think was meant for me. While prophesying, she said, "God says, even if He does not speak to us directly, we still need to worship Him." She also mentioned that young people need to worship God more.

In the dream, I remember listening keenly to the little girl and saying to myself, "He said He might not speak to me directly." I remember speaking to someone in the dream about the prophecy and telling the person that God says young people are not worshiping Him enough! He said, "They need to worship Me because I am God!"

I woke up from this dream, saying to myself, "God says young people need to worship Him more . . ."

Interpretations of Prophetic Vision of God's Heart for Young People

Dream

I saw a little girl about the age of thirteen years.

Interpretation

The Bible says:

". . . and a little child shall lead them.

—Isaiah 11:6

Dream

She was hearing directly from God and was prophesying. How do I know that it was from God? There was a great rumbling sound from the heavens whenever she spoke.

Interpretation

Many Scriptures in the Bible speak of the voice of God sounding like thunder and the sound of many waters. Psalm 29:3 speaks of the voice of the Lord. It says, "The voice of the Lord is upon the waters: the God of glory thundereth: the Lord is upon many waters."

Dream

Dr. Marlene Brown

I remember speaking to someone in the dream about the prophecy and telling the person that God says young people are not worshiping Him enough! He said, "They need to worship Me because I am God!"

Interpretation

In our world today, we see the enemy's plan to take over society's youth to destroy them. The enemy is focusing on the youth because young men and women are full of passion and energy. Whatever they are involved in, they do to the utmost, and they should devote this passion and energy to worship, for our Father God is jealous. The Scripture says we must love Him with all of our heart, soul, and strength. So, the Father is saying that young people need to turn to Him in body, mind, and soul while strong to overcome the wicked.

Ecclesiastes 12:1 says, "Remember now thy Creator in the days of thy youth, while the evil days come not, nor the years draw nigh when thou shalt say, I have no pleasure in them." First, John 2:14 also says: "I have written unto you, fathers, because ye have known him that is from the beginning. I have written unto you, young men, because ye are strong, and the Word of God abideth in you, and ye have overcome the wicked one."

His Second Coming

Chapter 46
Prophetic Vision of His Spoken Word

Seventh Heavenly Dream

Is not my word like as a fire? saith the Lord; and like a hammer that breaketh the rock in pieces?

—*Jeremiah 23:29*

These are the amazing visions/dreams that I, Marlene, had on March 16, 2001. These took place on the same day as the vision/dream in chapter 43 but in the afternoon. I woke up from this dream and immediately went into a second one. The time was about 5:30 p.m. when I was fully awake from both of these visions/dreams.

I dreamed that I saw the Lord. The place was partially dark, and He was on earth. I am unsure if His feet touched the ground, but He was very close to the earth.

Jesus was quoting some Scriptures, and as He spoke, I saw that the actual things to which He was referring kept happening in the air as if the spoken words had become tangible objects. I remember looking at Him, watching Him speaking to His Father with His face toward heaven. Whatever Bible Scripture He would quote, the manifestation of it would take place in the air.

I was so amazed in the dream, looking at the actual things happening in the air. I then looked at Him . . . it seemed as if there was a bit of doubt in my mind. Suddenly, a Scripture came to my mind. I am not sure if this was the quote: "Rivers of living water..." However, Jesus read my mind, and I was in for a surprise.

It began to rain down on my head, water pouring from the sky. I found myself on the ground, flattened beneath the water. I was shaking and staggering beneath this water!

I looked at Him, and He smiled at me and told His Father to stop the rain because I could not manage it. Then it stopped pouring.

It is important to note that whenever Jesus speaks, His mouth is not open. It was totally Spirit to Spirit. I could understand Him, and He could understand me without either of us opening our mouths to speak.

I immediately left this dream and went into the second one, where I saw the Lord again.

Interpretation of Prophetic Vision of His Spoken Word

Dream

Jesus was quoting some Scriptures, and as He spoke, I saw that the actual things He was referring to kept happening in the air as if the spoken words had become tangible objects. I remember looking at Him, watching Him speaking to His Father with His face toward heaven. Whatever Bible Scripture He would quote, the manifestation of it would take place in the air.

Interpretation

Word: A spoken sound having meaning.

The Bible tells us that whenever the Word of God is spoken, we see the physical manifestation of His Word. I saw Jesus display his power and authority over nature and creation (Matthew 8:23-27). He depicts a king ruling over his kingdom. The Scripture says, "For by Him all things were created, both in the heavens and on earth, visible and invisible, whether thrones or dominions or rulers or authorities—all things have been created through Him and for Him" (Colossians 1:17). This same Jesus existed with God as the "Logos" of God, the "Word." The Bible says in the beginning, He created the heavens and the earth: And God said, "Let there be light," and there was light." And God said, "Let the water under the sky be gathered to one place, and let dry ground appear." And it was so. Then God said, "Let the land produce vegetation: seed-bearing plants and trees on the land that bear fruit with seed in it, according to their various kinds." And it was so. And God said, "Let the land produce living creatures according to their kinds: the livestock, the creatures that move along the ground, and the wild animals, each according to its kind." And it was so (Genesis 1:1-24). Jesus was displaying his power over creation as God. He speaks the word, and it was so.

The Word of God says, "In the beginning was the Word, and the Word was with God, and the Word was God. All things were made by him; and without him was not anything made that was made" (John 1:1, 3).

The Word of God also declares:

> By the Word of the Lord were the heavens made; and all the host of them by the breath of his mouth. He gathereth the waters of the sea together as an heap: he layeth up the depth in storehouses. Let all the earth fear the Lord: let all the inhabitants of the world stand in awe of him. For he spake, and it was done; he commanded, and it stood fast.
>
> —Psalm 33:6–9

Jesus says, "The words that I speak unto you, they are spirit, and they are life" (John 6:63). Proverbs 1:23 declares, "I will make known my words unto you."

Dream

Dr. Marlene Brown

I was so amazed in the dream, looking at the actual things happening in the air. I then looked at Him. It seemed as if there was a bit of doubt in my mind. Suddenly, a Scripture came to my mind. I am not sure if this was the quote: "Rivers of living water." However, Jesus read my mind, and I was in for a surprise.

Interpretation

Isaiah says:

> So shall my word be that goeth forth out of my mouth: it shall not return unto me void, but it shall accomplish that which I please, and it shall prosper in the thing whereto I sent it.
>
> —Isaiah 55:11

Dream

It began to rain down on my head, water pouring from the sky. I found myself on the ground, flattened beneath the water. I was shaking and staggering beneath this water!

Interpretation

Isaiah 44:3 can interpret this section of the vision, which says:

> For I will pour water upon him that is thirsty, and floods upon the dry ground: I will pour my spirit upon thy seed, and my blessing upon thine offspring.

I believe the downpouring of the water meant the anointing of the Holy Ghost. As I heard an anointed man of God say once, this body is not able to take too much of the anointing from God. The Scripture says, however, we will be blessed with a new body to stand before

His Second Coming

our Savior. We shall be changed from mortal to immortal. "For this corruptible must put on incorruption, and this mortal must put on immortality" (1 Cor. 15:53). Proverbs 1:23 says, "I will pour out my spirit unto you, I will make known my words unto you."

Blessed be your name, Lord. Your name is worthy to be praised.

Dr. Marlene Brown

Chapter 47
A Prophetic Dream Within a Dream

This is the second dream I, Marlene, went into immediately after the dream with the downpouring of water.

... For the testimony of Jesus is the spirit of prophecy.

—*Revelation 19:10*

In this dream, Jesus suddenly appeared. He was walking by me. This is what He said to me: "I am the Lord. I came to do the work of My Father." He continued to say, "The church is divided, and I do not like it when people speak against the church."

I remember that in the dream, a man was asking Him how to receive the Holy Spirit. When he asked this question, Jesus looked at him, suddenly turning His face sideways toward the man without answering him. In my mind, I was saying to myself, *doesn't he know how to get the Holy Spirit? Doesn't the Bible tell him how?*

Suddenly, I woke up from both dreams. When my spirit woke from these two powerful dreams of seeing Christ, my body still slept. Then, I went into an earthly dream with my mother and sister in the dream. I dreamed that I woke up and went outside of the room, where I saw my mother. I began telling her of the two powerful dreams I had just had of seeing Christ.

I then woke up from this earthly dream. I was confused at first. I just lay still on the bed, remembering the magnitude of the dreams. I ran to the computer and began to type out the visions/ dreams, not wanting to forget the details.

His Second Coming

To Jesus be all the glory, honor, and praise. Bless His holy name. I pray that He never lifts His hands from me. Amen.

It is not unusual for one to have a dream in a dream or a vision in a dream. An example of this can be found in Daniel 7:1, in which Daniel had a dream and visions in his dream: "In the first year of Belshazzar king of Babylon Daniel had a dream and visions of his head upon his bed: then he wrote the dream and told the sum of the matters."

Dream

> *In this dream, Jesus suddenly appeared. He was walking by me. This is what He said to me: "I am the Lord."*

Interpretation

This interpretation can be found in Exodus 6:2–3. In these verses of Exodus, God was speaking to Moses:

> And God spake unto Moses, and said unto him, I am the Lord: And I appeared unto Abraham, unto Isaac, and unto Jacob, by the name of God Almighty, but by my name Jehovah was I not known to them.

Dream

> *"I came to do the work of My Father."*

Interpretation

In John 5:17, Jesus declares, "My Father worketh hitherto, and I work." He means that His Father is always working, so He will work also. The Scriptures continue to say, "Therefore the Jews sought the more to kill him because he not only had broken the sabbath but also said that God was his Father, making himself equal with God" (John 5:18).

Then Jesus answered and said to them, "Verily, Verily, I say unto you, The Son can do nothing of himself, but what he seeth the Father do: for what things soever he doeth, these also doeth the Son likewise" (John 5:19). "I can of mine own self do nothing: as I hear, I judge: and my judgment is just; because I seek not mine own will, but the will of the Father which hath sent me" (John 5:30).

The interpretation continues throughout the New Testament. Jesus declared in his message:

> All that the Father giveth me shall come to me, and him that cometh to me I will in no wise cast out. For I came down from heaven, not to do mine own will, but the will of him that sent me. And this is the Father's will which hath sent me, that of all which he hath given me I should lose nothing but should raise it up again at the last day.
>
> And this is the will of him that sent me, that everyone, which seeth the Son, and believeth on him, may have everlasting life: and I will raise him up at the last day.
>
> —John 6:37–40

In John 7:16, Jesus answers and says to them, "My doctrine is not mine, but his that sent me." In verses 28–29, Jesus continues by saying, "Ye both know me, and ye know whence I am: and I have not come of myself, but he that sent me is true, whom ye know not. But I know him: for I am from him, and he hath sent me. Then they sought to take him: but no man laid hands on him, because his hour was not yet come" (John 7:28–30). In verse 33, Jesus says unto them, "Yet a little while am I with you, and then I go unto him that sent me."

In John 10:36–38, Jesus says unto them, "Say ye of him, whom the Father hath sanctified, and sent into the world, Thou blasphemest; because I said, I am the Son of God? If I do not the works of my Father, believe me not. But if I do, though ye believe not me, believe the works: that ye may know, and believe, that the

Father is in me, and I in him. Therefore, they sought again to take him: but he escaped out of their hand" (John 10:36–39)

Prophetic Vision of Unity Within the Church

Though the church has been divided for so many years, I believe there is coming a time when the church will be together as one. Remember that Jesus's word to the Father was for the church to be one as He is one with the Father (John 17:20–21).

The Lord Jesus, in His kindness, showed me in a vision on August 25, 2001, the church coming together as one, fulfilling the prophetic prayer that He made in John 17.

In this vision, I saw different types of churches from different denominations marching together. They started from different locations and then met together at one focal point. I was amongst the group. Somehow, however, I lost the group. On my way home, I told myself, "The Lord must be so pleased to see all churches come together as one." Jesus's face then appeared in the sky . . . it was beautiful, gloriously beautiful. I saw many colors on His face. I then saw a rectangular-shaped box appear with writings in it. The box and the writings were filled with the glory of God. In the box were many writings on the inside, but I could only memorize two of the writings before they disappeared.

I saw "The Word 1–5." I repeated, "The word? The word," I asked the Lord as I looked at His beautiful face. Then I said to Him, "Oh, you mean John 1:1–5!" I also saw Philippians 4:1–4.

The Lord was speaking to me and saying He was pleased. In another area of the sky, Mary appeared. She had a heavenly glow above and around her.

I find it quite interesting that I would see Mary, the mother of our Lord Jesus was in the sky at that moment.

Dr. Marlene Brown

When I woke up, I began to read the Scriptures given. In John chapter 1, the Scripture reads:

> In the beginning was the Word, and the Word was with God, and the Word was God. The same was in the beginning with God. All things were made by him; and without him was not anything made that was made. In him was life; and the life was the light of men. And the light shineth in darkness; and the darkness comprehended it not.
>
> —John 1:1–5

Then I read Philippians 4:1, 3–5. It reads:

> Therefore, my brethren dearly beloved and longed for, my joy and crown, so stand fast in the Lord, my dearly beloved And I intreat thee also, true yokefellow, help those women which laboured with me in the gospel, with Clement also, and with other fellowlabourers, whose names are in the Book of Life. Rejoice in the Lord always: and again I say, Rejoice.

I believe that this Scripture speaks of my call to ministry. Not only am I chosen to minister to those whose names are in the Book of Life, but also to women throughout the nations of the earth. I find it fitting that Mary would be there as she represents the first woman who ministered to the Lord.

His Second Coming

Chapter 48
Prophetic Vision of Heaven (the Marriage Supper)

A dream that I, Marlene, saw on April 9, 2001.

I woke up at 8:30 a.m.

Aad it shall come to pass in the last days, saith God, I will pour out of my Spirit upon all flesh: and your sons and your daughters shall prophesy, and your young men shall see visions, and your old men shall dream dreams.

—*Acts 2:17*

On Sunday, April 8, 2001, when my husband and I were about to doze off to sleep, I began to speak to the Lord. I then turned to my husband and said, "My name is written in the Lamb's Book of Life!"

And he replied, "Yeah. . ." I then said to him, "No, my name is written in the Lamb's Book of Life!" Then there was silence, and we both drifted off to sleep. At about 2:00 a.m., our son, Brandon, awakened us. I managed to put him back to bed. I went to my prayer room to pray. I mentioned certain things to the Lord, which were just too personal between us both to write about here, then I went back to bed. In the morning, I woke up from the most amazing dream.

I dreamed that my husband, my eight-month-old son, Brandon, and I were in a particular country. The country seemed like a country or one of those countries that do not respect human life. In other words, they will kill you in a minute if you say or do something wrong.

We were walking along in this country . . . just walking, talking, and smiling, going along like tourists in a foreign city. The big question is, what exactly were we talking about? The answer is I do not remember. However, it seems as if we said something inappropriate about the people. Suddenly, a man appeared before us out of nowhere. He was short and medium-built. His square-looking face had a serious look to it, almost an angry look. He stopped and said that one of us had to die because of what we had said.

I turned to the man and said, "What did I say?" He looked at me and said that he could not say exactly, but one of us had to die. My attitude was: "You cannot tell us what was being said that was wrong, but one of us has to die?" He then walked away, leaving my husband and me standing still.

When I realized that he was serious that one of us had to die, I turned to my husband and said, "Well, the Bible says absent from the body, present with the Lord! They can only kill the body, but you will be with the Lord!"

My dear husband started to get really upset with me for saying that. This was his response: "What do you mean they can't kill us . . . if they kill the body, we are present with the Lord? If they kill us, we are dead!"

But I said to him, "This is only a body! The real you is on the inside! Your soul! This is just a body! If they kill the body, you will be with the Lord!"

He was so mad to know that one of us was going to die he would not hear of it.

I began to say to him, "Well, I don't think they would kill me, because they see I have a young baby." I continued, "All you need to do is believe that Jesus is the Son of God!"

His Second Coming

By this time, the man came back to us. I then asked the man which one of us he would kill.

To my surprise, the man said, "You." I looked at my husband. The man then left us. He went a little distance away to a tree, which had a huge, thick trunk. This tree also had long ropes or vines hanging down from it.

The man began to cut the ropes to tie my hands with.

At this time, I made use of the opportunity. I began to let my husband know that he should care for himself spiritually and Brandon so that I could see them again.

I then saw the man appear with long strings to tie my hands; a thought suddenly ran through my mind: "What if there is any doubt in my mind and I am not with Christ when they kill my body?"

Suddenly, I heard myself scream out, "Jesus! I believe that You are the Son of God!" I was then bound, and I am not sure if he cut my head off or what, but I found myself in another world.

This world was not on earth or under the earth. This world was somewhere in the air or the heavens. In this world, I saw a couple of people that I know. Everyone was seated around the tables. They were seated in various groups. The place was slightly dark, as if there were limited light, but I could clearly see the people who were close up.

As far as the eyes could see, the people were all seated around different tables as if they were waiting for some great festivity to begin. It reminds me of when Christ was seated at the table breaking bread, something similar.

I then turned to the two persons who were beside me, whom I knew very well on earth. In the dream, I knew them very well, but now that I am awake, I cannot see or tell who they are. The only two persons who died on earth that were close to me as a family were my grandmother and my brother. My brother died at the young age of thirty-five. It is important to note that I was not seated among my family. I was standing behind them while they were seated. I then mentioned to them that we should go for a walk.

They got up from their table. I looked over to another table and saw a man I knew on earth. My response was: "He is here? He made it?" We continued walking . . . "Oh, I know that person," I was pointing over to someone that was standing by a table. "He made it?" I was referring to another person that I recognized.

We continued walking until we reached a very long, narrow road. We began to walk on this road. Now, on either side of the road were tables with people sitting around them, and these people were waiting for the festivities to begin.

I continued to point out people that I knew as I went along. Some people that I saw, I was surprised that those persons really made it.

Finally, we reached the end of the road. At the end of the road, what I saw was most amazing!

A distance away was another city. It was also in the air. From where we stood at the end of the road, there was a wide gap of nothingness. It was total space, and it was looking pitch dark. If we had tried to go any further to reach that city, we would have fallen into empty space. The space of nothingness separated us from where we stood in this beautiful city. I was saying to myself, "Why is everyone all seated when there is such a beautiful city to look at?"

This city looked indescribably beautiful. The city was lit up. The light of the city was very soft, and it also had a glow. There was a bright light in mid-air. This bright light was not from the sun or the moon. I also saw a spiritual form or shape. My head began to turn slowly to my right, where I saw a building going up in the air like a temple. I called this structure a temple.

His Second Coming

The temple I saw was made with glass or crystal; it was too beautiful to capture the exact material from which it was made. I am not sure if Crystal describes it exactly. The material was transparent, white, soft, shiny, and glassy.

It was certainly a temple that man has never seen or can attempt to build on this earth, gloriously beautiful!

While looking through the temple, I saw someone move and begin to walk gently and slowly. If this person had not moved and began to walk, I would not have known someone was standing there. His outfit was just as white as the temple.

While the person continued walking, he took a left turn toward the entrance of the temple. As I continued to look through the temple, I saw a white chair like a silver throne at a distance.

The person continued to walk with such grace. He was so gentle and calm. He walked as if he were gliding along in slow motion. I was watching him through the transparent temple. He was coming toward the temple entrance, where I could see him much plainer.

We all knew that it was Jesus. We just stood there watching Jesus in all His glory. I cannot tell what His face looked like because my eyes were fixed on His clothing.

The color of His gown was the purest white I have ever seen. The word in English is not good enough to describe the whiteness of His gown. It was whiter than snow, pearl, or any white color that man had ever seen on earth. It was gloriously white, and it flowed softly. It had several layers of material to it because it had a puffy look at the waistline coming down like a wedding gown . . . but very soft looking.

He continued to walk with a very gentle, smooth glide and stepped outside. Now outside, leading from the temple, the ground looked like glassy, crystal water. It seemed very thick and glassy with a very white color. It had the purest white I have ever seen.

He then stepped outside and slowly lay down on His back in the water.

"Why is He lying down in the water?" I asked curiously.

Suddenly, I felt my eyes flutter in my bed. I opened my eyes and found myself lying on my back with my face toward heaven.

At this point, I did not know whether I should be happy or sad, based on my experience of being killed in the dream. I really thought that I was dead! The fluttering of my eyes brought me back to consciousness.

Now that I have the time to reflect on what I saw, I am thrilled that the good Lord has given me such an opportunity to see the pearly white city and the crystal river.

Words cannot describe the pearly white city that I have seen. The majesty and beauty that I have seen is beyond our understanding or the knowledge of man. This is indeed encouragement to the church and great encouragement for me!

Oh, Jesus, you are so wonderful! You are so amazing! You are gloriously wonderful!

Dream

> When I realized that he was serious that one of us had to die, I turned to my husband and said, "Well, the Bible says absent from the body, present with the Lord! They can only kill the body, but you will be with the Lord!"
>
> My dear husband started to get really upset with me for saying that. This was his response: "What do you mean they

> can't kill us... if, they ill the body, we are present with the Lord? If they kill us, we are dead!"
>
> But I said to him, "This is only a body! The real you is on the inside! Your soul! This is just a body! If they kill the body, you will be with the Lord!"

Interpretation

The Word of God declares that: "We are confident, I say, and willing rather to be absent from the body, and to be present with the Lord" (2 Cor. 5:8).

Dream

> My dear husband started to get really upset with me for saying that. This was his response: "What do you mean they can't kill us... if, they ill the body, we are present with the Lord? If they kill us, we are dead!"

Interpretation

The Word of God declares that we should not fear the one that can kill the body only, but rather the one that can kill both body and soul in hell. So, the Word of God says:

> And I say unto you my friends, Be not afraid of them that kill the body, and after that have no more that they can do. But I will forewarn you whom ye shall fear: Fear him, which after he hath killed hath power to cast into hell; yea, I say unto you, Fear him.
>
> —Luke 12:4–5

> And fear not them which kill the body, but are not able to kill the soul: but rather fear him which is able to destroy both soul and body in hell.
>
> —Matthew 10:28

Dr. Marlene Brown

Dream

I then saw the man appear with long strings to tie my hands; a thought suddenly ran through my mind: "What if there is any doubt in my mind and I am not with Christ when they kill my body?" Suddenly, I heard myself scream out, "Jesus! I believe that You are the Son of God!"

Interpretation

The Word of God says:

He that believeth on the Son of God hath the witness in himself: he that believeth not God hath made him a liar; because he believeth not the record that God gave of his Son. And this is the record, that God/hath given to us eternal life, and this life is in his Son. He that hath the Son hath life, and he that hath not the Son of God hath not life. These things have I written unto you that believe in the name of the Son of God; that ye may know that ye have eternal life and that ye may believe on the name of the Son of God

—1 John 5:10–13

But these are written, that ye might believe that Jesus is the Christ, the Son of God; and that believing ye might have life through his name.

—John 20:31

Dream

In this world, I saw a couple of people that I know. Everyone was seated around the tables. They were seated in various groups. The place looked slightly dark, as if there were limited light, but I could see the people who were close up clearly.

His Second Coming

As far as the eyes could see, the people were all seated around different tables as if they were waiting on some great festivity to begin. It reminds me of when Christ was seated at the table breaking bread, something similar.

Interpretation

Revelation 19:9–10 can interpret this great festivity, which speaks of the marriage supper to come:

> And he saith unto me, Write, Blessed are they which are called unto the marriage supper of the Lamb. And he saith unto me: These are the true sayings of God . . . for the testimony of Jesus is the spirit of prophecy.
>
> And I heard a voice from heaven saying unto me, Write, Blessed are the dead which die in the Lord from henceforth: Yea, saith the Spirit, that they may rest from their labors, and their works do follow them.
>
> —Revelation 14:13

Dream

We all knew that it was Jesus. We just stood there watching Jesus in all His glory. I cannot tell what His face looked like because my eyes were fixed on His clothing.

The color of His gown was the purest white I have ever seen. The word white in the English language is not good enough to describe the whiteness of His gown. It was whiter than snow, pearl, or any white color that man has ever seen on earth, and it flowed softly. It had several layers of material to it because it had a puffy look at the waistline, coming down like a wedding gown . . . but very soft looking.

Interpretation

The white gown seen is mentioned in Revelation 3:4–5, which says:

> Thou hast a few names even in Sardis which have not defiled their garments; and they shall walk with me in white: for they are worthy. He that overcometh, the same shall be clothed in white raiment; and I will not blot out his name out of the book of life, but I will confess his name before my Father, and before his angels.

Dream

The city was lit up. The light of the city was very soft; it also had a glow. There was a bright light in mid-air. This bright light was not from the sun or the moon. I also saw a spiritual form or shape.

Interpretation

Revelation 21:23 describes the city perfectly:

> And the city had no need of the sun, neither of the moon, to shine in it: for the glory of God did lighten it, and the Lamb is the light thereof.

Dream

My head began to turn slowly to my right, where I saw a building going up in the air like a temple.

Interpretation

This temple can be found in Revelation 7:15, which says:

> Therefore are they before the throne of God, and serve him day and night in his temple: and he that sitteth on the throne shall dwell among them.
>
> And the temple of God was opened in heaven, and there was seen in his temple the ark of his testament: and there

were bolts of lightning, and voices, and thunderings, and an earthquake, and great hail.

—Revelation 11:19

Dream

The temple that I saw was made with glass or crystal; it is too beautiful to capture the exact material that it was made from. I am not sure if crystal describes it exactly: The material was transparent, white, and soft, yet shiny and glassy.

Interpretation

And he carried me away in the spirit to a great and high mountain, and shewed me that great city, the holy Jerusalem, descending out of heaven from God, Having the glory of God: and her light was like unto a stone most precious, even like a jasper stone, clear as crystal.

—Revelation 21:10–11

Dream

Now outside, leading from the temple, the ground looked like glassy, crystal water. It seemed very thick and glassy with a very white color. It was the purest white I have ever seen.

Interpretation

This crystal, glassy water can be interpreted by Revelation 22:1, which says:

And he shewed me a pure river of water of life, clear as crystal, proceeding out of the throne of God and of the Lamb.

Dr. Marlene Brown

We thank God for the apostle John, who saw so much and described to us what he saw in Revelation. We also thank the Lord Jesus for showing first the apostle John the reality of the New Jerusalem and the marriage supper. If it had not been for the apostle, I would think that what I saw was too beautiful to be real. Saints of God, the Bible is indeed true. His promises are for us today. Certainly, He is coming back just like He said. And yes, heaven is real. The marriage supper is also real. It is that which is to come.

When I saw Jesus stepping outside and slowly lying on His back in the water, I responded, "Why is He lying down in the water?" I believe that what He did was very prophetic.

I believe the Lord is revealing that we need to lie down in the river of God and become saturated in His presence. This is when the anointing will begin to flow through us. We will begin to experience signs and wonders within the body of Christ as well as have prophetic visions and dreams.

I now know that we are in the winding up of the Scriptures. We are now in Revelation. I also know that we are in the very last days. I can feel His coming. His coming is much closer than we think. These signs that I have seen in the heavens are clear indications of how close His coming is.

We do not have time to play church; these are serious times that we live in. The Scripture says he will be coming at any time now, even as a thief in the night. This is now the time to be on the watch.

May the peace of God be with you all . . . Amen!

His Second Coming

Chapter 49
Preparing for His Second Coming

He who testifies to these things says, "Yes, I am coming soon." Amen. Come, Lord Jesus.

—*Revelation 22:20*

I believe that many of us pastors and leaders have become vain in our own thinking. No longer, to live is Christ, and to die is gain. We believe that if we live for Christ and stand up for Him, it will mean poverty, but it is the opposite. To live for Christ means blessings and prosperity. Yes, we can stand for Christ and still have it all. Jesus Christ says, "I came that you might have life and have life more abundantly." (See John 10:10.) This means both in this world and the one to come. Jesus told Peter that he would have everything restored 100 percent with persecution if he gave up all to follow Him. So yes, the tangible blessings will be there, but persecution will also follow if we preach Christ and not a gospel that is filled with hype and emotions mixed with man's psychology and the wisdom of man—but not of God.

In the early church days, the Scriptures declared that the apostles dedicated themselves to prayer, fasting, and the reading of God's Word. No wonder they had such great revivals among them. No wonder they saw such miracles, signs, and wonders amongst them, as the Scripture says, and great fear fell on all the churches.

Today, the church is less feared and less effective. Why? Could it be that more pastors and leaders are being caught up with the ideology of man and not with that of God? Could it be that we have become men-pleasers and not God-pleasers, not wanting to offend any with the Word of God? Could it be that we have lost the Spirit of the gospel and are left with the theology of the gospel? As a result, not allowing the Holy Spirit to reveal righteousness and to convict the heart of sin? However, God still has a remnant that has not bowed to Baal, a set of people who will walk in obedience and authority to His Word. A set of people who are chosen—as He declared in His Word, that many are called, but few are chosen—those whose hearts have been circumcised by the blood of Christ.

In Revelation 3, Jesus speaks to the church about being an overcomer. Not only does He want us to overcome the hour of temptation, which shall come upon all the world, to try them that dwell upon the earth—this includes both sinners and Christians, from the pulpit to the pew—but He also promises rewards in heaven if we overcome.

Jesus says in verses 11–13:

> Behold, I come quickly: hold that fast which thou hast, that no man take thy crown. Him that overcometh will I make a pillar in the temple of my God, and he shall go no more out: and I will write upon him the name of my God, and the name of the city of my God, which is new Jerusalem, which cometh down out of heaven from my God: and I will write upon him my new name. He that hath an ear, let him hear what the Spirit saith unto the churches.

His Second Coming

About the Author

Reverend Dr. Marlene Brown is an ordained minister and itinerant international speaker. She is the founder and president of Residence for Christ International Orphanages and Outreach Relief, Inc., a non-profit organization registered in Canada.

Rev. Brown was brought up in a Christian home, with her father being a pastor. She is a PK (Pastor's Kid). She knew about the Lord Jesus from the Bible but never knew Him. The apostle Paul declared, "That I may know Him and the power of His resurrection" (Philippians 3:10). Therefore, her desire is for the body of Christ to get to know Jesus personally, through His Word, and through visitations in visions and dreams. Rev. Brown was baptized at fourteen but left the church at sixteen. She became highly rebellious towards God and church and lost all interest in and desire for Jesus. She experienced success with her husband, but her soul was empty and dry. She began to yearn for a relationship with the living God. Rev. Brown then had an experience with Jesus that transformed her life.

In the year 2000, she was invited to church. There was an altar call, so she went up. The pastor began to prophesy to her concerning what the Lord Jesus was saying to her that day. He began, "The Lord said to tell you that He loves you, He loves you. He loves you! He said to tell you His hand is upon you, and as of today, you will never be the same again!" The pastor then went on to speak about more personal things about her life and promises that she had made that only she and the Lord Jesus knew about. She left the altar feeling rejuvenated in her spirit and knowing that the living God knows her personally and loves her. She began to reread the Bible, but this time with a hunger and a thirst to know the living God. She wanted to know all the Lord Jesus said in His Word. Rev. Brown wanted to ensure her life aligned with God's Word. Even then, she did not feel satisfied in her soul. There was still a thirst in her soul.

The greatest miracle occurred when Rev. Brown watched the Jesus film movie on YouTube. At the end of the movie, there is a sinner's prayer. Rev. Brown repeated the sinners' prayer out loud with the conviction of every word that was spoken as she repented of her sins and invited Jesus Christ into her heart to be the Lord of her life and Savior of her soul. At the end of the prayer, Rev. Brown testified of the joy she received in her heart. From that day onwards, she has the joy of salvation.

Furthermore, within four months of being saved, Jesus Christ, the Son of God, began to visit her in prophetic visions and dreams to confirm the prophecy's word. She started having encounters with Jesus for four consecutive years. He has visited her over fourteen times within those years. During those years of visitations, Jesus showed her a preview of His Second Coming, a vision of the Rapture of the church, a vision of heaven, and the marriage supper, among other visions and dreams. These visions/dreams are interpreted by the Word of God line upon line and precept upon precept, making them extremely prophetic in nature. Her prophetic encounter with God fulfilled what the prophet Joel said: "And it shall come to pass afterward, that I will pour out of my spirit upon all flesh; and your sons and your daughters shall prophesy, Your old men shall dream dreams, your young men shall see visions" (Joel 2:28 NIV).

Jesus confirms this truth concerning the work of the Holy Spirit by saying He, the Holy Spirit, will show us things to come, and He will glorify Him (Jesus). Jesus continued by saying, "All things that the Father hath are mine: therefore said I, that he shall take of mine, and shall shew it unto you" (John 16:14–15). Therefore, the Holy Spirit has shown her the Father's heart and the plan for his Son's

His Second Coming

imminent return to earth. The Scripture says, "Indeed, the Sovereign LORD never does anything until he reveals his plans to his servants, the prophets" (Amos 3:7).

In a vision of the night, Dr. Brown heard the voice of God say to her, "You are called to be a prophet to the nations." Then, to confirm the prophetic mandate given to her by the voice of God, approximately three years after that dream, Jesus Christ came in a vision of the night in His glory in the heavens and commissioned her to go to the nations to preach the gospel. At first, she saw an angel in the sky with a sword drawn. Then Jesus appeared in the heavens and said to her through words written in the sky: "If you are going to the nations of the earth, you need to go "NOW." The word "NOW" was written in capital letters. Then He left, showing it is a matter of great urgency for her to release the visions of Him and His Second Coming to the nations, for the church to know that "NOW" is the time to be on the watch! Revelation 16:15 states, "Behold, I come as a thief. Blessed is he that watcheth, and keepeth his garments, lest he walks naked, and they see his shame."

Consequently, in a prophetic class, the power of God slew Rev. Brown, and Jesus began to speak to her once more, saying, "Run, run like the wind; take MY gospel to the nations!" Furthermore, the Lord kept repeating this over and over in her head. She now blesses the church with the prophetic visions and dreams.

Dr. Marlene Brown

In Conclusion

Reverend Brown believes Christ desires His bride to have experience with the bridegroom. She believes Christ desires this relationship like never before as His coming draws so much closer. Rev. Brown's eyes have seen His glory over fourteen times. During these visitations, Jesus showed her a preview of His Second Coming, which was so real that she thought it was happening at that moment. She exclaimed that there was a feeling of urgency in the atmosphere. Why such urgency, one might ask? Jesus wants the body of Christ to be prepared for His Coming all through the nations of the earth! He is not willing for any to perish but for all to come to repentance. He wants us not to lose interest in His coming but to be on the watch.

"But of that day and hour knoweth no man, not the angels of heaven, but my Father only. Watch, therefore: for ye know not what hour your Lord doth come" (Matt. 24:36, 42).

Jesus says in the book of Revelation:

> And, behold, I come quickly; and my reward is with me, to give every man according as his work shall be. I am the Alpha and Omega, the beginning and the end, the first and the last. Blessed are they that do his commandments, that they may have right to the tree of life, and may enter in through the gates into the city. For without are dogs, and sorcerers, and whoremongers, and murderers, and idolaters, and whosoever loveth and maketh a lie.

His Second Coming

I, Jesus, have sent mine angel to testify unto you these things in the churches. I am the root and the offspring of David and the bright and morning star.

And the Spirit and the bride say, Come. And let him that heareth say, Come. And let him that is athirst come. And whosoever will, let him take the water of life freely.

—Rev. 22:12-17

She now blesses the church with these prophetic revelations by the Holy Spirit, in Jesus's name.

To Contact the Author

For speaking engagements and ministry, Dr. Marlene Brown can be contacted via one of the following media:

Marlene Brown Ministries

Residence for Christ International Orphanages and Outreach Relief, Inc.

(A non-profit organization registered with the Canadian government)

www.ResidenceforChrist.org
MarleneBrown@ResidenceforChrist.org

Website: https://www.spiritualformation.online/spiritual-formation

Social Media Networks

YouTube Channel: Spiritual Formation Center (SFC) – YouTube

Blog: SoloScriptorium.com

Podcast: Spiritual Formation Online Podcast (buzzsprout.com)

Instagram: @DrMarleneBrown

Facebook: SFCDevelopment

www.ingramcontent.com/pod-product-compliance
Lightning Source LLC
Chambersburg PA
CBHW031058080526
44587CB00011B/736